FIGHTER, WORKER, AND FAMILY MAN

German-Jewish Men and Their Gendered Experiences in Nazi Germany, 1933–1941

D1564655

When the Nazis came to power, they used various strategies to expel German Jews from social, cultural, and economic life. *Fighter, Worker, and Family Man* focuses on the gendered experiences and discrimination that German-Jewish men faced between 1933 and 1941.

Sebastian Huebel argues that Jewish men's gender identities, intersecting with categories of ethnicity, race, class, and age, underwent a profound process of marginalization that destabilized accustomed ways of performing masculinity. At the same time, in their attempts to sustain their conceptions of masculinity these men maintained agency and developed coping strategies that prevented their full-scale emasculation. Huebel draws on a rich archive of diaries, letters, and autobiographies to interpret the experiences of these men, focusing on their roles as soldiers and protectors, professionals and breadwinners, and parents and husbands.

Fighter, Worker, and Family Man sheds light on how the Nazis sought to emasculate Jewish men through propaganda, the law, and violence, and how in turn German-Jewish men were able to defy emasculation and adapt – at least temporarily – to their marginalized status as men.

(German and European Studies)

SEBASTIAN HUEBEL is a faculty member in the Department of History at the University of the Fraser Valley and head of the Department of Humanities at Alexander College in Vancouver.

GERMAN AND EUROPEAN STUDIES

General Editor: Jennifer L. Jenkins

FIGHTER, WORKER, AND FAMILY MAN

GERMAN-JEWISH MEN AND THEIR GENDERED EXPERIENCES IN NAZI GERMANY, 1933-1941

SEBASTIAN HUEBEL

UNIVERSITY OF TORONTO PRESS
Toronto Buffalo London

© University of Toronto Press 2022
Toronto Buffalo London
utorontopress.com
Printed in Canada

ISBN 978-1-4875-4123-1 (cloth)   ISBN 978-1-4875-4126-2 (EPUB)
ISBN 978-1-4875-4124-8 (paper)   ISBN 978-1-4875-4125-5 (PDF)

Library and Archives Canada Cataloguing in Publication

Title: Fighter, worker, and family man : German-Jewish men and their gendered
    experiences in Nazi Germany, 1933–1941 / Sebastian Huebel.
Names: Huebel, Sebastian, author.
Series: German and European studies ; 43.
Description: Series statement: German and European studies ; 43 | Includes
    bibliographical references and index.
Identifiers: Canadiana (print) 20210264942 | Canadiana (ebook) 20210265027 |
    ISBN 9781487541231 (cloth) | ISBN 9781487541248 (paper) | ISBN 9781487541262
    (EPUB) | ISBN 9781487541255 (PDF)
Subjects: LCSH: Jewish men – Germany – History – 20th century. | LCSH: Gender
    identity – Germany – History – 20th century. | LCSH: Masculinity – Germany –
    History – 20th century. | LCSH: Marginality, Social – Germany – History – 20th
    century. | LCSH: Jews – Germany – Identity – History – 20th century. | LCSH: Jews –
    Germany – History – 1933–1945. | LCSH: Germany – History – 1933–1945.
Classification: LCC DS134.23 .H84 2022 | DDC 305.892/4043 – dc23

The German and European Studies series is funded by the DAAD with funds from the
German Federal Foreign Office.

DAAD Deutscher Akademischer Austauschdienst
German Academic Exchange Service

This book has been published with the help of a grant from the Federation for the
Humanities and Social Sciences, through the Awards to Scholarly Publications Program,
using funds provided by the Social Sciences and Humanities Research Council of
Canada.

University of Toronto Press acknowledges the financial assistance to its publishing
program of the Canada Council for the Arts and the Ontario Arts Council, an agency of
the Government of Ontario.

Canada Council   Conseil des Arts
for the Arts   du Canada

ONTARIO ARTS COUNCIL
CONSEIL DES ARTS DE L'ONTARIO
an Ontario government agency
un organisme du gouvernement de l'Ontario

Funded by the   Financé par le
Government   gouvernement
of Canada   du Canada

Canadä

MIX
Paper from
responsible sources
FSC
www.fsc.org   FSC® C016245

I dedicate this work to my children, Ellie and Jasper.

Contents

Figures

Acknowledgments

To have come this far, I feel deeply indebted to family, friends and colleagues. When I first became interested in German history – as a teenager in Germany watching Guido Knopp's Hitler documentaries on television – I felt strongly that my calling was to become a historian one day. My years as an undergraduate student in Canada, at Thompson Rivers University, were formative and laid the groundwork for learning how to think like a historian. At the graduate level, I found Marion Kaplan's seminal work *Between Dignity and Despair* most influential, and I consider my work as a continuation of the still evolving field of German-Jewish historiography, with a narrower focus on Jewish masculinity. Benjamin M. Baader was kind enough to forward to me the introduction to the edited volume *Jewish Masculinities: German Jews, Gender, and History* when he, Sharon Gillerman, and Paul Lerner were in the final stages of preparing publication. The editors' claim in 2012 that insights into the lived experiences of German-Jewish men during the time of Nazi Germany were scarce was an inspiring prod towards my research. The present text follows the spirit of this historiographical critique.

I am immensely grateful to my parents who have stood by my side and supported me throughout my endless years of being a student. Special recognition also goes to Dr. Christopher R. Friedrichs for his mentoring support and who, in tandem with Richard Menkis and Kyle Frackman, all at the University of British Columbia, shepherded me through this project. I would also like to extend my appreciation to Franziska Bogdanov, at the Jewish Museum in Berlin, who was most accommodating during my research in 2015. I am also grateful to my colleague Ian Rocksborough-Smith at the University of the Fraser Valley for providing invaluable pointers that helped me prepare the manuscript for submission. I extend my gratitude to Amber Nickell at Purdue University for her help with the historiography outside of German-Jewish history. Immeasurable gratitude is also due to Stephen Shapiro at University of Toronto Press, whose guidance and encouragement have been of the utmost help, as well as Robin Studniberg, Margaret Allen, Ruth Pincoe, and the three anonymous readers who helped me immensely in revising, copy-editing, and indexing my book. Finally, my greatest appreciation is for my wife, Lindsey, who not only had to make numerous sacrifices during the years of my research but who remained loyal on the frontline of proofreading my coarsely written chapters and spotting a myriad errors, all the while raising two tiny and wonderful human beings.

FIGHTER, WORKER, AND FAMILY MAN

Introduction

On 1 April 1933, Richard Stern (Figure 1) put on his World War I medal during a Nazi-staged boycott that targeted Jewish businesses and firms. Walter Bendix, when banned from the German lawyer's association in 1935, opted to find some niche employment as a legal consultant, instead of applying for an emigration visa.[1] As a form of escaping Nazi violence and arrest during the infamous night of Broken Glass, 9 November 1938, eleven Jewish men hid in a villa of an "Aryan" merchant; some of them did not even know the proprietor. And in a tiny cigar shop – about nine square metres in size – owned by another "Aryan," two Jews spent fourteen consecutive nights, sleeping on chairs.[2]

This book is about stories, stories written by German-Jewish men and about German-Jewish men in the Third Reich. It is about men who put on their World War I medals at the time when German Jews were expelled from the military and their public standings were challenged. It is about men who were deemed hyper-sexualized race defilers of German women. It is about working men who faced existential economic struggles in Nazi Germany and challenges in fulfilling their roles as fathers and husbands. It is also about Jewish men who were singled out as men and often brutalized in their homes and in prewar concentration camps. In short, this book is about the gendered experiences, challenges, victimizations, reactions, and negotiations of German-Jewish men who saw their masculinities stifled by the Nazi regime. How did Jewish men come to perceive the onslaught of Nazi antisemitism in the Third Reich as men? How did they experience and cope with the radical dislodging of their roles as proud and patriotic war veterans who had hitherto cultivated close emotional ties to their country? How did Jewish men adapt to economic restrictions and hardships in their roles as breadwinners and providers for their families? How did Jewish men as husbands and fathers perform the roles of protectors of their

Figure 1. Richard Stern standing in front of his store in Cologne, 1933,
publicly displaying his World War I medal as a form of anti-Nazi defiance.

families? How did they experience the sudden exposure to physical violence on the street and in Germany's prewar concentration camps?

Few other fields have received the kind of scholarly attention and witnessed such an enormous output of literature as the Holocaust and World War II. With the turn to women's history in the 1970s, there has been a palpable growth in the study of oral histories of survivors and victims, which in turn has led to an impressive corpus of literature on the Jewish experience. As Saul Friedländer has rightly postulated, "The voices of the victims are essential if we want to attain an understanding of the past."[3] As part of this process, gender history has witnessed an astounding output of literature on women in the Holocaust, and today we know substantially more about particular challenges and forms of torture (rape and forced sterilizations to name two) but also about the gender-specific responses and forms of resistance that women developed during the Nazi era.[4] Yet strikingly, the study of Jewish masculinities under Nazi rule remains an underresearched area. The literature is reticent on aspects of the Jewish male experience and does not fully take into account Jewish men and their experiences under a torturous, murderous regime, especially outside of Nazi concentration camps. As Benjamin Baader, Sharon Gillerman, and Paul Lerner have astutely noted, "we have far too little insight into the psychological impact of Nazi propaganda and policy, or of the experience of street violence, physical intimidation and humiliation, deportation and life in the concentration camps on masculine self-identity in those years."[5]

This silence around questions about manhood has been grounded in a widely shared view in the 1990s and early 2000s that archival sources were bereft of explicit content related to the male gender, thus questioning the utility of men's studies. Others have argued that such undertakings would produce trivial or irrelevant results – especially in the historicity of the Holocaust that, so the argument goes, should illuminate and explain *universal* Jewish suffering. Yet, as Björn Krondorfer has poignantly stressed, scholars have falsely assumed masculinity as standard and normative. In reality, we have limited understanding of the male gender, including past habits, practices, and experiences amongst the many *different* groups of men and women who have engaged in constructions and negotiations of images of masculinity. Krondorfer contends that men's studies is a "slippery category" that requires a fine reading behind and between the lines of the sources. Ironically, then, we might have asked the wrong questions, mistaking men as unmarked beings. In a sense, men's lives, narratives, and experiences have been hiding in plain view from us.[6]

In her revealing, interview-based study, Nechama Tec writes, "The Germans put ... almost impossible challenges in the fulfillment of [the role] of the breadwinner. When Jewish men found themselves unable to do what traditional society expected of them, they frequently became demoralized and depressed."[7] References to the Jewish male experience and to Jewish masculinity, however, typically do not transcend brief anecdotal excursions. As a result, the few references to Jewish gender during the Holocaust have taken on a myopic and distorted character, and conclusions pertaining to Jewish men and masculinity in the Third Reich remain tenuous, a desideratum that the following study hopes to partially fill.[8]

The field of men's studies is heavily indebted to feminist theory and scholarship. In the following chapters, German-Jewish masculinities are conceptualized as an identity configuration established through processes of identification and differentiation. Signifiers like cultural symbols, social practices, and physical bodies connote masculinity in relation to femininity. Such configurations are embedded as cultural norms as well as social practices and relationships of power. Because definitions of masculinity are dependent on understandings of femininity, and vice versa, it is essential to incorporate definitions of femininity as well as women's views and their contributions to constructing masculinities. Gender is a concept of difference, always preoccupied with the instability in power relations between and within the sexes. German-Jewish men's (often self-perceived) erosion of male authority and change in status in the years 1933 to 1941 was no different, as it occurred in a social context of power relations that only acquired meaning in the presence of women and other groups of men. German-Jewish men's gradual loss of control over their own and their families' lives signified a loss of authority and created feelings of powerlessness that were intricately linked to conceptions of masculinity. As a relational category, however, gender does not exclusively rely on a masculinity-versus-femininity formula. Alternative, competing configurations *within* one gender also produce inequality. Masculinities are multiple and variable, and their formative processes are ongoing. In the Third Reich, Jewish men constituted their sense of Jewish masculinity by orientation to an elusive yet manifest mainstream masculinity, something George Mosse calls "stereotypical masculinity."[9] Within German society, masculinity was increasingly defined by racial doctrines, by physical markers such as strong bodies, and by the cultivation of a militarized type of masculinity evinced by the celebration of values like bravery, discipline, and obedience. At the same time, previous definitions of masculinity, featuring monogamy and heterosexuality, for instance, were sustained.

Thus, to understand the evolution of German-Jewish masculinities, one needs to understand prevailing concepts of non-Jewish masculinities as well.[10] As Michael Kimmel and Michael Messner phrase it, "Men are not born. They are made."[11]

Hoping to remain part of such an imagined hegemonic community that defined ideal manhood, Jewish men were marginalized, pushed to the edge by implicit and explicit attempts of the state, civil society, and other agencies of power in the Third Reich. All denied Jewish men their continued practice and adherence to hegemonic markers of masculinity. This marginalization occurred in a social context in which the state, the media, and society celebrated the creation of a *Volksgemeinschaft* – a people's community – that centre-staged the strong, healthy, and soldierly "Aryan" male and that made Jewish men feel especially excluded. The centre of attention in this study, therefore, is not a singular model of masculinity but the *processes* of marginalizing a loosely defined group of Jewish men who sought to resist their emasculation, and their reactions to this process, including acceptance, submission, and resignation, but also contestation, negotiation, and defiance.

Critics might say that the process of marginalization allocates considerable control to the state and deprives Jewish men – whose lives, it seems, were radically changed *by* the Nazi regime – of agency. This study, however, circumvents this caveat by incorporating Judith Butler's innovative theory of "gender performativity," which liberates the gendered subject, returning agency to the individual.[12] The multiple voices that take on a visible presence in this book demonstrate the heterogeneity of perceptions that German-Jewish men had and that pertained to the socio-economic, cultural, and political changes happening in the Third Reich. Moreover, these sources witness the remarkable resilience and restraint German-Jewish men exhibited, trying to sustain or regain control over their and their families' lives. Giving a voice to these actors of the past eschews another construction of Jews as passive victims of Nazism. Yet, creating a patchwork of myriad excerpts of Jewish men's records and their attempts to sustain a normal life brings with it the risk of overemphasizing individual agency. Performance of a gender is compelled by norms that none of us choose. We work within the norms that constitute us as individuals. These norms are the condition for our agency, but they also limit our agency.[13] As Butler has made clear, performance does not mean "that the meaning of the performance is established by the intention of the actor – hardly. What are being performed are the cultural norms that condition and limit the actor in the situation."[14]

Thus, German-Jewish men unveiled an array of different responses, with their actions being largely performative, and thus part autonomous and part preprogrammed. When Jewish men, for instance, resorted to behaviours of demonstrating their Germanness in 1933 by visibly showcasing their World War I medals or publicly referencing their war contributions, they chose to do so voluntarily. At the same time, Jewish men relied on pre-existing and embedded socio-cultural norms and values over which these individual men had little control. German-Jewish men were the products of their time and place, and their demonstrations of military masculinity (see chapter 1) were a direct reflection of the prevailing socio-cultural milieu.

Even though gender analysis comes to fruition only in relational contexts, with multiple conceptions of femininity and masculinity at all times working with and against each other, other categories – most notably race, class, and ethnicity, but one needs to add age as a category as well – are equally crucial. The working definitions for categories such as Jewishness, Germanness, class, and age are the following: for the first, definitions of Jewishness, this book relies on Harriet P. Freidenreich's categorization of Jews as religious Jews, whom she calls "Jewish Jews" or pious Jews; less religious Jews, whom she refers to as "just Jews" or Jews who would attend the synagogue only on important religious holidays; and "former Jews," who had once belonged to but left their Jewish communities, but whom the Nazis, nevertheless, classified as Jews.[15] Jewish men of all three groups are subject to this study, though the majority of men this study looks at belonged to the second and third categories, as highly assimilated German Jews. It will become evident that while for some men their gender identity intersected with their religious identities, for many their Jewishness was primarily a category that the perpetrators used and that had less direct impact on their gender identity.

In terms of citizenship, the author will look at German-Jewish men who identified themselves as German subjects, regardless of their formal status. For instance, east-European Jews who had moved to Germany in the early twentieth century (and who would have fought on the German side during World War I) but who technically lacked a German passport are included along with German Jews who did possess official documents. Class, too, could strongly vary in contextual importance. While the struggle of upper-middle-class men to maintain their socio-economic positions might have been more pressing and humiliating than it was for lower-class Jewish men, in terms of military masculinity, for instance, Jewish men demonstrated their national belonging and pride for their country regardless of economic background, and class thus seemed to be of lesser importance. Finally, age is of essential importance, a persistent blind spot in Holocaust historiography, as

Doris Bergen has pointed out.[16] Judith Gardiner rightly argues that gender should always be understood developmentally in terms of change over the life course and in historical rather than in static terms.[17] While some Jewish men could share a unifying war memory that transcended class barriers, their commemoration was evidently exclusive to a certain age group. Many of the men in this study had reached their status as "full men" by the time the Nazis came to power; they were established in social and economic terms, were married, had families, and had previously adopted a militarist-nationalist canon of values that they had internalized in the war and the army. For these men, of the generation born at the end of the nineteenth century, it was undoubtedly more challenging to let go of their accomplishments and harder to contemplate emigrating from Germany.

Only if partnered with other signifiers is gender capable of highlighting a diversity of and inequality in social relations and practices. Therefore, in order to write an integrated history, I utilize gender as a category of intersectionality that conceptualizes the oppression of Jewish men in the Third Reich not exclusively as gendered subjects but as men with a cumulative identity in which the categories of nationality and citizenship, their religiously/racially defined Jewishness, as well as their class backgrounds and age, are all indispensable.[18] Thus, masculinity, like gender in general, strongly intersects with other categories of identity and only in a glued-together fashion can it offer us valuable insights into people's past lives. As R.W. Connell argues, in order to understand gender, we must constantly go beyond gender.[19]

Though this study's goal is to construct a "messy" canvas of complex and intersecting categories of identity, it is, as Elissa Mailaender has pointed out, a real challenge to simultaneously investigate the politics of femininities and masculinities within and between classes, ethnic groups, and sexual orientations.[20] To keep this project of a manageable scope, and also because of the scarcity of sources on sexual matters, the book does not extensively address German-Jewish male sexualities including homosexuality. Sexuality was a common taboo in men's narrativities, especially in the prewar years when Jewish men tended to (re-)construct normalized lives (that would include normative – yet absent in the sources – sexual relations), since they were either not (yet) segregated from their spouses and women in general (as they would be later on in the camps during the Holocaust) or were not (yet) subjected to sexualized forms of violence in the camps. Because of this, I consider this a study of cultural constructs of and social experiences by German-Jewish men, including their contested gender roles in a vibrant, complex matrix of power relations within German Jewry and vis-à-vis the

Nazi state. As sexualities did not dramatically change in the prewar years for most German-Jewish men, the sources this study has looked at are relatively silent compared to women's camp narratives from the time of the Holocaust. German-Jewish male sexualities in the prewar years, including homosexuality, thus remain a desideratum that yet needs to be filled.

In the following chapters, the author hopes to maintain a balance of scholarly breadth and depth. This study explores German-Jewish masculinities in case studies by contextualizing and historicizing German and German-Jewish masculinities, often inflected by racist and antisemitic discourses, that had emerged and been consolidated in the nineteenth century. The following chapters thus strive to cover a chronological as well as a thematic range of topics that examine German-Jewish military masculinity (chapter 1); Nazi antisemitism and propaganda in the realm of Jewish sexuality and race (chapter 2); the bourgeois concept of work masculinity (chapter 3); Jewish men as husbands and fathers (chapter 4); street violence and its ramifications outside the Nazi concentration camps (chapter 5); and Jewish men's adaptation to and survival in Nazi prewar concentration camps (chapter 6). To realize adequate breadth and depth, this study follows a methodological approach of simultaneously working on three different layers: the cultural level of discourse and ideas; the level of legal and social practices; and the level of individual subjective experiences, perceptions, and identities.[21]

On the cultural-discursive front, the gendered nature of discourses, texts, and propaganda images by Nazi racial "experts" and newspapers, which, for instance, elaborated on Jewish men's alleged abnormal sexuality and their criminality in defiling the German race pool, are examined. On the second level, the focus will be on the legal and social implications of such cultural productions. For instance, the discursive questioning of Jewish men's military masculinity in newspapers and their portrayal as alleged cowards and physical weaklings led to their *de jure* exclusion from the Wehrmacht as well as the closing of the Jewish veterans' organization. The underlying methodology of this work hopes to demonstrate that it was not discourses and words in the media alone that affected (or not) Jewish masculine identities but the conversion of ideas into practices by the state. Above all, however, the focus of this study is on the third, subjective level of personal experience as recorded in short-term accounts (diaries) and long-term memories (memoirs) of Jewish men and women. It examines Jewish men's and women's reactions, adaptations, and contestations of the cultural-discursive and social-legal intrusions into the existing gender order of German-Jewish masculinity.

Diaries and memoirs occupy a position of importance in this study, though with an inevitable caveat: this study realizes that it relies on written texts that overrepresent certain groups. Diary writing has traditionally been a middle- and upper-class exercise in which proletarian, blue-collar workers tended to less engage.[22] To counter an ensuing hyper-focus on class-based sources, the author has made wide use of memoirs that were often written decades after the events and were thus usually written by elderly men and women less determined by their class background who hoped to pass on their life stories to their descendants. The use of both diaries and memoirs has yielded invaluable information about a cross-section of German Jews of all ages and different classes who lived in the Third Reich.[23]

The following discussion seeks to establish a more differentiated picture and to paint a wider canvas of the Jewish male experience and gender negotiations in the Third Reich than has hitherto been available. Accordingly, this study argues that in their attempt to defy emasculation and maintain ties to hegemonic norms and practices of masculinity, German-Jewish men experienced a profound marginalization of their masculinities while simultaneously exhibiting considerable degrees of resilience and agency. Subject to gender-specific hardship and suffering, Jewish men were and perceived themselves to be emasculated; but such configurations were momentary, situative, and shifting. Jewish men could act despairingly, as historians have suggested; yet the anecdotal evidence of this book shows that many German-Jewish men were equally capable of adaptation, negotiation, and individual practices of resistance in order to perform, albeit in different ways, a degree of manhood.

Chapter One

Unsoldierly Men? German Jews and Military Masculinity

We have to fight with all our energy against the odium of cowardice and weakness that is cast upon us. We want to show that every member ... is equal to every Christian ... in any physical exercise. Physical strength and agility will increase self-confidence and self-respect, and in the future, nobody will be ashamed of being a Jew.[1]

As part of the process of morphing into a nation-state in the nineteenth century, the various German states professionalized their militaries. The idea of a civilian army consisting of conscripted young males was intricately tied to modern conceptions of citizenship. Enlightenment philosophy of the eighteenth century viewed the (male) individual no longer as a passive subject who needed governance by absolutist monarchs or an infallible clergy but as a participant in a state that required the citizen's active contribution for it to prosper. As a quid pro quo, European states began a process of granting men some gender-exclusive citizenship rights in return for their military service.

Over the course of the nineteenth century, the German state militaries increased their visibility and importance in society. As Ute Frevert has argued, the revolutionary message of conscription was the blurring of borders between the military and civilian spheres.[2] Men's mandatory service in the army – often following years of attending cadet schools – resulted in a type of military socialization in the barracks that affected the structures and mentality of civil society at large. As the young male conscripts entered the barracks for one to three years, they began to learn military values that they later would carry into civilian life and that would have a sustained socio-cultural effect. Recruits were taught discipline, punctuality, orderliness, respect for the law, courage, valour, stoicism, and strong will. Through the state's introduction of the symbols, rituals, and language of national belonging, such as the Iron Cross (a military award medal), a cult of the fatherland developed that, according to Karen Hagemann, culminated in a new and heightened nationalism.[3]

Military service not only correlated to the concept of citizenship but also had significant ramifications in the realm of gender relations. As part of a character-building exercise, the conscript entered the barracks as a young man and left as a "complete man," a matured citizen who was prepared for an adult male life. Military service thus created within German men a sense of national belonging and political importance and significantly contributed to the construction of military masculinity.[4]

Seeking social inclusion and acculturation as well as economic improvement, starting in the late eighteenth century the majority of German Jews had come to accept and aspire to the idea of emancipation and notions of German citizenship (*Bürgertum*) with the full palette of commensurate rights and duties. This included acceptance of conscription and participation in the citizen army. For German-Jewish men, the army became a keystone in their civil and gender identity.[5] German citizenship was constructed as a privilege to be earned rather than a right of birth.[6] In the Austro-Hungarian Empire, the law stipulated that men could not vote until the age of twenty-four and first had to fulfil their military service. The law rested on the motto "Duties first."[7]

German Jews, particularly the more secularized elements, accepted the idea of an exclusively male sphere of the military. German Jews internalized the discourse of serving in the military in the hope of proving (and improving) their physical aptitude as soldiers and, more importantly, their worthiness as German citizens.[8] Gregory Caplan has termed the Jewish entrance into the military sphere, something traditional Jewish orthodoxy had long rejected, as the highest form of Jewish acculturation.[9] This longing for social inclusion and acculturation was reciprocated by calls from non-Jews who demanded that Jews partake in fulfilling civic duties. As the writer Ernst Schaeffer, for instance, claimed in 1897, "Military recruitment is needed, so it is in the interest of Jewry itself to eagerly fulfil the duty of the soldier: obligation to itself and the German state by taking full advantage of the military as a school of masculinity."[10]

The Jewish adaptation to and construction of military masculinity, however, did not originate in an uncontested vacuum, detached from other cultural and social developments in German society. While German Jews had tried to find ways of acculturating to a "military spirit" that Nahum Goldmann defined in his *Der Geist des Militarismus*[11] (1915), since the late eighteenth century non-Jewish politicians, scholars, and

Figure 2. An early nineteenth-century antisemitic postcard from Germany that belittles a Jewish male (left corner), questioning his physical aptitude to join the military.

writers had long begun to raise doubts about Jewish suitability for the military. Some codified Jewish men as unmanly and effeminate. Indices for neurological disorders (nervousness, hysteria, passivity, cowardice) as well as physical features (flat feet, small composition, obesity, and weak stature) placed Jewish men in a corner with women (Figure 2).[12] The pamphlet *Israel im Heere* (1879), which appeared in several editions, reported that

> Jewish men lack bodily strength and active temperament ... Their entire skeleton is defective. The breast is not broad and is arched, shoulder not straight and flat, neck and head not upright ... It is an annually recurring affair that the Jews offer a much smaller contingent of usable military recruits than the rest of the population, and they make up a highly disproportionate fraction of those who cannot complete marches and maneuvers ... Such physical inferiority is rarely the foundation of warrior-like bravery.[13]

By the turn of the century, antisemitic caricatures had become a strong weapon in influencing attitudes towards Jews. Particularly following Germany's defeat in World War I, accusations of Jewish war shirking manifested themselves among conservative, nationalist associations. Authors such as Alfred Roth, who under the pseudonym Otto Armin wrote *Die Juden im Heer* (1919), or periodicals such as the *Kreuzzeitung* repeatedly accused German Jews of not having participated as staunchly in the war as German Christian men had done (Figure 3).[14]

Figure 3. A caricature from the Austrian newspaper *Wiener Arbeiterzeitung* depicting a demasculinized Jewish male dressed in women's clothes, 1919. The image insinuates that Jews were cowards and war shirkers and thereby betrayed the German-Austrian nation.

In the postwar era, a common antisemitic trope orbited around the idea of the Jewish traitor who had backstabbed the German nation; such disdainful use of scapegoating lingered into the years of the Third Reich. In his 1925 *Mein Kampf*, Adolf Hitler charged Jews with having avoided front line service entirely: "Nearly every clerk was Jewish and nearly every Jew a clerk."[15] The amalgam of national citizenship, masculine gender identity, and militarism started to disintegrate for Jewish men at a time when military values began to recapture social momentum in the late 1920s with a burgeoning Nazi party.

The marginalization of Jewish men in the cultural-military realm was, however, not a field left uncontested by German Jews. Starting in the late nineteenth century, Jewish associations such as the *Centralverein Deutscher Bürger jüdischen Glaubens* (Central Association of German Citizens of Jewish Faith) had taken it upon themselves to respond to the various discourses and imageries of Jewish military ineptness. Jewish men, in response to antisemitism prevalent in places such as universities, founded their own Jewish student fraternities and thereby carved out their own sites to perform military masculinity through, for instance, the act of dueling.[16] Some Jewish intellectuals and reformers such as Max Nordau (1848–1923), who coined the term *Muskeljudentum* (muscular Jewry), saw it as imperative for Jews to physically and morally regenerate through athleticism and thus counteract the antisemitism of the day. As a result, German Jews established their own clubs and chose names of Jewish war heroes from antiquity like *Bar Kochba* (a Jew who had revolted against the Roman Empire). These male-exclusive associations were used for regenerating the Jewish body, especially for the youth, and cultivating a martial manliness characterized by the soldierly values of bravery, courage, and aggression.[17]

Many German men, including Jewish men, had come to pride themselves on their participation in military training and service, even after the war was lost in 1918. For an entire male generation, the military had become a school of life, a point of identification that men would carry with them in their post-military civilian lives including in the Third Reich.[18] Nationalism and masculinity had become deeply entangled in Germany.[19] Like Gentile men, Jewish men viewed military accomplishments as proof of their manliness, which in turn demonstrated their worth as Germans. One's military record and its associated symbols were codified as means to the end of amalgamating military masculinity, Jewish identity, and German citizenship.[20]

The Nazi State and the End of Jewish Military Masculinity, 1933–1941?

Beginning in 1933, the Nazi state intensified efforts to dishonour and marginalize German Jews by "demilitarizing" them. While in the immediate postwar era accusations of Jewish war-shirking might have attracted, appealed to, and satisfied certain segments of society – such as the disillusioned war veteran who had joined one of the many conservative-völkisch associations – in the Third Reich, with a renewed emphasis on the military as a socially important institution, antisemitic propaganda became canonic.

Censored newspapers launched blunt attacks on Jewish men's wartime service (Figure 4). Under the title "Jewish Frontline Soldiers?," the *Völkische Beobachter* pursued this theme in April 1933:

> Front soldiers. This is the newest catchphrase … Suddenly, all Jews are frontline soldiers. We old war veterans know that the Jews … even in their military units were most of the time behind a desk, employed in logistics (*Baggage*) … If they had the bad luck of being temporarily stationed at the front, they generally spent very little time there, but found themselves sooner or later further behind the front or even at home (*Heimat*). The fact that a few Jews died at the front is certainly not an extraordinary merit of the Jewish race. After all, there was general conscription and not every Jew was able to shirk … Some even had the ambition to become an officer and then move up into a better position at home. In this time, Jews did not only enjoy all the same rights as German citizens, but also procured additional major privileges … But we will have even less use for the people of Moses in the defense of our German soil than in the world war …
>
> These are Jewish frontline soldiers? Let's not fall for the old trick of the Centralverein with its pamphlets "Jewish war veterans," "Jewish physicians," "Jewish intellectuals" … Now everyone is a war veteran; now they fetch their Iron Crosses which they had illegally acquired (*erschoben haben*). Now they pride themselves in their war wounds and the dead in order

Figure 4. An antisemitic caricature from *Kladderadatsch*, 1934, showing a World War I memorial to the ten million dead of World War I. Two male Jews stand beneath. One says: "Why shouldn't we risk a war? We won't have to fight in it."

to capitalize on them ... It is impossible to determine who the few Jewish war veterans, based on Aryan blood mixing (*Blutvermischung*), were ... For fifteen years they have spit on (*bespieen*) war service, scorned it and dragged it into the mud.[21]

Literary and graphic assaults like the one by the *Völkische Beobachter* intended to disparage German Jewry *in toto*. However, the specific accusations that Jews had not contributed importantly to the German war effort and should therefore not be included in the German *Volksgemeinschaft*, the people's community, had strongly gendered connotations. The lack of military virtues made Jewish men into war shirkers, cowards, and traitors. Because of their "un-German" character, German-Jewish men were denied Germanness, and repudiation of their contributions in World War I made *all* Jews decidedly un-German. The tale that Jewish soldiers had spent most of the time in the war behind desks or even at home suggested that Jewish men intrinsically shared a sphere with women that some Gentiles considered female. The desk was used as a metaphor for menial, secretarial work that was considered especially suitable for women. The metaphor alluded to the notion that war-making was a male honour and responsibility, while living a safe distance apart from military action was a privilege reserved for women, children, and the elderly – one that was misused by the Jews. When the Nazis could not avoid acknowledging Jewish combat service (which German Jews repeatedly pointed out by show-casing war medals and the like), the argument was made that Jews had only self-interest but not the nation's interest at heart.[22] The Nazis chose to attack and degrade German Jews where Jewish men felt most emotional and were culturally most vulnerable, the cultural realm of military masculinity.

The rise in cultural marginalization of Jewish men coincided with attempts to imbue military norms and values in German society. The Nazis reinvigorated such attempts in the 1930s and idealized the German male as the global standard of the model soldier. The masculinization of social role models resulted in the grouping of male soldier-heroes who were presented as the manliest of men.[23] Raewyn Connell has outlined that the Nazi regime was strongly gendered and, in its public face, intensely masculinized: "National Socialism presented to the world a seamless front of dominant masculinity: hard, decisive, armed, modern."[24] In the Third Reich there was an increased presence in the German media of the Aryan male body with strong connotations of physical prowess and militarism.[25] The new images of the ideal German male as a man of action and deed, of aggression and force, had developed into a conformist tenet of militarist values and part of the general cultural norms in the Germany of the 1930s.[26] The new hero was the SA trooper and the Wehrmacht soldier (Figure 5).

The militarization of society coincided with legal steps to emasculate Jewish men, in addition to the discursive efforts of ostracizing Jews. The Nazis excluded Jews from all things military. In March 1935, Hitler reintroduced mandatory conscription for men. With the founding of the Wehrmacht, German Jews were by law excluded. Despite some major protests, the Nazi state remained steadfast in its attempt to thereby dishonour and emasculate Jewish men. Because the Nazis paid great attention to military traditions and symbols, the newly founded Wehrmacht was propagated with much media fanfare and propaganda. The rejection of Jews was especially humiliating to Jewish men who had come to identify with and internalize the military values of Wilhelmine Germany. Besides the ruling that German Jews – who were legally denied German citizenship following the Nuremberg Race Laws of 1935 – were not worthy of being part of a German national army, further discriminatory measures included prohibiting German Jews from possessing guns. The Gestapo and other local and federal police agencies argued that Jews with guns would endanger (*gefährden*) the German population.[27] The "untrustworthy" Jew was depicted as a potential aggressor – of course an illogical image that stood in contradiction to the image of the war shirker who was afraid of violence

Figure 5. A Nazi propaganda poster depicting military masculinity, date unknown, by Hans Schweitzer (who used the pseudonym Mjölnir). An SA man stands next to a soldier: "The guarantee of German military strength!"

and incapable of using a gun but one that nevertheless had an immediate and dramatic effect on German Jews. Even sabres and rapiers had to be surrendered to the police eventually.[28] Symbolically, Jewish men, who were denied the acquisition of new weapons while weapons they already possessed were confiscated, were emasculated. While the new German hero was the young male in SA or Wehrmacht uniform, Jewish men were made to look weak and defenceless, antonyms to the German ideal of military masculinity.

In addition to the physical exclusion of Jews from the military and the laws prohibiting Jews from owning weapons, the state used further symbolic ways to deprive German-Jewish men of military gender identity. During the *Heldengedenktag*, the annual commemoration of the fallen in World War I, state authorities forbade any Jewish participation and curbed the inscription of names of Jewish war casualties on memorials.[29] To the consternation of many Jews, Jewish names were even removed from existing war memorials.[30] Further regulations banned Jews from hoisting the German flag, another symbol of military importance. In 1936, the Jewish veterans' organization (*Reichsbund jüdischer Frontsoldaten* [*RjF*]), founded in 1919, could no longer associate itself with all things military. Other Jewish militarist-nationalist associations (though minuscule in membership numbers) that represented militarist and at times even fascist principles, such as the Black Squad (*Schwarzes Fähnlein*), the Association of German National Jews (*Vereinigung deutsch-nationaler Juden* [*VdnJ*]), the New Front of the German Jews (*Neue Front der deutschen Juden*), and the German Vanguard (*Deutscher Vortrupp, Gefolgschaft der Juden*), were banned outright.[31] Further rules outlawed the wearing of sport badges and wartime medals. Jews could no longer purchase hunting licences or explosives.[32] Through such concerted efforts, Nazi authorities turned this group of formerly proud German-Jewish war veterans, and the younger generation of Jewish men who through physical exercise and athleticism had adopted and internalized an equivalent militaristic ethos, into unsoldierly pariahs.

The Jewish Experience: Military Masculinity in the Third Reich

In their diaries and memoirs, many Jews started to observe the increased militarization of German society. In her 1930s diary, the physician Hertha Nathorff (1895–1993) of Berlin expressed her revulsion, noticing ever more proud Nazi soldiers walking around with their brides and naming Germans "a uniform-friendly people. Exercising and parading, this is the new time."[33] The businessman Walter Tausk (1890–1941) of Breslau also reflected in his diary that strong SA formations of eighteen-year-old "snotty-nosed brats" (*Rotzlöffel*) were marching every day with much fanfare and equipped with guns.[34]

Paradoxically, while some Jewish observers were evidently appalled, if not terrified, by a society that was armed to the teeth and that had just de facto legalized antisemitism, the majority of Jewish records rather testify to a welcoming of a newly reinvigorated German militarism. Most Jewish war veterans accepted the Nazi renewal of soldierly masculinity because many could directly identify with such images through their own previous experience in the army and find a compatible solution to sustain their Jewishness and German patriotism. The example of Julius Meyer represents the standpoint of many German Jews – men in particular. In his memoir, the author reminisced that many German Jews had stayed in Nazi Germany because of their deep-rootedness in Germany, a quality they and their ancestors had acquired and proven in military battle. Because of their identification with military and nationalist values, they simply could not leave Germany.[35] The literary critic and member of the Jewish *Kulturbund* (Cultural Federation) Kurt Baumann (b. 1907)[36] recalled that his father was opposed to emigration because he was certain he would be needed again in the next war.[37] The Breslau-based teacher and historian Willy Cohn (1888–1941) noted in his diary as late as 1939 that he was ready to fight for

Germany.[38] As Alfred Wolf (1898–1981), economist and businessman, remembered, "I lived in a country for which to fight I had given my parents sleepless nights, for which 12,000 Jews had been killed during action in the war 1914 to 1918."[39]

According to their own perceptions, having proven their loyalty, fulfilled their duty to the nation, and exhibited military virtues such as bravery and courage, Jewish ex-soldiers tried to preserve their accomplishments through an organized association whose influence would penetrate the general public. Through public acts of commemoration and attempts to educate the general public about the Jewish contribution in the war, the Jewish veterans' organization RjF (*Reichsbund jüdischer Frontsoldaten*), founded in 1919, actively sought to demystify antisemitic attacks and simultaneously construct an image of a Jewish soldierly masculinity. In the 1920s, the *RjF* had started to promote military values within the sports and youth organizations that were attached to it.[40] The members of the *RjF* believed themselves to embody a masculine ideal, and by incorporating the symbols and imageries of a Jewish military tradition into the discourse of German militarism they infused the German-Jewish commitment to self-improvement with the values born of service at the military front.[41] As Leo Löwenstein (1877–1956), former captain in the war and co-founder of the *RjF*, proclaimed, it was the highest goal to stand up as men to the challenge (*mannhaft die Stirn bieten*) and protect the honour of Jewish veterans.[42]

In the 1930s, the *RjF* expanded its scope, trying to represent the entirety of German Jewry. The *RjF* believed that the predicament that German Jews were in could only be solved through faith in military attitudes and virtues. For this reason, it launched a strategic publicity campaign, printing millions of pamphlets, postcards, and memorial books that listed German-Jewish accomplishments, including *Die Jüdischen Gefallenen des deutschen Heeres, der deutschen Marine und der deutschen Schutztruppen, 1914–1918* (1932); *Gefallene deutsche Juden: Frontbriefe, 1914–1918* (1935) (Figure 6); and *Heroische Gestalten jüdischen Stammes* (1937). This process of associating German Jews with the fatherland and their contribution to the German military and to the war effort reflected a continuity of reactions to antisemitic agitation. The *RjF* printed letters from the front, for instance, in 1935, following the establishment of the Wehrmacht and the concomitant exclusion of Jews from it. By publishing such works, the *RjF* and its members sought relief from their perceived humiliations. Holding on to cultural reference points – soldierly duty and honour – helped them to preserve a sense of national as well as gender identity. Felix Theilhaber's bestseller on Jewish World

Figure 6. The first two pages of *Gefallene Deutschen Juden: Frontbriefe 1914–18*, an anthologized collection of frontline letters written by German-Jewish men during World War I. It was published in 1935 by the Jewish veterans' organization *RjF*.

War I pilots, *Jüdische Flieger im Weltkrieg: Ein Buch der Erinnerung*, which had come out in 1919, was reprinted in 1935 in response to popular (Jewish) demand.[43]

Most significant, however, were the frequent articles published in the Jewish weekly newspapers, such as *Der Schild*. In them, the authors repeatedly referenced the military, World War I, and the Jewish contribution to both. In a general statement on the title page, Löwenstein wrote on 26 January 1934 that the *RjF* had learned that "every community, as its basis for its very existence, has the necessity for soldierly education in order to create a soldierly and disciplined spirit ... No regulation can stop us from avowing ourselves to the German nation and home (*Heimat*) for which we have risked our lives ..."[44] Clearly, the *RjF* and affiliated associations were active in the perpetuation of nationalist ideals that were meant to further a sense of national belonging of Jews in Germany. Through public acts such as their own commemorative ceremonies for the fallen soldiers,[45] the *RjF* constructed a German-Jewish identity that was meant to encompass and protect all Jews but that was closely based on the gendered conceptions of the masculine military ideal.

The efforts of the *RjF* shared many attitudes with other (liberal and integrationist) Jewish organizations and institutions. Influential liberal Jewish periodicals and newspapers with high print circulations, such as the *C.V. Zeitung*, echoed – albeit in a more muted tone and less frequently – acceptance of military values. In an article of 6 April 1934, the *C.V. Zeitung* asked its readers to remain steadfast and to persevere: "Our fathers have endured their fate with heroism and inner dignity.

Let us learn from them."[46] Even more explicit was the article a week later, arguing that

> in 1914 a German national unity had been forged; 100,000 Jewish soldiers participated in the war; 12,000 died; these were not single cases (*Einzelschicksale*) but proof of communal values (*Gemeinschaftswerte*) that all Germans shared. The duty to serve (*Wehrpflicht*) was the noblest expression of citizenship.[47]

Strikingly, the language of German nationalism, patriotism, and militarism was not a temporary phenomenon on the periphery of German-Jewish society but penetrated the mainstream of Jewish thought and social life. German Jews generated and then relied on a generational consciousness that was predicated on the utilizing of World War I memories. In the early years of the Third Reich, having served in the military was still considered an honourable, noble attribute that testified to Jewish masculinity.

Besides its media campaign to counter the increased marginalization of Jews from society, the *RjF* requested privileged treatment for its members by the German government. It directly advocated for its members by establishing a line of communication with German government offices and even with President von Hindenburg and Hitler. Its three goals were to prevent economic harm and maintain employment for its members; to prevent harm to the families of war veterans (including their children and spouses); and to advocate for a strong Jewish presence in the German military.[48] The first goal was realized through the intervention of President von Hindenburg when the Law for the Restoration of the Professional Civil Service was introduced in April 1933. The law mandated the forced dismissal of Jewish and politically unreliable civil servants, but exemptions were made for any veteran and civil servant whose father or son had been killed in the war. Clearly, preferential treatment of some groups of German Jews was legitimated by the elevated status that the Nazis still ascribed to Jewish men who were connected to the military.

To obtain such an exemption, was, however, a high hurdle to jump. The notary Karl Friedländer (b. 1882) remembered the confusion when the law came into effect.[49] The lawyer and notary Siegfried Neumann (b. 1895) recalled that the Nazis made it clear soon enough that in order to qualify for an exemption, the male candidate had to actually submit evidence of having participated in at least one actual battle (*Kriegshandlung*).[50] The construction of Jewish military masculinity was thereby instantly reaffirmed, while so-called Jewish war shirkers and "desk employees" who had worked in the army in administrative functions (even as physicians) were exempted from the exemption. Indoctrinated by their own propaganda, the Nazis probably anticipated that most applications for exemption would fail, as they presupposed that most Jewish men had not been enlisted in the army and certainly did not participate in any frontline battle. According to Saul Friedländer, however, the initial application of the civil service laws was "relatively mild." For instance, of the 4,585 Jewish lawyers and 717 judges in Germany employed in 1933, 3,167 and 336 respectively remained in their posts because of their military service records (or because they had been employed prior to August 1914).[51] Of the 5,000 or so Jewish civil servants, around half were able to remain in office.[52] The *RjF* gained further privileges relating to the second goal of protecting veterans and their families. For a number of years, veterans' children were exempted from the law against "overcrowding" in German schools. Peter Gay (1923–2015) recalled that because of his father's wartime service and injury, he was spared a dismissal in 1933.[53]

While the *RjF* could realize some temporary yet important gains, it could not reach its third objective. The establishment of the Wehrmacht in 1934 was met with rejoicing and ardent support from the more patriotic members of the Jewish communities in Germany. Hans-Joachim Schoeps (1909–80), founder of another pro-military, anti-Zionist Jewish organization and professor-to-be of religious history, stated with much pathos:

> We young German Jews feel compelled to express our satisfaction with this step. Just as our forefathers fulfilled their duty to the Fatherland in 1914–1918, so are we prepared today for military service, in loyalty to our motto: ready for Germany.[54]

As part of identifying with the military, the *RjF* again requested Hindenburg's support. Exclusion of Jews from the armed forces would deprive them of the greatest duty and the greatest right of the homeland, namely an education in toughness and a readiness to put everything on the line for the fatherland. With Hindenburg's death on 2 August 1934, however, Jewish veterans lost the one central figure in whom they had placed their faith. After the subsequent exclusion of Jews from the military, a number of protests were drafted. Repeated calls to allow Jewish youth into the army for them to perform the highest honourable duty (*Ehrenpflicht*) and to have the honourable right (*Ehrenrecht*) ultimately fell on deaf ears.[55] More than a thousand former Jewish officers wrote in a note of protest to the minister of war, Werner von Bloomberg, that their honour had been wounded, followed by a declaration of *willingness* to nevertheless serve again in the future:

> We do not want to push ourselves forward [*aufdrängen*] for the active military service that we are not entitled to, but to express that we are not going to drop the claim for future Jewish participation in the honourable duty in arms and, thereby, have the right for a dignified existence.[56]

As this quotation illustrates, there was an emphatic commitment to military masculinity, collectively performed and celebrated, amongst German Jews in the Third Reich. After the culmination of violence and aggression against German Jews during *Kristallnacht* in 1938, however, most Jewish organizations and institutions were dissolved. The *RjF* was one of the very last ones permitted to exist, but it was no longer allowed to engage in active politics or in the education of youth; as its last function, it was restricted to the care of war casualties and the maintenance of Jewish cemeteries, even after deportations had begun in 1941.[57] As a sign of resignation but perhaps also of defiance, the *RjF* proclaimed its intention to continue to cherish its soldierly ideals and beliefs by remaining in a state of defence without bearing arms (*Wehrhaftigkeit ohne Waffen*), and to protect the community, despite the weakening of the organization. As it stated in 1938,

> With failure, an internal emigration now is recommended. The German Jew has to experience the restriction of military service (*Wehrbeschränkung*) imposed upon him as a soldierly test of character (*charakterliche Wehrerprobung*) in the deepest sense of soldiering: to act tightly (*straff*), faithful and trusting ... What we have always wanted is now expected from us: willingness to sacrifice, bravery, decisiveness and readiness for responsibility ... Integration and commitment for the community.[58]

The once 50,000-member-strong and confident organization (out of a total German-Jewish population of 525,000 in 1933) was reduced to symbolic insignificance.[59] Yet, the *RjF* constituted an important part of German-Jewish life in the prewar years of the Third Reich. The organization's *esprit de corps* encapsulated a nationalist flavour and praised a manly and soldierly spirit, demonstrating bravery, courage, decisiveness, and toughness of will, values to which all men in Nazi Germany were supposed to adhere. More than anything, the story of the *RjF* underscores how German Jews collectively – and initially quite successfully – negotiated with, protested against, and resisted the new regime; it also provides insight into a gendered analysis of German Jews, both men and women, who used the gendered identities of Jewish males as self-understood patriotic military men, in the past and in the present, in order to maintain inclusion for themselves and their families and to resist their emasculation and marginalization. With the disappearance of a strong, centralized, and collective voice in the late 1930s, however, Jewish veterans and their families were increasingly left to themselves to make sense of and adapt to their new situations.

Through identification with military social values, Jewish men and women hoped to eliminate barriers of religio-racial difference that the Nazis were (re-)creating. Even though a collective organization such as the *RjF* could have a decisive impact on Jewish everyday life and could use its influence in the public sphere to steer public German opinion in the mid-1930s, processing the changes in their lives and making sense of the new order under Hitler was first and foremost an individual act that each and every German-Jewish person had to go through. As part of negotiating and reconstructing their sense of belonging to the German state, culture, and society, German-Jewish men and women relied on individual strategies, some of which were intended to prove their loyalty to the fatherland through men's past military contributions. Military accomplishments had mattered to several generations of German Jews who had grown up in the Wilhelmine period, who had become accustomed to military values, and who had experienced war itself. This tradition of values with its gendered ramifications did not simply represent a cultural residue that lingered on in the weekly beer-hall gatherings of some veterans' organizations. The military identity German-Jewish men cultivated was principally – while also affirmed collectively – an individual attempt to assign gender identity. Jewish military masculinity, therefore, transcended efforts by the *RjF* to live up to the standards of the military. Military masculinity (like gender in general) was part of one's public and private life, culturally expressed and physically embodied. Starting in 1933, it became an integral part of making sense of the Third Reich. According to the historian Judith Gerson, referencing service mattered because by doing so Jewish men hoped to secure their rights to citizenship and to bestow honour on them and their families. Military service, according to Gerson, represented "the pinnacle of acceptance as German men and German citizens – a definition of masculinity, which simultaneously linked national identity to gender identity."[60]

Two ways of referencing military masculinity stand out. Firstly, German Jews related to the military and military norms as part of a self-identification process. At a time of turmoil and uncertainty, many German Jews actively reminisced about their own military service and achievements as part of responding to and simultaneously defying Nazi threats and intimidation. By trying to preserve military masculinity as part of their identity, Jewish men constructed a self-image that helped them fend off, even deny, the divergent identity that the Nazi state imposed on them. Secondly, German Jews used military masculinity as way of affirming other men's masculine identities. Honour, status, and respect were often – as in the pre-Nazi years – assigned to individuals who had either served in the army or the war or who had come to demonstrate and exhibit military virtues. As displayed in letters, diaries, and memoirs, assigning military masculinity to themselves and others was one of the most common and visible response strategies German Jews utilized in the Third Reich.

Jewish men developed strategies to respond to Nazi intimidation and threats starting in 1933 by utilizing symbolic language and gesture to perform military masculinity. Typically, such behaviours took the form of a direct reaction to a specific attempt by the Nazis to discriminate against Germany's Jews. On 1 April 1933, the Nazis staged a nationwide boycott as one of their first efforts to ostracize German Jews, intimidate them, and hurt them economically. Placing paramilitary units, typically SA men, in front of stores and businesses, desecrating shop windows, intimidating passers-by and customers from entering into Jewish-owned stores, as well as verbally and physically injuring Jewish store owners were all part of the April boycott.[61] In response to the boycott, many Jewish businessmen decided to open their stores on 1 April. In defiance, many store owners "stood their ground" and displayed, only weeks after the Nazi seizure of power, some of the military attributes that German society had to come to internalize for decades: bravery, courage, steadfastness, and perseverance.

Many decided to "decorate" their stores with war memorabilia, displaying sabres, rapiers, knives, and other personal war memorabilia in their store windows. Others wore the war medals that they had been awarded in World War I, including the Iron Cross and other honorary military badges. Edwin Landau (b. 1890) of Deutsch-Krone, western Prussia, vividly recalled the day of the boycott:

I took my war decorations, put them on, went into the street and visited Jewish shops where at first I was also stopped. But I was seething inside and most of all I would have liked to shout my hatred into the faces of the

barbarians ... This land and this people that until now I had loved and tre-
asured had suddenly become my enemy. So I was not a German anymore,
or I was no longer supposed to be one ... I approached ... one guard whom
I knew and who also knew me and I said to him, when you were still in
your diapers, I was already fighting out there for this country.[62]

Born in 1925, Fritz Ottenheimer grew up in a family that owned a
textile store in Constance. He remembered his father's reaction on the
day of the boycott:

My father went to our little store one morning ... He saw trucks cruising
through Constance ... After my father had arrived at the store, he saw a
uniformed SA guard in front of the door. My father turned around, went
back home and returned ... with a little bag. This time he passed the
Stormtrooper and unlocked the door. He took the shirts, socks and ties out
of the shop window and spread out his World War I medals in their place.
He then stepped outside, stood next to the Stormtrooper and pulled up his
right shirt sleeve, exposing his war injury. He did not have to wait very
long. A number of people who knew my father's military record stepped
up to the Stormtrooper and explained that Ludwig Ottenheimer was a
good German, a disabled war veteran who had done more than just his
duty for his country ... More and more people arrived ...[63]

The journalist Max Reiner (1883–1944) recalled how some Jewish
store owners wrote in white letters on their shop windows the duration of their war service, the number of times they had been injured,
and the decorations they had received.[64] The businessman Erich Leyens
(1898–2001) went so far as to print a pamphlet to be distributed on the
day of the boycott:

I outlined the patriotic services of generations of my family to their
country ... I [also] had put on my old uniform with my war medals ...
[H]ere is what the local newspaper [the following day] wrote: "When people in uniform attempted to block the entrance to the commercial building of the firm Leyens and Levenbach, one of the owners, Erich Leyens,
a frontline volunteer and recipient of the Iron Cross First Class, put on his
field uniform and medals, placed himself next to the SA men and distributed the following leaflet: 'Our Reich Chancellor Hitler, the Reich Mini-
sters Frick and Goering have repeatedly made the following statement:
Anyone who insults a combat veteran in the Third Reich will be punished
with imprisonment. All three Leyens brothers served as volunteers on the
front. They were wounded and were decorated for courageous action.

Their father Hermann Leyens had been a volunteer in the fight against the Spartacists. His grandfather was wounded at Katzbach during the wars of liberation. With such a record of past national service, do we now have to be subjected to public humiliation? Is this how the fatherland today expresses its gratitude, by placing huge pickets in front of our door with the demand not to buy from our house? We regard this action, which goes hand in hand with the dissemination of slanderous accusations all over town, as an attack on our national and civic honor as well as a desecration of the memory of 12,000 German front soldiers of the Jewish faith who have lost their lives in action. Furthermore, we regard this provocation as an affront against every decent citizen. We do not doubt that, even today, there are citizens in Wesel who have the courage of their convictions, which Bismarck once called for, and exemplify German integrity which, especially now, stands steadfastly by our side.'"[65]

Such gestures of military masculinity were not exceptional in the early years of the Third Reich, nor were they limited to the boycott in April 1933. The Breslau teacher and historian Willy Cohn (1888–1941) confessed in his diary on 1 May 1933, one month following the boycott, that going to work was unsettling for him because he did not know if he might not be sent home again. So he stuck the ribbon of his Iron Cross through the buttonhole of his jacket: "Perhaps it is a good thing as a Jew to make a show of this right now."[66]

Even a few years after Hitler's rise to power, Jewish men clung to their military identities, which they thought corresponded to the masculine identities of mainstream Nazi society. In one of their many contradictory decisions, when the Nazi government decided in 1934 to introduce a further military decoration for World War I veterans, German-Jewish veterans were not excluded. Cohn wrote in his diary, "Submitted to the police my application for the Front Fighters' Cross!"[67] A few months later, in February 1935, Cohn did not have to think twice about visiting a Nazi government building to pick up the piece of paper that he *thought* partially (re)-established him as a man: "Went to the police station to receive the Front Fighters' Cross … the Police Chief gave a short speech in which he pointed out that wearing the Cross is an honor."[68] The merchant Alfred Schwerin (b. 1892) recalled that in the 1930s he too always wore his military badge because "all men are wearing some kind of badge."[69] The emblems served as markers for German-Jewish men, and through references to military service these men made themselves appear to conform to the general standard of identifying with the military, a process all German men were supposed to partake in. Even the rabbi of Hannover, Emil Schorsch (1899–1982), deemed it important enough in his memoir to remember the same recognition he received from Hitler's government in 1935.[70]

Jewish men widely practised making explicit reference to their military service, either in the public sphere through symbolic gestures like putting on their uniforms and medals, or in the more private sphere through the act of writing in a diary. Clearly, German-Jewish men constructed a mental map consisting of what they considered their previously established military honour, national citizenship, and gender identity, and the current crisis that threatened to deprive Jewish men of their intersecting identities. Because German Jews – represented by men – had participated in the war, had made significant sacrifices, had proven their loyalty to the fatherland, and had demonstrated courage and bravery as attested by war medal rewards, they anticipated in the early years of Hitler's reign that German society at large would (continue to) honour these deeds and achievements and, as a result, would respect them and their families as equal, fellow citizens. As Michael Geheran has stressed, these hopes often came true. Germans continued to acknowledge German-Jewish war contributions. Many non-Jewish veterans stayed in touch with their Jewish ex-comrades. Such a persistence proves that *local* relationships within communities between Jews and non-Jews could trump ideological considerations years into the Third Reich.[71] The performativity of military masculinity represented a binding agent that kept alive social relationships among Jewish and non-Jewish Germans.

It is striking that this paradigm of spontaneous reactions took place all over the country and included Jewish men of all ages, of different class backgrounds, and of different levels of religious observance. There was no planning, cooperation, or coordination among German Jews on 1 April. Public displays of military masculinity were not prescribed by an institution like the *RjF*. Reactions were typically single acts by individuals that in their totality, however, constituted a pattern of gendered behaviour. Upholding military norms and referring to military achievements testified that German-Jewish men and their families – in their own view – were honourable and respected citizens.

While these cases exemplify specific intent with a desired outcome, and some did indeed generate positive results, Jewish men also made assertions of military masculinity – at the time and in retrospect – in more prosaic ways and general contexts. Many still thought that as soldiers themselves they knew what it meant to face and endure danger. Through evoking military virtues such as perseverance, discipline, and stoicism, many Jewish men perceived the Third Reich as a storm to be weathered, a temporary predicament – similar to a war – which they would have to endure. The Königsberg lumber merchant Arthur Propp (1890–1965) recalled that "perhaps one could have seen the danger clearer if there had not been four years of war ... One was used to the immoral life. War and inflation had passed."[72] The neurologist Hermann Pineas (b. 1892), in his 1945 memoir, recalled that in 1933, as a wounded war veteran, he thought nothing could happen to him.[73] Clearly, German Jews' behaviour, attitudes, and judgments were shaped by, among other factors, their or their relatives' identities as military men. Because Jewish men, as cemented in their memory, had endured and persevered in times of crisis, with their lives at stake, many thought they had the prerequisites necessary to endure another "storm," while others presumed that, as deserving veterans, they would not be subjected to the Nazis' antisemitic laws.

The self-identifications with military masculinity and the concurrent attempts at normalization, however, did not simply frame Jewish men's symbolic responses to Nazi intimidation with the hope or intention of reversing the negative trends in German-Jewish everyday life. Jewish men used self-identifications, especially in the second half of the Third Reich, as expressions of frustration, helplessness, and despair. Juxtaposing past times when military service was performed and masculine honour and respect were gained to the present time in which the military value system was disintegrating for Jews, Jewish men and women voiced their disillusionment and incomprehension. In almost nostalgic passages, authors such as the language professor Victor Klemperer (1881–1960) portrayed World War I as a time of risking one's life but also of camaraderie and respect:

> I compare this dread of death with that in the field. This here is 1000 times more horrible. There it was at worst the field of honor, there I was certain of every assistance were I to be wounded ... It is a thousand, a thousand times more horrible than all my fear in 1915.[74]

Klemperer further noted: "I often tell myself that I was also in mortal danger in 1915. But here death threatens me in a more awful form." On 1 August 1942, he wrote, "Tomorrow, outbreak of war in 1914 ... what a decent business the last war was, how little it horrified me in comparison to this one." On 30 October 1942, he asserted, "It is unimaginably dreadful, not to be compared with any memory of Flanders, or any mortal fear I have ever experienced."[75] The elderly Albert Herzfeld also expressed his frustrations relating to a perceived loss of identity as a German-Jewish man. In November 1938, he grumbled that "I have defended my fatherland as a volunteer in the war, have endured all, but now I am not allowed to cast my vote. I cannot understand this!"[76] Klemperer's and Herzfeld's statements exemplify the connection between Jewish claims of citizenship, military service, and the construction of masculinity. As a man who had served for years in war and peacetime, Herzfeld considered himself an honourable German – a citizen-soldier of the type that had originated in the nineteenth century – who had fulfilled his duty and who deserved the full rights of any German citizen, including the right to vote.[77] A similar diary entry of disillusionment from Dr Max Cohnreich (1882–1949) read, "German Jews have not only offered their skill and knowledge but sacrificed their wealth and lives to the Fatherland and the Fatherland's thankfulness drove them after unspeakable cruelties, crimes, pain and torment fifteen years later into the wilderness!"[78]

Even years after the events, some authors juxtaposed their war services to the inconceivable injustice they had experienced under Hitler. Edwin Halle of Saarbrücken (1895–1967) complained in an appendix to his diary that after serving the fatherland he was "kicked in the butt," even though he too had received the honorary certificate from Hitler; only luck, he explained, saved him from the gas chambers, a fate even the bravest of his comrades who had been decorated with the highest honours faced as a reward for their services.[79] Joseph Adler (b. 1895) recalled in his memoirs that in the immediate aftermath of *Kristallnacht*, after his home had been destroyed by rioters,

> during my military stint in France, I saw much devastation. Houses and apartments that were destroyed by shell fire, burning, charred and scattered property, but such a picture of barbaric annihilation, I have never seen.[80]

German-Jewish men were products of their times, of the world they had grown up in. As a way of comprehending the violence they and their families were experiencing, many responded by making reference to military norms, norms that had previously guided their lives, provided orientation, and generated rewards in the form of reciprocated honour and status in society. This previously established frame of reference was used as a safety net, as a last resort, by Jewish men and women to reverse unjust treatment and reinstall the previous status quo that had guaranteed (at least some) level of integration and respect within German culture. In their growing desperation and state of incomprehension, German Jews made extra use of men's military identities. Juxtaposing the norms from a time when they had acquired social and cultural capital to the current (or subsequently remembered) time of

Nazi dictatorship allowed Jews, and men in particular, to express their protest and indignation. Trying to justify their gendered identities as military men or men who adhered to military norms, Jewish men used diaries and memoirs to express their profound frustration over being ostracized from German society and its commonly shared values, and their vague, implicit hope to re-enter it.

In addition to projecting military masculinity onto themselves, German-Jewish men assigned it to others, thus perpetuating the normative catalogue of military-like behaviours and values. Many sources describe how individual German-Jewish men reacted to Nazi discrimination by recalling their personal military history, while other memoirs and family accounts describe a family member (father, brother, son, husband, in-law) or close friend who also was a war veteran. Typically, such references are made in the context of describing the perceived unjust treatment of these individuals. Similar to self-identifications, references to others' military masculinity juxtaposed the victimization of the individual to his actual military merits and military identity. The referencing of military service and values was meant to return deserved honour and respect to the individual, a symbolic countermeasure to the attempted emasculation of Jewish men.

In his meticulously kept diaries, Victor Klemperer, an outgoing, well-known intellectual in Dresden, frequently described his personal encounters with others. Klemperer, who was a veteran but who as an intellectual had not associated with the military, sports, or even political organizations that celebrated military virtues, still habitually described the men he met based on the standards of military accomplishments. He labelled a Jewish physician in Dresden, Dr Katz, as someone who kept a World War I photo of himself in uniform, on horseback, wearing a monocle and the Iron Cross, First Class, in his waiting room. On another occasion, he wrote, "Yesterday at Marckwald's. There we met Bernstein, a scraggy man, in his 50s, corn merchant, ended up as a medical orderly in the war, now male nurse." Describing his female co-worker in the factory, he wrote, "My Frau Rudolph is a harmless creature. Her father fell in August 1914." In the cellar during an air raid on Dresden, Klemperer met a Mr Kautzsch, "an upright warden … former sergeant major (silver wounded-in-action medal, long decorations bar)."[81]

Klemperer's detailed descriptions related to people he hardly knew; however, in most memoirs and diaries, Jewish men and women made primary reference to family members who, endowed with military masculinity, were depicted in a more respectful, honourable fashion than individuals who were not associated with things military.

Already on the first page of his memoir, Ernst Hausmann (b. 1929) explained that

> We did not leave Germany because we were unpatriotic citizens. During World War, I my father had served four years at the front in the trenches around Verdun, France, and received the Iron Cross in recognition of his service to his country.[82]

The toolmaker Walter Besser (b. 1911) of Coburg remembered how honoured his father, a World War I veteran, felt when he was awarded an honorary military badge (*Frontkämpferabzeichen*) in 1935.[83] The family chronicle of Hans Wolfes (b. 1876), commissioned in 1936, read, "As in previous wars, the Wolfes family placed their sons at the disposal (*zur Verfügung gestellt*) of the defence of the fatherland during the World War of 1914–1918." The chronicle then lists all family members who had died on the "field of honour."[84] Harvey Newton (born as Hermann Neustadt in 1920 in Breslau) started his 1995 memoir with his birthdate and birthplace, followed by, still on page one, his father's military voluntary service in 1901.[85] Fritz Ottenheimer, born in 1925, began his history, also written in 1995, with his male relatives who had participated in World War I,[86] and the 2015 memoir by Zvi Aviram (born in 1927 as Heinz Abrahamson) states that,

> At the beginning of my memoirs, I would like to place the story of my father Arthur Abrahamson, who was a soldier in World War I. It is important for me to begin my memories this way ... After my father had committed himself to war and Kaiser for many years, as a sign of gratitude he received a kick in the butt (*Tritt in den Hintern*).[87]

Larry (Lothar) Orbach (1924–2008) recalled in his memoirs how his father in the early 1930s was the proud president of the local chapter of the *RjF* in Falkenburg and recorded that his father would never leave the house without his military badge. Once, his father even got involved in a pub fight in response to some antisemitic jokes. Larry remembered how proud he was to tell his mother about his father's "heroic deed" (*heroischer Kraftakt*).[88] All these cases demonstrate how family members, such as sons, were so poignantly affected by their fathers' past accomplishments, their enactments of military masculinity, that decades later they would still remember these episodes in their memoirs. Clearly, the self-identification of Jewish men as war veterans and adherents to a military code of behaviour in civilian life was echoed by others, including the friends and families of veterans and soldiers. These writers transported Jewish men's military masculinity into their memoirs and thereby reaffirmed these men's gendered identity in the eyes of their families or other acquaintances. They projected other men's military service into texts that helped consolidate those men's identities as German-Jewish men.

Importantly, this reciprocal process of reaffirming one another's gendered identity through military service was not only limited to men. Various primary sources indicate that military masculinity – as a constituent element of masculinity – was performed and demonstrated not only by men but also by women. The cultural constructions of gender are in a constant flux of reaffirmation and negotiation, and the cultural definitions of what it means to be a man (or woman) get internalized and reproduced by both men and women.[89] Thus, Jewish women, too, used the military as a gendered reference point for defining masculinity. While a few referred to themselves in masculine, military terms, such as the physician Hertha Nathorff, who called herself in her diary "a soldier in battle,"[90] much more common was women's practice of assigning Jewish men a degree of military masculinity. Marga Spiegel (1912–2014) remembered that during the Nazi years her family thought that because of her father's and grandfather's military service in World War I the family would not be harassed.[91] In her memoirs, the educator Elizabeth Freund (1898–1992) introduced her brother-in-law as a World War I officer decorated with the Iron Cross.[92] And Frieda Friedmann wrote the following letter, addressed to President von Hindenburg:

> I was engaged to be married in 1914. My fiancé was killed in frontline combat in 1914. Two of my brothers, Max and Julius Cohn, were killed in frontline combat in 1916 and 1918, respectively. My remaining brother, Willy, came back from the field, blinded in a hail of shrapnel ... In 1920, I married a disabled soldier with whom I live in a very unhappy union because of his handicap ... All were decorated with the Iron Cross for service to the Fatherland. And now it has come about in our Fatherland that pamphlets are being circulated in the streets, demanding *Juden raus*. There are public incitements to pogroms and acts of violence against Jews. We are Jews and did our unreserved duty for the Fatherland. Should it not be possible for your Excellency to bring some relief and to remember what the Jews, too, did for the Fatherland? Are these incitements against Jews courage or cowardice when the Jews constitute 1 percent of the 60 million inhabitants in the German state?[93]

In writing letters or remembering male relatives' contributions, Jewish women perpetuated the social standard of male honour through military achievement. The purpose of mentioning their relatives' military past was to retroactively assign to them the respect and acknowledgment that they deserved and thereby define them as reputable men in a situation of powerlessness. While some references were brief and limited to World War I, other women went into more detail, solidifying their men's military identity. Charlotte Hamburger recalled how in the 1920s her husband, the judge Hans Hamburger (1891–1953), belonged to a fraternity where he was able to create a sense of belonging, practise subordination (*unterordnen*) to the will of the group, and develop a martial spirit through fencing, all of which helped him to live a manly life (*betonte Männlichkeit*).[94] Statements like these demonstrate that military masculinity was equally internalized, accepted, and reproduced by (Jewish) women, who came to see an honourable man as someone who had succeeded in life. To these women, the men to whom they referred were manlier because they had already proven their manhood in the past.

Aside from discursively constructing military masculinity through their writing, women's attempts to validate men as warrior-like figures could translate into tangible results. Marion Kaplan illustrated how in the aftermath of *Kristallnacht*, in late 1938 and early 1939, Jewish women persistently negotiated on their husbands' behalf to secure their release from concentration camps (and subsequently from Germany). Some of these women utilized a gendered strategy of assigning their Jewish husbands, relatives, or friends a status of military masculinity, hoping it would ensure and expedite the men's discharge from imprisonment. Charlotte Stein-Pick entered the Nazi Party Headquarters in Munich on numerous occasions in 1939 to request her husband's freedom based on his status as a war veteran. Her actions implied that her husband, as a patriotic German, had made sufficient sacrifices for his country during the war and was therefore entitled to privileged treatment. Her actions further suggested that she considered her husband to be more of a man than other Jewish men, as her husband had participated in the war and thus deserved to be among the first to be released. More than anything, Stein's behaviour exemplifies the fluid state of gender construction. Masculinity was not a monolithic, one-dimensional form of ideal manhood. A plurality of masculinities existed; military masculinity, by definition, differentiated men from women, but also from other types of masculinity. In a sense, Stein implicitly validated the Nazi discourse of the effeminate man by the insinuation that the imprisoned Jewish men who had not participated in the war were less manly. This differentiation among groups of men (military men versus non-military men) is central to conceptualizing masculinity as a cultural construct that consists of multiple types that each contend for a dominant status.[95] As military masculinity had become hegemonic in the late nineteenth century and was even more elevated in the Third Reich, military masculinity was produced not only by the state and its organizations and institutions but by society as well. The militarization of society was a gender-producing process in which women and men equally participated.

Conclusion

The German military was of major importance to many Jewish families and individuals in the Third Reich. Some Jews and half-Jews (*Mischlinge*), as Bryan Rigg has shown, were even able to enter the Wehrmacht in the 1930s and hide their Jewish identities; a few thought it was so honourable to serve in the German army that they blatantly ignored the rampant antisemitism that was apparent in Germany.[96] While the cases of Jewish Wehrmacht soldiers may have been rare and exceptional, they still illuminate the military as an institution of social importance and the pervasiveness of military values within German society. For some time, Jewish men continued to be part of this trend of militarization in society, with many coming to accept Nazi foreign policy, the rebuilding of a strong army, and the promise of avenging the supposed injustice that had happened in Versailles in 1919. As war veterans and German nationals, many German-Jewish men and women identified themselves through men's military service and an adherence to military norms as equal members of society. The belief in such values had developed prior to 1933, but its importance increased after the Nazis' rise to power and continued even when German Jews had been deported to the East.[97] German Jews' performative reliance on military masculinity unfolded on two fronts: the collective, institutional level, embodied through the *RjF*, as well as the personal, individual front with German Jews responding publicly and privately to the antisemitic discourses that had developed in the nineteenth century and that saw Jews as unfit for the military. Jewish men and women had come to internalize the military value system and the gender construction of men as military-like and drew tangible benefits from it, including employment and other privileges or initial exemptions from getting deported.[98]

The story of Jewish military masculinity as part of gender identity construction and negotiation was never a static one, and it is clear that Jewish men's demonstrations of military masculinity were age-specific and especially resonated among members of the war generation, the

men and women who had previously internalized Wilhemine militarism and experienced a war. Moreover, adhering to a military value
system was performative and occurred in a larger social-cultural context that celebrated Germany's return to political and military strength
and that swayed many German-Jewish men to participate in this wave
of excitement. Thus, military masculinity gained performative meaning especially in the early years of the Third Reich when German Jews
still had hopes for a continued existence in Germany. Over time, however, with the continued economic, social, and cultural ostracization
that German Jews faced, incentives to hold on to the understandings
of military masculinity declined in frequency and importance. Demonstrations such as the ones on 1 April 1933 and subsequent calls for Jewish integration into the new army ceased after 1938. Franz Memelsdorff
(1889–1958) remembered that following his release from the concentration camp in 1938, he stopped wearing the Iron Cross medal.[99] Such
gestures reveal that the aspiration to sustain a membership in Hitler's
Volksgemeinschaft dissipated when it became apparent that no Jewish
existence was possible.

As the following chapters will demonstrate, however, even following
the decisive events of 1938, a spiritual presence of Jewish military masculinity continued as part of Jewish men's identity. During an air raid
on Dresden in June 1944, when truly one should have feared for one's
life, Victor Klemperer described a little band of people in the Jewish air
raid cellar, very few men among them:

> Cohn, Eisemann senior, Neumark chat to one another. Naturally about
> their war experiences 1914–1918. A grotesque conversation really in a
> Jew's cellar. But it goes without saying that each one of us is attached to the
> German army of the First World War ... with the same degree of passion.

Klemperer called it "the Jews' favorite topic."[100] What he meant was
the Jewish *men's* favourite topic.

Chapter Two

The Question of Race and Sex: Jewish Men and Race Defilement

By 1900, antisemitism had evolved from a religious-based ideology to one based on modern pseudo-science and racial discourse. To stigmatize, ostracize, and discriminate against Jews, the National Socialists invested considerable energy in canonizing some of the established textual and figurative variations of racial antisemitism. Using mass media, the Nazis hoped to increase an awareness of Jewish "otherness." This chapter examines one such antisemitic discourse: Jewish race defilement and the effects it had on Jewish masculine identity. The Nazis misused the Jewish male body and allegedly criminal mind to convince German society of a Jewish sexual-racial threat. At the same time, German Jews internalized and processed this Nazi form of branding, with some Jewish men even modifying their social demeanours. A conspicuous allegation in Nazi propaganda, a recurrent indictment in German courts, and an agonizing, personal experience of criminalization that many Jewish men faced, the theme of Jewish race defilement was one of the most visible motifs in the media and an essential element of antisemitism in the Third Reich.

Discourse and Race Defilement

European cultural constructions of normative manhood – measured by men's stronger muscle strength and willpower – classified men as the stronger sex, more active and with a potential of aggression. The militaristic society of fin-de-siècle Germany had defined masculinity in soldierly terms. After 1918, *Freikorps* members and politically conservative *völkisch* associations, as Klaus Theweleit has shown, continued in their belief in a German-soldierly masculinity that was defined by physical male prowess and aggression and the subordination of women.[1] Delineating his utopian masculinized state, Hitler wrote in *Mein Kampf:*

[M]y beautiful youth! Is there a more beautiful generation in the entire world? Look at these young men and boys! What material! It will be the foundation of a new world order. My education system will be hard. The weak must be hammered away. In my castle a generation of young men will grow up who will be the terror of the world. I want forceful young men majestic, awesome, and fearless, able to withstand pain, without weakness or gentleness. The free wild beast should stare from their eyes. I want my young men to be strong and beautiful. They should have a physical preparation in all sports. I want them to be athletic ... This way I have the pure material of nature in front of me.[2]

Hitler's idealization of a strong, physical masculinity echoed some of the scientific beliefs of the time that intertwined questions of proper sexuality with questions of racial and national health.[3] It was in this context, the constructed idealization of a bodily-soldierly masculinity as the epitome of racial health, that the image of the Jewish male as a non-normative man emerged. In an attempt to exclude Jews from public, male-exclusive institutions such as the military or the political realm, nineteenth-century antisemitic demagogues had predominantly relied on constructed and easily recognizable Jewish male profiles, stigmatizing them as unmanly, particularly because of their alleged military inaptitude (see chapter 1).[4] Common nineteenth-century anti-semitic stereotypes described and depicted Jews initially as the untrustworthy, extorting peddler (*Wucherer*), dressed in shaggy rags; later on as the obese banker, dressed in expensive suits; as the fully bearded *Ostjude*, caricatured in a religious kaftan dress, hat, and long black payot (sidelocks), frequently exposed as a homeless, filthy-looking wanderer (*Wanderer*); and as the seemingly assimilated urban intellectual, typically a journalist with horn-rimmed glasses or a physician in a doctor's coat. Yet, it was the Jewish male race defiler that would come to prominence in the Third Reich, and it was the sexualized imagery of Nazi propaganda that tangibly resonated in many Jewish and non-Jewish circles.

The sexualized form of antisemitism originated when modern science superseded the influence of religion, and Nazi ideology became inundanted with racist, völkisch subtexts. According to contemporary eugenicist schools of thought, the world consisted of different human races that competed for finite space and resources that were vital for a nation's survival.[5] For groups of the political right with dreams of German (imperial) dominance in the world, the question of Jewish "otherness" turned into one of racial distinction and medical importance because Jews represented an inherently different and irreversibly inferior genetic makeup.[6]

To make nineteenth-century antisemitic racism more comprehensible and popular, images and caricatures in particular were used, making the Jewish body recognizable and visible.[7] These images relied on such physiognomic features of the Jewish male as abnormally large hands, flabby lips, and noses and black curly hair and crooked posture, and depicted the Jewish body in unhygienic, dirty ways. Using artistic techniques for making the Jew distinguishable was, thus, an imperative, as antisemites had to circumvent the fact that most German Jews had long assimilated in dress, speech, and lifestyle to German society.[8]

The Jews' disordered outward appearance signaled, however, not only an inferiority in bodies and thus an unsuitability for joining the military but also a different and inferior Jewish mindset. Jews were regarded as un-German, alien to German national culture and traditions. Jews (and others), thus, were not only assigned a racially different body type, but perhaps more importantly, their characters and behaviours were also defined through race. In a highly polarized gendered context, Jewish men were questioned as to masculine virtues such as courage or hardiness, as analysed in chapter 1.

Combining scientific and racist sexism, notions of protecting the German nation by way of regulating sexual relations and preserving the racial purity of the nation satisfied medical experts, eugenicists, and antisemites alike. To justify the need for protecting Germany from within, an image of an internal threat was thus created. The notion of "Jewish ineptitude," propagated within military circles and expressed in caricatures, no longer sufficed. By 1900 Jews were increasingly portrayed as unbalanced and entirely controlled by their *eros*, their sexual lust.[9] Using the new medical interest in and knowledge of sexual matters, antisemitic writers classified Jews as sexually lecherous and driven by animalistic instincts. The writer Theodor Fritsch (1852–1933) in his 1897 *Antisemitismus Katechismus* defined the restriction of sexual intercourse with Jews as the most imperative of the "Ten German Commandments."[10] By the time the Nazis came to power, a discursive seedbed of racial antisemitism, intertwined with notions of Jewish sexuality, had been planted.

Nazi Propaganda and the Discourse of Jewish Sexuality

Trying to unveil and make "the Jew" visible, in order to persuade German society of a Jewish threat, antisemites before and after 1933 turned to discursive strategies that linked invented physical and mental

Jüdische Jagd auf Freiwild

Figure 7. An antisemitic caricature subtitled "Jewish Hunt for Women" that appeared in Kurt Plischke's 1934 book *Der Jude als Rassenschänder* [The Jew as a Race Defiler].

features to visual representations of the Jew. To legitimize their racism, Nazi propagandists, thus, demonized Jewish male sexuality, creating a metaphor of Jewish sexual threat and racial destruction of the "Aryan" nation, commonly referred to as race defilement. To visualize the invisible processes of racial degeneration and defilement, the Nazis came to rely on the effective use of imagery that annotated such processes by depicting exclusively Jewish men in an aggressive state (Figure 7).[11]

The Nazis defined "race defilement," *Rassenschande*, as the purported and perfidious crime by Jewish male "predators" who defiled the German race by lusting after blonde women, having sexual intercourse with them, and thereby mixing their inferior and putatively diseased Jewish blood with that of "Aryans."[12] As the Institute for the Study of the Jewish Question (*Institut zum Studium der Judenfrage*) claimed in 1939, there could be no doubt that Jews had a distinctively sensual lust of a sexual nature in their blood.[13] The message in Nazi propaganda depictions of Jewish race defilement, thus, was that a strong people like the Germans could only stick together, be strong, and survive if the people heeded the principle of protecting the most essential and basic element of their organism, their blood.

To educate German society about the Jewish sexual threat, the Nazis used a plethora of print materials. No other print magazine could rival Julius Streicher's *Der Stürmer* in its fervour to disseminate notions of Jewish race defilement. With persistent regularity, its caricatures indicated how centrally important race defilement had

Figure 8. An antisemitic caricature, "Legion of Shame," printed in 1935 in *Der Stürmer*. The caption reads: "Ignorant, lured by gold. They stand disgraced in Judah's fold. Souls poisoned, blood infected. Disaster broods in their wombs."

become in the Nazi mind.[14] The caricatures suggested a pervasiveness of race defilement by Jews, who did not single out specific women but targeted German women *in toto* (Figure 8). According to the Nazi author Kurt Plischke, author of the pseudo-scientific monograph *Rassenschande*, the list of tricks Jewish men used to defile women was extensive. Luring women into his luxurious car, for instance (Figure 9), the Jew was portrayed as a lecherous seducer going after innocent, beautiful women whose bodies he savagely raped and afterwards "discarded (*wegwerfen*) like a squeezed lemon," leaving them to their fate as infertile, worthless women in misery whose only remaining option was to prostitute themselves.[15]

Even in children's books, the Jewish male was illustrated as a sexualized threat (figures 10 and 11). Like other printed sources in the Third Reich, they had the common goal of stereotyping Jews, making them visually recognizable through their dress code, facial features, and gestures indicative of inherently evil behaviour. If the Germans did not heed the warnings by Plischke (and other Nazi "experts"), the message cautioned, the German nation would face an existential crisis, with infertile women of inferior, degenerate blood. To inhibit further racial

Figure 9. An antisemitic caricature, "The Beginning and the End," suggesting that Jewish males were sexual aggressors in the form of rapists and race defilers. This 1930 caricature was printed in the Nazi newspaper *Der Stürmer*.

destruction, Nazi propaganda made use of the most simplistic visual and textual language to make it easy for every German citizen to recognize a Jew by *his* looks and *his* behaviour (Figure 12).

In seemingly more scientific literature, such as *Rassenschande*, the author queried,

> Who does not know him, the oriental youth with his flat feet, dark curls, the cigarette in his flabby lower lips (*schlaffen Unterlippen*) under a crooked nose – dressed too colourfully, who with his brazen smiles wanders on the streets of the big city? He is lurking for blonde, young girls; once he has found one that is appealing enough for his oriental appetite, he starts his attack (*fest aufs Korn nehmen*).[16]

Following cake, fine liquor, and a visit to the cinema and a tavern, the Jew takes the girl to some cheap accommodation or the nearby park to do his deed. Plischke insistently cautioned German girls through words and images that if they did not listen to this warning, they would devalue themselves and forsake the greatest happiness that awaited all German women: motherhood (Figure 13).[17]

In order to embed a social awareness of the alleged Jewish crime of race defilement into German consciousness, the Nazi representations of Jewish men as rapists and race defilers needed to be a constant, unchanging theme, repetitively recurring in the papers, in the form of short articles with simple language, brief descriptions, and a clear appeal to emotions through exaggerated caricatures and graphic dramatization.[18] The pictures and photos thereby took on a performative and persuasive force.[19] They represented visual texts that were complementary to the written texts.[20] Particularly the emotional component was crucial. Antisemitic texts and images galvanized a sufficient number of Germans to bring their behaviours into line with the messages of Nazi propaganda. It became common practice for some Germans to denounce Jews, especially couples living in mixed marriages. The typical target was a Jewish

Hinter den Brillengläsern funkeln zwei Verbrecheraugen und um die wulstigen Lippen spielt ein Grinsen.

Figure 10. An antisemitic image suggesting that Jewish male doctors were rapists and race defilers. The image was printed in Ernst Hiemer's 1938 children's book *Der Giftpilz* [The Toadstool]. The caption reads: "Two criminal eyes flashed behind the glasses and the fat lips grinned."

Figure 11. An antisemitic caricature insinuating Jewish male sexual deviance in the children's book *Trau keinem Fuchs auf grüner Heid und keinem Jud auf seinem Eid* [Trust No Fox on his Green Heath and No Jew on His Oath] by Elvira Bauer, 1936.

man and sometimes a non-Jewish German woman – accusing both of race defilement and exposing them to social humiliation by making them march through the streets wearing self-incriminating signs (figure 14). According to Alexandra Przyrembel, cultural imagery and social experience were both part of a process of assigning shame to the victims that helped create feelings of enmity toward Jews within society.[21]

The Nazis hoped to achieve their goal of raising social awareness of the pathological and criminal Jewish male not only through the use of caricatures but by referring to real-life cases, commonly reported in local and national German newspapers (Figure 15).[22]

Antisemitic sexual discourses with their graphic imagery did not occupy a marginal presence in socio-cultural life, instigated by a few state-owned print magazines such as *Der Stürmer*, *Der Angriff*, or *Völkischer Beobachter*. Instead, the use of body images (*Körperbilder*) that Nazi antisemitism relied on became hegemonic.[23] The vilification

Figure 12. An antisemitic caricature in *Der Stürmer* labelled "Children drawing the Jew," 1938. The propagandized features in this caricature centre on the alleged phenotype of male Jews in an attempt to identify Jews in general.

Figure 13. A Nazi propaganda poster saying, "German Woman: Keep your blood pure. Foreign forces must not reach for you," 1944.

Figure 14. A staged photograph of Oskar Dankner with his alleged girlfriend, 1933. Both were subjected to public shame and forced to walk through the city of Cuxhaven wearing signs around their neck. Dankner's sign reads: "As a Jewish man [Judenjunge], I only take German girls to my room."

of Jewish male race defilers – among other antisemitic discourses – penetrated deeply into the media landscape of Nazi Germany and inevitably had a lasting effect on many readers and listeners.

The film industry, too, produced specifically themed antisemitic pro-paganda, camouflaging it as documentaries, of which *Der Ewige Jude* (Figure 16) was an example.[24] Entertainment films such as *Jud Süß* – which Saul Friedländer coined "the most effective of all Nazi anti-Jewish films" – further enhanced such monolithic images of Jews.[25] *Jud Süß* was popular, drawing more than twenty million viewers into the theatres. The scene in which the movie's protagonist, the Jew Süß Oppenheimer, rapes a young woman seems to have had a powerful effect upon the audience. Some people were so moved, according to Robert Herzstein, that after the show, they screamed curses at the Jews: "Kick the last Jews out of Germany."[26]

Key to the enforcement of racial legislation, as Robert Gelately has shown, was "the volunteered provision of information by the popula-tion at large about instances of disapproved behaviour."[27] A 1937 Ham-burg case exemplifies how far people's participation that the Nazis relied on went when a seventeen-year-old filed charges against an unidentified individual because he had witnessed a "Jewish-looking man with black hair, hooked nose and horn-rimmed glasses hug and take to his side a twelve-year-old girl."[28] Evidently, public participation

Figure 15. The Nazi newspaper *Die Nationalzeitung* of Gelsenkirchen printed this photograph of Julius Rosenberg, who was denounced for being in a relationship with an "Aryan" woman, in August 1935. The couple was subjected to public humiliation and persecution. Rosenberg's sign reads "I am a race defiler, J. Rosenberg," followed by his street address. His girlfriend's sign reads "I am a blonde angel and slept with this Jewish boy, Elisabeth Makowiak," followed by her street address.

and state propaganda were two sides of the same coin. Official antisemitic discourse reverberated sufficiently in society for it to take on a social dynamic of its own.

The impact of antisemitic racial-sexual propaganda in the Third Reich is telling not only for how it infiltrated social-cultural life in Germany but also for how it indirectly constructed an ideal image of proper non-Jewish gender norms. Depicting the Jew as a threat could only be effective and obtain contextual meaning if the Nazis could precisely define the side that was constructed as "normal" but threatened. Depicting Jewish men as threats reverberated with a general understanding of gender hierarchies in Nazi Germany. The sexually loaded graphics and texts connoted a gendered understanding of how the Nazis envisioned their patriarchal state. In the caricatures, the Nazis generally depicted German women as inherently helpless and in need

Figure 16. A film poster for the Nazi propaganda film The Eternal Jew, 1940. Visual markers of the Jewish male are striking.

of a male protector, who would faithfully provide for and protect his family. On the other hand, the behaviour of Jewish or non-Jewish men in using women only for their personal sexual pleasure, impregnating them, and then leaving them to their fate was disapproved of and socially condemned.

Paradoxically, while in military discourses (chapter 1) Jewish men were represented as effeminate, unmanly men who were inept at military service and thus not qualified to achieve military honours and respect, in the context of sexuality and race defilement, Jewish men were depicted and classified as hypersexualized and marked with a kind of animalistic, bestial aggression, strong will, and physical prowess. The German media cemented images of hypersexualized Jewish men in an effort to warn, even threaten, the public, and in particular unknowing youth and feeble-minded, easy-to-influence German women. The city of Konstanz, for instance, put up a poster at the Central Post Office in August 1933 with the following wording: "Christian maidens who consort with Jewish pigs will get photographed and published in *Der Stürmer*."[29] As Plischke elucidated in his book, "educating women is urgently warranted, as women [in 1934] are apparently still unaware of the menace of race defilement and what it could mean to them and their descendants."[30]

The hypersexualized images of Jewish male race defilers evidently challenged Jewish masculinity; yet Jewish men were depicted not as helpless, weak, and effeminate (unlike in chapter 1) but as quite the opposite: Nazi propaganda assigned Jewish men too much masculinity, thus distancing them further from the hegemonic centre of heterosexual norms. As Jewish men were hyper-masculinized and depicted as animals driven by uncontrollable instincts and perversions, they were made to seem not properly male. As putative race defilers, they were marginalized.

Race Defilement, Policy, and Jewish Masculinity

Cultural images of the Jewish sexual aggressor were perpetuated in the Third Reich. This discursive emasculation through an animalistic hyper-sexualization of Jewish men by the Nazis intruded on the realm of legal discourse and policy. Nazi leaders and decision makers who instigated and sanctioned antisemitic propaganda hoped to convert discourse into policy. To prepare society for legal changes, Nazi leaders publicly insulted Jewish men for their alleged sexual misconduct. As David Welch has noted, propaganda campaigns were intended to heighten people's awareness of their "Aryan" origins and characteristics.[31]

One of the most notorious propagandists, Julius Streicher, the Gauleiter of Franconia and editor-in-chief of *Der Stürmer*, claimed that defiling Gentile women was a holy act for Jews. To support his argument, the paper relied on a variety of dubious passages from the Talmud. In one of his many defamatory speeches on the topic, Streicher proclaimed in 1935 that

> Alien albumin is the semen of a man of another race. Because of intercourse, the male semen is partially or totally absorbed by the female body. A single incident of intercourse is sufficient to poison her blood forever. She has taken in the alien soul along with the alien albumin. Even if she marries an "Aryan" man, she can no longer bear pure "Aryan" children, but only bastards in whose breasts dwell two souls and who physically look like members of a mixed race ... Now we know why the Jew uses every method of seduction he knows to shame German girls as early as possible, why the Jewish doctor rapes his female patients while they are drugged ... The German girls, the German women, who absorb the alien semen of a Jew, can never again bear healthy German children.[32]

Adolf Hitler, too, harboured an obsession with alleged Jewish sexual perversion. In speech and writing starting in the 1920s, he accused Jews of being the primary beneficiaries of prostitution and the cause of spreading sexually transmitted diseases. Hitler stressed in *Mein Kampf* that "the adolescent Jewish male lurks for hours, hoping to defile the blood of the young women. With all possible means, he tries to spoil the racial foundations of the people that he tries to enslave."[33] Based on the emphasis on Jewish sex crimes by leading National Socialists and Hitler himself, the introduction of racial legislation, the Nuremberg Race Laws of September 1935 in particular, constituted a predictable and logical step on the road to radical antisemitism with direct implications for Jewish masculinities.

The increasing concerns about sexual relations, intermarriage, and miscegenation among Germans and Jews promoted calls for government intervention, and the Nuremberg Race Laws not only provided a de jure definition of Jewishness; one of the laws, the "Law for the Protection of the Hereditary Health of the German People," stipulated a ban on marriage and sexual relationships between Jews and non-Jews.[34] The laws were intended to determine and shape Germans' understanding of and public and private behaviour towards their Jewish fellow citizens.

Even though the Nuremberg Race Laws were intended to segregate all Jews from non-Jewish Germans, regardless of sex and gender, as Patricia Szobar has shown, according to the laws' stipulations, only men were liable for prosecution. Upon violating the laws, women – both "Aryan" and Jewish – were not accountable for criminal prosecution and could be charged only as witnesses in race defilement proceedings (similar to law 175 that outlawed homosexuality but only prosecuted male homosexuals).[35] Some of the racial legislation by the Nazi state stood in a direct relationship to the sexualized discourses and the propaganda that had developed in the late nineteenth century and that had centred on representations of hyper-sexualized Jewish men.[36] Parallel to the stigmatization and criminalization of Jews in graphic caricatures as well as in text, the promulgation of racial legislation and the enforcement thereof was grounded in a culture of conceptualizing the male as the aggressor and the female as the victim.

There were several reasons for an enforcement that differentiated between the sexes. On the one hand, as a German state attorney of the Third Reich stated,

> Man's greater moral (*sittliche*) responsibility as well as the stronger self-control (*Beherrschung*) and resistibility (*Widerstandskraft*) in sexual matters vis-à-vis the easily manipulable (*beeinflussbare*) woman is the cause for the asymmetry of the law for the protection of the German blood.[37]

Typically, women were spared prosecution in race defilement trials, as they were deemed by nature to be passive in sexual activities and easily manipulable. Female transgressions, such as entering into liaisons with Jewish men, were trivialized as somewhat natural and understandable. Guided by patriarchal principles, the Third Reich made the prosecution of Gentile women less central and important.[38]

On the other hand, as Patricia Szobar has stressed, "representations of Jewish women as sexually dominating would have rested uneasily alongside images of a powerful and aggressive 'Aryan' masculinity."[39] Thus, it was vital for the Nazis to enhance patriarchal notions and bipolar images of male-female gender identities in order to build a strong, masculinized state in which men took central leading roles. The Nazis depicted "Aryan" masculinity as naturally dominant.[40] Furthermore, because men were viewed as the stronger sex, in control physically and mentally and equipped with a stronger and more rational mind than women, vilifying Jewish women for sexual transgression would have quintessentially meant that women could also act as seducers. It would have suggested that men – in this case the "Aryan" men who were portrayed in the media as the heroic soldiers, the protectors of family and fatherland – could fall victim to female Jewish seduction. In short, "Aryan" masculinity would have been undermined; "Aryan" men would have appeared as passive, weak, and seducible. For this reason, to uphold the image of strong "Aryan" soldierly masculinity, Jewish women were left out of the understanding of racial legislation and enforcement. As men were the central figures in the campaigns of an idealized "Aryan" society, the counterpart to such an envisioned utopia was also male: the Jewish male race defiler. Constructions of "Aryan" and Jewish masculinity were therefore mutually co-dependent.

The prosecution and enforcement of the Nuremberg Race Laws took a high toll on German Jews, with sentences for Jewish men of up to four years of penal servitude.[41] Nikolaus Wachsmann calculated that between 1936 and 1939, about 420 men annually were sentenced to prison for race defilement, with the great majority being Jewish men, who generally received longer sentences than convicted non-Jewish men.[42] This number, at first glance, might seem relatively small compared to the total Jewish population of over half a million in Germany. Furthermore, it is plausible to surmise that the actual number of court cases was artificially high because many of these investigated cases were based on denunciations or hearsay. Nevertheless, antisemitic propaganda that orbited around Jewish transgressive sexuality cannot be measured by the number of court cases only. The cultural impact that Nazi caricatures and laws had on society must have been much greater. The Nazis regulated their propaganda and disseminated their messages aggressively and perpetually, reaching millions of Germans. The pervasive images of Jewish race defilement, therefore, implicitly contributed to shaping Germans' generally negative attitudes toward their Jewish neighbours.

Finally, throughout the 1930s, the German press intensified its efforts to publicize court hearings, and newspapers like *Der Stürmer* increasingly reported on court cases that dealt with Jewish race defilement. As inflammatory as the earlier drawn caricatures, newspaper reports with photographs of court cases vilified the Jewish male, and these antisemitic representations were able to reach a large audience and readership outside the actual courtroom. Until 1938, state prosecutors had to report every trial of a Jew to the press division of the Reich Ministry of Justice, and many of them were then broadcast and publicized.

The Jewish Experience of Race Defilement

The propaganda of Jewish criminal male sexuality and the implementation of antisemitic legislation that differentiated between the sexes essentially contributed to the cultural emasculation of Jewish men, who were constituted as the antithesis to normative definitions of German masculinity. But how did Jewish men internalize this discursive and legal sexual antisemitism?

Notably, an adaptation in Jewish men's behaviour in direct relation to antisemitic sexualized discourses began prior to the promulgation of the Nuremberg Race Laws that in 1935 would prohibit sexual relations between Jews and non-Jews. In 1933, the Nazified press increasingly focused on the issues of racial ideology and racial hygiene. It was at this time that the personal safety of German Jews in public institutions such as swimming pools and saunas started to become precarious. Starting in the 1920s, Nazi and other *völkisch* papers had reported on alleged cases of sexual misconduct by Jewish men in public baths. Jewish men were accused of luring and approaching "Aryan" women, followed by inappropriate behaviour. In his memoir, Ernst Marcus (b. 1890), a notary and lawyer in Breslau, recalled that

> The Jewish question reached a new stage. It suddenly turned into a problem of sexuality (*Sexproblem*). It started with incidents in public bathing houses. Jewish visitors were thought to have molested "Aryan" girls ... Strangely enough, these cases occurred in a short time frame all over the country. Everywhere, Jews importuned "Aryan" girls ... An "Aryan" seamstress told my wife that she had noticed unobtrusive and despondent Jewish men in the baths keeping themselves to the sides. Her acquaintances have had the same impression ... At the same time, *Der Stürmer, Das*

Schwarze Korps and other Nazi papers opened the barrage (*Trommelfeuer*).
The reader of such papers had to ask himself how the Jews had all the
time to betray the German people of its possessions and wealth if they
apparently and uninterruptedly were preoccupied with seducing German
girls and women.[43]

Though Marcus mocks the problem of race defilement, his comment
represents a rare case of an observation by a non-Jewish individual, a
seamstress in this case, who noticed a discernible change in behaviour
and attitude among Jewish men specifically and in the context of Jewish sexuality. Public places like pools, where men and women partially
exposed their bodies, were constructed by the Nazis as an opportune
habitat for Jewish men to lure, ogle, and seduce female patrons. Due to
staged public outcries in the press related to stories of alleged sexual
misconduct in public pools,[44] Jewish men reacted to the indictments
of their sexual misbehaviour and modified their conduct accordingly
either by staying away from pools altogether or, as Marcus's recollection indicates, by trying to appear as inconspicuous as possible.

Yet Jewish adaptation, if it was even noticed, did not stop the Nazis
from further introducing antisemitic regulations. In the early to mid-
1930s, Nazi propaganda deprived Jewish men of a normative masculinity, depicting them as sexual delinquents and pushing them to the
margins of social life. The Nazis assigned such importance to notions
of racial health and hygiene that public pools became one of the first
places in Germany that prohibited Jews from attending. As they were
seen as sexual predators, their traditional "hunting grounds," the public pools, were closed to them.[45]

Unlike earlier when it was municipalities taking the initiative, with
the promulgation of the Nuremberg Race Laws in September 1935, the
federal government took the centre stage, subjecting German Jews to
regulations, state prosecutions, and police violence. As Robert Gelately has shown, however, the practicability of the laws rested on volunteered information from Germans. Hundreds of Jewish men were
denounced for violations of the Nuremberg Race Laws. The reasons
for denouncing Jewish citizens were complex and ranged from cases of
economic self-interest to outright antisemitic hatred.[46]

The circumstances that could lead to arrest varied and were often
of an arbitrary nature. In one case, a married Jewish man riding his
bicycle accidentally collided with a female pedestrian. Apologizing for
his inattention and as a form of compensation for the inconvenience
he had caused, he invited the young woman for a cup of coffee. His
misfortune was that a local Nazi party boss had witnessed the incident

and reported him. His punishment was two months in jail.[47] Jacob Georgsohn recalled that he too was denounced anonymously for race defilement in 1936. After two weeks in pre-trial custody (*Untersuchungshaft*), he was transferred to the concentration camp Hamburg-Fuhlsbüttel, though evidence did not suffice for an indictment.[48] In other cases, when the available evidence did not suffice, or did not exist in the first place, the use of torture could force the accused to confess his crime. The Frankfurt wine merchant Frederick Weil (b. 1877) recounted such a story. When a sixty-year-old married Jewish male acquaintance of Weil was arrested for race defilement allegations, the Gestapo mistreated him so badly that he agreed to sign a declaration in which he confessed his criminal deed.[49] Max Augenreich (1915–88) was arrested by two SA men when they spotted him and an "Aryan" girl in a movie theatre. He was sentenced to six months in jail in 1937, followed by forced labour assignments.[50] Another Jewish man was convicted of race defilement for glancing at a young "Aryan" girl across the street. The court ruled that "although the man had no physical or verbal contact with the girl, his glance had a clearly erotic basis."[51] Finally, in more extreme cases, particularly during the early war years, courts did not shy away from delivering death penalties, regardless of the lack of evidence. As one verdict read,

> The fact that he pretended to be an "Aryan" to bypass the restrictions for Jews can be understood to some degree. But that he did not live in solitude and humbleness, but misused as much as possible the position that resulted from his camouflaging, is a Jewish impertinence ... He unscrupulously had a go (*heranmachen*) at German women and girls and did not care if they were engaged or married. During intercourse, he did not make use of any protection and not only willfully accepted the possibility of conceiving a Jewish bastard but called such an outcome desirable.[52]

As these cases demonstrate, a considerable number of race defilement cases were entirely based either on denunciations, vague assumptions, and hearsay or on fabricated indictments. Even cases of race defilement that allegedly had occurred *prior* to the passing of the laws in 1935 could be investigated.[53] All cases demonstrate that the introduction of legal steps in 1935 and the enforcement thereof were meant to ostracize and segregate Jews from "Aryan" Germans, following a cultural, discursive tradition that had previously focused on and personified the "evil Jew" as a male. When the Nazis began to codify and enforce their racially based laws in the 1930s, in their formulation and enforcement the laws had strikingly gendered connotations and ramifications, with Jewish men at the centre. The Nazis not only formulated racial legislation based on intertwined sexual and racial fetishes but also implemented them radically and often without any real substantive grounding.[54] Looking at a woman, greeting a woman on the street, or going to the theatre with a female friend could be construed as sexually promiscuous and therefore illegal behaviour.

As criminal investigations of race defilement, often of an arbitrary nature, proliferated, German Jews began to observe, record, and gradually internalize the new social realities. The elderly Albert Herzfeld noted in his diary on 15 November 1935 that he knew Jewish men who were extorted to transfer over their businesses if arbitrary accusations of race defilement were not to be filed.[55] The businessman Alfred Wolf (1898–1981) of Heilbronn also recalled in his 1969 memoir how his brother-in-law, Manfred Levy, the co-owner of an embroidery factory in Berlin with several hundred employees, was accused by one of his female employees of "pinching her buttocks." He remembered how he and his wife perceived this as a deadly serious charge. "It was a matter of life and death. If Manfred would be found guilty, he would go to jail and from there to a concentration camp … The tension was unbearable." Later, the judge acquitted Levy, upon which his wife "broke down and screamed."[56]

In a similar case, the businessman Erich Leyens (b. 1898) of Wesel was accused of *Rassenschande* on two separate occasions in 1936. In his memoir, he recalled that

> I was summoned to appear in court … In the first case, a young "Aryan" woman had filed a suit charging me with being the father of her child. However, when she was confronted with me in court she declared, "But I have never seen this man in my life." … As the courtroom erupted in laughter the charges were immediately dropped and I was allowed to go free … The second charge against me was more dangerous … [Only] the [accuser's] fiancée's courage saved me.[57]

As Leyens's and the other cases demonstrate, in the years preceding the Holocaust, race defilement was a commonly used strategy for discriminating against Jewish men by damaging their military and business reputations in society, sexually criminalizing them through court convictions, and brutalizing them in jails and concentration camps, where they would face especially harsh defamation, extortion, and brutalization.

Contemporary Jewish accounts also evince the hysteria about race defilement. A 1934 compendium of reported antisemitic cases in Germany, edited by émigré Jews from Germany, cited the *Frankfurter Zeitung*, which in turn had cited press releases by the Hessian police:

> Jews had lost all the warranted restraints toward German women and tried to approach them, causing uproars within society. The political police were therefore compelled to arrest and take into custody the guilty or those known Jews to whom public enragement could be addressed ... All Jews therefore are again strongly advised to demonstrate natural (*selbstverständlich*) restraint.[58]

A few days later, again relying on police press releases, the *Frankfurter Zeitung* announced that, despite repeated warnings, several Jewish men had been arrested and sent to concentration camps. "Again, a local Jewish merchant has tried in obnoxious (*anstößig*) ways to approach a Christian girl. The accused, like several of his racial comrades (*Rassegenossen*), was taken to the concentration camp Osthofen."[59] As the historian Kim Wünschmann has analysed, these men convicted of race defilement (or merely being investigated for it) were often brutally treated in such camps, sometimes resulting in death.[60]

The Nazi discourses on race defilement directly and indirectly affected the lives of many Jewish men and women. The actual impact of the Nazi hunt for Jewish male race defilers, however, cannot be determined from a study of court cases alone and the sentenced individuals who ended up in court, prison, or concentration camp. An analysis of diaries, testimonies, and memoirs validates the argument that the Nazi discourse on Jewish sexual delinquency had a palpable and radical impact on the lives of Jewish men and women.

The merchant Alfred Schwerin of Pirmasens (b. 1892) pointed out in his memoirs that the purveyors of print media in the Third Reich had been collectively organized by the Nazi press office and were instructed to sell Nazi papers in the most visible manner, at the best location within their stores and kiosks. Particularly *Der Stürmer*, according to Schwerin, was always visible and had a not-to-be-underestimated influence on the uneducated and less educated in society. Most of all, however, it impacted the youth, who were already hungry for erotic images and scandalous stories.[61] In a similar fashion, Alfred Wolf evoked the effect Nazi propaganda had on him:

> Nazi newspapers excelled in dirt and filth. They talked about circumcised pigs. It is very difficult to imagine the level to which these people descended and the atmosphere that surrounded us. The feeling of being isolated,

watched, avoided is utterly depressing ... Once a Gentile lady stopped me on the street, which was as kind as it was courageous. I said you don't have to talk to a circumcised pig.[62]

These examples demonstrate that the propaganda efforts at sexualizing Jews did not occur in a social vacuum unnoticed by German Jews. The introduction and sanctioning of graphic antisemitic vulgarity and slander by the state was noticed, processed, and internalized by Jewish and non-Jewish Germans. Time and again in postwar memoirs, German Jews made references to the pervasiveness of (sexualized) antisemitic imagery in Der Stürmer and other mass media. The act of observing the radicalization in antisemitic propaganda, with its often sexualized content, was a central element of the Jewish experience in the Third Reich and manifested itself as part of Jewish and Gentile consciousness.

Besides triggering personal reflections in diaries and memoirs, sexualized propaganda had further profound effects on Jews, transcending mental internalization and starting to alter patterns of actual behaviour among German-Jewish men. As part of the linguistic violence of Nazi propaganda that intruded into people's everyday lives, the term "race defilement" itself took on a pervasive, mystical force.[63] Some came to fear potential, arbitrary accusations against them for violations based on the new and common usage of the language of race defilement. Some Jewish men began to anticipate possible scenarios if they were caught in this maelstrom of sexual antisemitism. Alfred Meyer (b. 1920) remembered the impact the Nuremberg Race Laws and Nazi propaganda had on him:

I remember one case. A Jewish man had a female friend who was "Aryan." He went to great pains to avoid all physical contact with her, but was accused of having masturbated in her presence while she was undressing. Convicted of having defiled the "Aryan" race, he was sentenced to years in the penitentiary and castrated. Whether true or false, such stories impressed me deeply, in consequence of which I hardly dared during the years of my sexual awakening to even look at female persons. For a boy between 13 to 19 years of age that is not altogether easy.[64]

The adolescent Salomon Perel, born in 1925, while hiding his Jewish identity in the Hitler Youth in wartime Germany, remembered how fearful he was about his Jewish identity and about having his peers discover his circumcision, and how he shied away from meeting girls when his buddies, in their free time, met with girls from the Bund Deutscher Mädel, the young girls' equivalent of the Hitler Youth.[65] The later famous TV quiz-show master Hans Rosenthal (1925–87) similarly recalled how the concept of race defilement had had a direct and immediate impact on his social behaviour. Around 1941 in Berlin, not wearing the Yellow Badge, the teenager Rosenthal met a girl of his own age whom he liked:

> What a madness! ... [In this moment] I completely forgot in what situation I was. I started to have doubts. Race Defilement! Prison! Death Penalty! Terms that one could read in the press every day buzzed through my head. I, the race defiler![66]

Rosenthal, ridden by fear, decided to cancel the date that he had planned for the following night.

Whereas Perel and Rosenthal in their postwar memoirs remembered their fears and placed them in the context of Jewish criminal behaviour and race defilement, the journalist Max Reiner (1883–1944) went into even more detail in his contemporary account:

> I was told that there were women who made it their business to invite Jewish men to make excursions (*Ausflüge*) or a visit to a café in order, under threat of reporting them to the police, to ask for greater amounts of money ... [One day] I noticed ... in the evening, walking home in some side streets that were frequented by women of the demi-monde (*Halbwelt*), that women who did not look like their profession, what the French call *faire d'amour*, addressed me. They did not even suggest a tender get-together, but both times, they lamented their miseries, asking for financial assistance. I sidestepped them quickly. I cannot claim that in both cases they were out for extortion, but I am not sure that if I had stopped and not given them anything or only very little, they would not have started to scream and approach other pedestrians for help from the Jew's race-defiling (*rassenschändischen*) overtures ... I am wondering whether some cases of alleged race defilement that were punished so gruesomely started and ended with such similar attempts by approaching money-hungry women.[67]

Like Rosenthal and Perel, Reiner exhibited an acute awareness of the centrality that the Nazis assigned to the concept of race defilement in 1930s Germany. Even more, he not only internalized the discourse but projected it onto his body, using it as a defining and salient feature of Jewish masculinity. He implicitly accepted that his appearance was Jewish and that women could also recognize him as a Jew. His body became a "site of experience," and this internalization had a profound impact on his demeanour and his self-understanding as a man.[68] Reiner altered his social behaviour by trying to avoid any contact with suspicious women in ominous situations such as being out at night in an empty street.

Even in the realm of prostitution, the enforcement of racial legislation did not halt. In one case, a Jewish man was arrested in Hamburg when he met up with a prostitute. In another case, in Frankfurt in 1938, a Jewish man was found guilty though no sexual intercourse had taken place. The court determined that the law was violated because the terms of the Nuremberg Laws involved the protection of German honour in addition to German blood. The accused was sentenced to two years and two months of jail with a possible extension.[69]

Finally, Jewish women, too, were directly affected by the Nazi criminalization of Jewish men as sexual aggressors. Some, like the physician Hertha Nathorff (1895–1993), simply noted the pervasiveness of talk about race defilement: "So many people are getting arrested for race defilement or attempt thereof. It is the catchphrase of the day. School children speak about and read about it in *Der Stürmer*." In another diary entry, she noted that "innocent men get arrested and ruined."[70] Isaak Behar (1923–2011) recalled how his mother was in constant fear for her son in wartime Berlin when he went out at night without wearing the badge and after he had fallen in love with a young "Aryan" woman at work.

> My mother, who hardly left the house ... was in constant fear ... I knew about my mother's fear. But I could not believe my luck. A young woman, a very beautiful one ..., was in love with me ... a woman who, even if it was just for two hours every Sunday, gave me the feeling of being a normal young man.[71]

Behar's mother, on top of her worries that her son was not wearing the required badge and was out after curfew, must have pictured her son getting seen or caught in the presence of his girlfriend and his subsequent punishment. Yet Behar, by going out, resisted the new gender order that the Nazis were imposing on Jewish men.

The 1930s Nazi discourse on race defilement could become a lived reality for many German Jews, even if the "crime" had not been committed. It effectively contributed to a reconfiguration of Jewish masculinity; depicted as sexual criminals, Jewish men were categorized as a threat by the state and a participating society, a process that in turn made Jewish men adapt to – or feel forced to adapt to – antisemitic imagery and social legislation. As Behar's memoir further demonstrates, the process of reconfiguring Jewish masculinity – as with Jewish military masculinity – was not a domain entirely reserved for men or to be used only by men. Jewish women – for example, mothers worrying about their sons or wives fearing for their husbands – also participated in this process of allocating men a new status.

An additional stipulation of the Nuremberg Race Laws forbade Jewish households from hiring "Aryan" maids under the age of forty-five as a measure to prevent sexual assaults by Jewish men.[72] Jewish memoirs and diaries are replete with references to this ruling by the Nazi state. As Peter Gay (b. 1923) remembered in his postwar memoirs,

> If this statute had not been so vicious in intent and disruptive in results, we could have laughed at this childishness, as though every male Jewish employer could be expected to rape his female "Aryan" employees as long as they were sexually attractive and capable of childbearing. This provision enacted into law the lewd fantasies that the *Stürmer* was peddling weekly and that cost us the services of Johanna Hantel, whom I much liked.[73]

Similarly, as the elderly Albert Herzfeld, born in 1865, noted in his diary on 7 December 1935,

> There are 200,000 Jews left in Germany, of which half [are] men, of which at least half are children or elderly, leaving about 50,000 adult males, who, in all seriousness, cannot seriously jeopardize a people of 66 million! How should they? They are content if they are left alone because they have enough to worry about.[74]

Conclusion

The centrality of racism and antisemitism in the endeavour of constructing a Nazi utopia defined by racial purity and health has been thoroughly researched by historians.[75] A historiographical shortcoming has been a lack of a detailed scholarly investigation that intersects Nazi antisemitism, propaganda, and Jewish gender and that pays particular attention to the experiences and perspectives of the central objects of the sexualized propaganda effort: Jewish men.

Antisemitic propaganda in the Third Reich was not exclusively about anti-miscegenation and Jewish sexuality but drew deeply on other historic discourses that were political, economic, and cultural in nature. Yet, as Marion Kaplan has rightly asserted, Nazi racism was never gender-neutral: "Propaganda castigated Jewish men as cheats and traitors, depicting them as greedy bankers and pimps."[76] The construction of propaganda that implanted racially and sexually intertwined fantasies of degeneration in the German public mind constituted an important and influential strategy in the definition and criminalization of German Jews and their isolation from non-Jewish Germans.[77] In their incessant references to ostensibly defending middle-class morals and norms of proper "Aryan" sexuality, the Nazis amalgamated antisemitic racism with discourses of sexuality, establishing a fear-mongering, desperate scenario according to which Jewish men through their hypersexualized nature were threatening the "Aryan" race. Such depictions of German-Jewish men were emasculating as they marginalized all Jewish men, regardless of age, class, or even ethnicity, depicting them as heedless of the accepted conventions and behaviours that defined hegemonic masculinity. Thus, constructions of promiscuous Jewish male sexuality did not occur in a vacuum, disconnected from other cultural discourses, but took place in a lively context of social relations.

To manifest images of evil Jewish masculinity, the media not only disseminated a negative image of the Jewish man but simultaneously propagated its counterpart, the exemplary "Aryan" male in his strong, healthy body. As Daniel Wildmann has justly pointed out, in the Third Reich the male "Aryan" body was not defined in its relation to the female body but in relation to the *non-Aryan*.[78] In their graphic and textual attacks against Jewish men and women, the Nazis could only succeed in reshaping ordinary Germans' views of Jews by instilling a counter-image to the "Aryan" hero. The Nazis thus relied on relational juxtapositions of idealized and vilified images of Good and Evil. In their propaganda, the Jew qua the Jewish man was generally ugly, unhealthy, obese, unathletic, and acting ominously in the presence of women and children, while the "Aryan" man was portrayed as trustworthy, hard-working, and possessed of an aesthetically beautiful body, showcasing strong muscles and resembling a Greco-Roman warrior.[79] Especially nakedness represented vitality, purity, and health, while Jewish men were depicted as dressed up, either in shabby clothes or businessmen's attire. Either way, the implication was that they hid their diseased bodies and deviant sexuality.

Jewish men came to process the idea of race defilement and adapted to the new social realities with a preponderance of news coverage of race-defilement trials. Yet, even though Jewish men's gendered identities were discursively marginalized in Nazi propaganda, and while in their reactions and social behaviours some certainly altered their public appearance and conduct, in their gendered self-understandings, Jewish men did not necessarily view themselves as emasculated or as a distinct group of sexualized victims. What had changed was the fact that because of the omnipresence of race defilement discourses and legislation, Jewish men were at greater risk and had to be more careful, particularly the ones who (thought they) looked Jewish.

It is crucial, in the end, to note that configurations of masculinities happen in a co-dependent relationship and can intersect with and impact one another. Though Jewish men were castigated as sexual threats, their military masculinity, which they had built over years and which the Nazis tried to take away, continued to matter and could even partially invalidate the discursive and legal assault on them. Some Jewish male "sex offenders" received lesser sentences because of their military service in World War I.[80] Militarism still carried meaning, even for so-called race defilers. On the other hand, in one case, a Jewish man was given an exceptionally harsh sentence because the woman he had an affair with was married to the most honourable type of man in the Third Reich, a Wehrmacht soldier. His "attack" on Aryan military masculinity resulted in seven years of imprisonment.[81]

Chapter Three

Work until the End? Jewish Men and the Question of Employment

In addition to depriving Jewish men of their cultural-military honour, while simultaneously targeting them through sexualized-racial propaganda, the Nazis threatened the vast majority of German Jews – both men and women – in material terms by depriving them of their ability to earn a living. Economic antisemitism tried to push the Jewish presence in the economic sphere to the margins and eventually eliminate it altogether. In dismissing Jewish civil servants and employees in private firms, as well as boycotting, vandalizing, and then "Aryanizing" Jewish businesses throughout the 1930s, the Nazis attacked Jewish economic existence, inadvertently prompting changes in the realm of gender relations as well as in the construction of German-Jewish masculinity. It is these changes that constitute the focus of this chapter.

Gender historians have been largely silent on the concept of work masculinity and its significance for Jewish masculine identity in the Third Reich, in particular Jewish men's struggle to stay in meaningful employment, and the gendered implications of their progressive exclusion from the workforce.[1] A closer look reveals that Nazi economic antisemitism violently challenged the majority of Jewish men in their roles as providers. For many, the loss of income and of the means to provide for their families, as well as their forced idleness and inactivity, implied a state of powerlessness and emasculation. As they could no longer work and provide, many felt they were no longer "real men." Yet, Jewish men's perceptions of this emasculating process of being denied the means to provide for themselves and their families varied significantly and could generate an array of alternative and defiant responses. While unemployment could signify a loss of status and respect that triggered in some middle- and upper-class men drastic changes in their demeanour ranging from withdrawal into self-isolation to the development of depressive behaviour and even suicide, for other men the prospect of losing meaningful work had less radical implications. Instead, they persisted in preserving their masculine identities as "working men" by taking the Nazi attacks on their socio-economic foundations as a challenge that called for the defence and preservation of their masculine roles as providers. By staging a successful fight to remain in their accustomed positions or acquiring different means to make an income for their dependants, and finally even finding some gendered dignity and pride in performing forced labour during the war, many Jewish men resisted Nazi emasculation by economic means.

By 1933, work was typically performed outside the home. The emergence of a working middle class apart from traditional, largely agrarian ways of living brought about significant changes in the dynamics of social and gendered life for Europeans in the nineteenth century. As part of this modernizing process, social reformers started to imagine an ideally functioning modern society that was based on, *inter alia*, definitions of masculinity and femininity. Experts negotiated and codified definitions of man and woman in literary texts, novels, reform and advice literature, and encyclopedias. The well-known *Brockhaus* encyclopedia, for instance, defined women throughout the nineteenth century as nature's true representatives of emotions and love and their primary roles as those of wife and mother.[2] Both the middle-class embourgeoised Jewish man and his Gentile counterpart were expected to acquire a respected profession (*Beruf*), wealth (*Besitz*), and education (*Bildung*). In nineteenth-century Europe, work and social standing acquired mutually reinforcing meanings for men.[3] Simultaneous to, if not preceding, the construction and propagation of images of the male citizen-soldier, work masculinity was essentially defined by men's ability to use their education, vocation, and wealth to create, provide for, and protect their families, thus establishing themselves as the heads of their families.[4] As a result, Jewish men increasingly obtained their sense of achievement outside of religion. As Paula Hyman has argued, "Men were to function in the public sphere, earning their family's living and being active in the world."[5] Seeking inclusion and acculturation, many German-Jewish families adapted to bourgeois standards, including the gendered division of labour and the concept of honourable work. As Dalia Ofer and Lenore Weitzman have stressed, in the 1920s and 1930s Jewish men and women lived in gender-specific worlds. As in most non-Jewish families, married men were primarily responsible (though not always exclusively) for the economic well-being of their families.[6] It was the prevailing gender model that was carried over into the 1930s.[7]

In 1933, 61.3 per cent of German Jews worked in commerce and business (as compared to 18.4 per cent of the total population in Germany), and 12.5 per cent in public services and free professions (as compared to 8.4 per cent of the total German population). Only 1.7 per cent and 1.4 per cent respectively were engaged in agriculture and domestic services (as compared to 28.9 per cent and 3.9 per cent of all Germans). A high proportion of Jewish university graduates were notaries and lawyers (16.2 per cent), doctors (10.8 per cent), and dentists (8.6 per cent). In the same year, 46 per cent of all working Jews were self-employed.[8] By 1933, German Jews seemed to have realized many of the aspirations that had defined the *Bürgertum* in the nineteenth century. However, their relative concentration in certain fields and independent professions meant that Jews, especially those in the professions, had become a conspicuous target in antisemitic circles that saw them as unwanted competition.[9] Even before the Nazis took power in 1933, antisemitic discourses had started to depict "the Jew" as only engaged in dishonest commercial or intellectual work, to the detriment of the manually hard-working German man (Figure 17).

In 1933, the Nazis had not yet developed a clear blueprint for a European-wide genocide targeting Europe's Jews and other minorities. In its first steps to exclude Jews from German life, the state used antisemitic propaganda to aggressively disseminate depictions of Jews as exploitive, anti-German manipulators of an international capitalist system.[10] In subsequent steps, the Nazi state implemented allegedly defensive measures by seeking to restrict and eliminate any Jewish economic presence in Germany. With measures ranging from anti-Jewish economic boycotts and the forceful dismissal of Jews from federal, state, or municipal employment to legally undermining Jewish businesses with the intention of taking them over (a process referred to as "Aryanization"), the Nazis started to use multiple means in 1933 to rid the German economy of any possible Jewish influence. As Avraham Barkai has noted, this was a silent and gradual process of economic expulsion and expropriation.[11] In the economic realm, the Jew had become an outcast.

As well as producing the alleged economic benefits that would follow from the curtailment of a Jewish presence in the economy, however, the attempt to dislocate Jewish economic influence also served a gender-cultural function: the construction and elevation of the honourable "Aryan" male worker. Texts and images that discussed the concept of male-exclusive work (and manual labour in particular) carried

Figure 17. An image from the children's book *Trau keinem Fuchs auf grüner Heid und keinem Jud auf seinem Eid* [Trust No Fox on his Green Heath and No Jew on His Oath] by Elvira Bauer, 1936. The author juxtaposes the manually hardworking German male in a muscled and healthy body with an obese, unkempt Jewish man depicted as a businessman.

connotations of pride, virtue, and honesty in *völkisch* discourse. These texts depicted a self-sufficient German working man as not reliant on anyone's charity or pity. In gendered discourses that were carried over into 1930s propaganda, the Nazis bestowed honour upon the "Aryan" working man and celebrated him as someone able to withstand the adversities of life – like a soldier – and who was capable of making a living for himself and his family. Indeed, next to "Aryan" soldierly masculinity, constructions of "Aryan" work masculinity demarcated by honest, hard labour in manufacturing and agriculture were praised (Figure 18). Not only did these men embody a sense of independence and achievement by fulfilling the gender norm of providing for themselves and their dependants; they were also lauded for their active

Figure 18. A Nazi poster representing the ideal of "Aryan work masculinity," date unknown.

contributions towards making Germany an economically strong nation, in which the collective, the German *Volk*, could live in prosperity and harmony.

Translating ideology into social practice, the Nazis spared no efforts to propagandize their successes in eradicating mass unemployment, bringing back millions of jobs to the Aryan people. In contemporary sources and postwar memoirs, Germans often linked their support of Hitler to his alleged achievements in the economy. Even Sebastian Haffner had claimed that among Hitler's achievements, his "economic miracle" outshone all.[12]

It was in this context, of a nation celebrating its revitalized economy and the end of the crisis associated with the Weimar Republic, that Jewish men must have felt particularly excluded and vulnerable to humiliation. In the Third Reich, the Nazis sought to deprive Jewish men of ways of identifying themselves with definitions of masculinity that centred on the notion of economic independence and productivity. Work, in short, transcended the necessity to obtain material rewards needed to live; work had become a gendered signifier for honour, respect, and virtue. It was for this reason that German-Jewish men were denied membership in the Reich Labour Service (*Reichsarbeitsdienst*), a six-month-long compulsory work service, introduced in 1935 that required German men, typically at the age of eighteen, to work in infrastructure and other projects (Figure 19).[13] In addition to their exclusion from the prestigious Wehrmacht, the highest and most honourable institution for men to join, Jews were deemed not even worthy of digging trenches and building roads.

While for non-Jews economic standards were slowly improving, over the course of the 1930s German Jews increasingly suffered from unemployment, a steady decline in incomes, material

Figure 19. Passport of Expulsion (*Ausschließungsschein*), Reich Labour Service, for Erwin Klotzsch, Berlin 1941.

destitution, and poverty. Already in 1935–6, 83,000 Jews accepted aid from the Jewish Winter Relief Organization.[14] In 1938, Jewish unemployment had reached over 80 per cent. Of the employed, over 70 per cent were considered self-employed, but this included people who were simply living off their remaining assets or significantly reduced pensions.[15] Thousands had become dependent on Jewish aid agencies.

Research by Nechama Tec has shown that the decline and eventual loss of work had a profoundly debilitating and demoralizing effect on men and the ways they constructed their gender identities. Citing a wealth of primary testimonies by Holocaust survivors, Tec asserts that the Germans posed almost impossible challenges to the fulfilment of the role of the breadwinner. "When Jewish men found themselves unable to do what traditional society expected of them, they frequently became demoralized and depressed."[16] At another point, the author argues that

> Men's coping skills were … affected by their past habits. Men … could not fulfill the traditional roles of protector and provider. This inability to meet accepted male obligations often had an emotionally paralyzing effect.[17]

Thus, masculine identity was closely tied to the concept of work. As wage-earners, men ensured part of their masculine identity. When the means to make an income were challenged, some Jewish men also felt threatened in their male identities. In his memoirs, Herbert Löwy, who had worked devotedly as a nurse, recalled that when he got laid off in 1933, "Suicidal thoughts crossed through my mind. What was I supposed to do at home, if I was no longer allowed to be the provider for my family?"[18] Max Krakauer (1888–1965) of Leipzig, owner of a movie business, was denied the mandatory membership in the Reich Chamber of Culture that was required for him to work. As he noted,

> But I had to feed my family, and the question how to master this tortured me and many of my comrades who shared my fate day and night. Whatever I tried, and I tried everything possible, failed due to the systematic agitation [Hetze] against us. The disappointments and losses were countless. Soon, I had to downsize our apartment.[19]

The department store owner in Hanau, Carl Schwabe (1891–1967), remembered how excruciating a time it was for him when his business declined. With too many commitments and too many bills to pay, he recalled that "I was suffering terribly."[20] Gad Beck (1923–2012) also recalled in his postwar memoir that the family's financial circumstances took a major turn for the worse in 1935: "My father, who was going on fifty, was still slaving away with his wholesale tobacco business so his two children could go to the college-track secondary school." Beck also recalled how "my father started feeling the effects in his business relations, but he never spoke to us about it." Eventually, Beck's father was no longer able to pay for his sons' schooling. After he had lost his business and the family had to move to a smaller, more affordable place, Beck's father became "absolutely devastated." He isolated himself for days. "He felt like a failure."[21]

In all of these cases, Jewish men's loss of employment or reduction of income from their established vocations led to an economic deterioration within German-Jewish households. It was not only the loss of material conditions of life, however, that was at stake. As John Tosh has rightly argued, "masculinity is inherently insecure because – among other factors – its social recognition depends on material accomplishments."[22] In the Third Reich, German-Jewish men faced major economic struggles to maintain the material lifestyles to which they and their families had been accustomed. Not being able to maintain such levels meant a palpable increase in existential concerns and fears. However, Jewish men's concerns caused by the loss of work gained a deeper meaning, transcending the fear of losing one's standard of living. It was not only the economic plight and a reduction in standard of living, which Jews might have been able to adapt to, that weighed on Jewish men. Instead, Jewish men were tormented by the inability to uphold their masculine identities, which had earned them much respect and authority within the family and in public. In his memoir, Krakauer spoke of countless disappointments and losses. Beck's father perceived himself as a failure. Löwy considered suicide.

Strikingly, the authors did not lament the decline in material conditions, the loss of money, or the painful increase in hunger or relative poverty that might have resulted from an acute shortage of financial resources. Löwy contemplated suicide not because of a possible deterioration of material living standards but rather because of his emotional desperation and perceived loss of face as head of the household. These authors palpably feared an erosion of their power within a system of gender relations in which they held key positions. As sole breadwinners, these men had dignity and authority, and now they experienced major disruptions in lives that had been significantly governed by gender relations.

Hilde Sonnet-Sichel remembered her husband's work-related debility:

The desperate feeling of being an outcast distressed him. He was unable to sleep at night. He stopped eating because – as he said – no one has the right to eat if he does not work. He eventually became so despondent that he slid into a major depression. He feared that we would all starve to death … He turned skinny and scraggy with deep furrows in his face. His entire self-confidence was gone. In the past, he always had such a friendly smile and a good word for everyone. Now he is changed … [he] does not see anyone anymore.[23]

Honnet-Sichel's memories about her husband, a lawyer, underline that it was not the reduction in standards of living that led to an emasculation of Jewish men. Her husband had enough to eat, but he refused to do so because it was the perceived attack on his gender identity that he was unable to cope with. Honnet-Sichel's husband and many others understood themselves to have fundamentally failed in their gender roles as breadwinners and providers.

Other texts explicitly relate to men's pain of being unemployed. With no work, some felt a lack of purpose. With no income and no sense of being productive and useful, Jewish men's identities changed. As Hamburg lawyer Kurt Rosenberg (1900–77) noted in his diary in 1936,

My work life is disquieting. Since 30 June, I am no longer allowed to give legal advice … I was finally barred from my arduously built and much-loved work. Even free-of-charge advice was outlawed. I felt the emptiness of the space I was pushed into.[24]

Following the realization that living in Germany according to the customs, habits, practices, and expectations to which German-Jewish men and women had been accustomed was no longer possible, some Jewish men – more so than women – slid into the passive, docile, and desolate behaviours and depression that Tec has referred to. Already in 1933, Rosenberg had noted in his diary that

> It has gotten very quiet in my office. There is too much to think about. Plans appear in my mind, vague and uncontrolled. There is no room for distractions ... You are tired and exhausted. You are looking for peace. You are avoiding people with similar fates who always want to unload their concerns and pessimism. You wait but don't know what you are waiting for. You almost hope fate will force you to make a decision.[25]

Zvi Aviram (formerly Heinz Abrahamson, born in 1927) recalled how deeply shaken his father was the day after the anti-Jewish boycotts of 1 April 1933; he became so depressed and fearful that he had to stop working as a shoemaker, falling into a passive state. Eventually, it was his mother who had to sell the business and provide for the family. His father turned into an unemployed, broken man. In retrospect, Aviram confessed how he disapproved of his father's psychological withdrawal, leaving all the responsibility to his mother.[26] Yet what was likely hard for a teenaged boy to discern at the time was that Aviram's father was not simply hit hard financially by the boycott of his business. Being unable to provide for his family went much deeper and had serious repercussions for his identity and self-understanding as a man. From being in control and actively supporting the family, Aviram's father became a different person, a man of passivity and lack of initiative. Similarly, Inge Deutschkron (b. 1922) remembered how her father, a teacher until 1933, hung around with other unemployed men, playing cards all day long.[27]

Aviram's excerpt is insightful as testimony from a son who remembered the change in his father. Like Honnet-Sichel, Aviram was an observer of the emasculation of Jewish men in the Third Reich. As gender identities are in constant flux, in a process of being negotiated and contested, it is crucial to realize that having Jewish wives and children witness their husbands' and fathers' losses indirectly contributed to the emasculation of some Jewish men. Only in social relationships, within the family and society, did men's new roles and identities gain relational meaning, as Marion Kaplan – in her analysis of Jewish women's role in stepping up and taking active control of work in and outside the home – has shown. Jewish women's and even children's increased work responsibilities in response to men's disappearance in the work force underlines this.[28]

While Jewish economic victimization was certainly not exclusive to Jewish men, it was men who came to experience the pressure of conformity to be the breadwinners. Such pressures could lead not only to physical deterioration and ill-health but also to behavioural change, including desolate, depressive behaviours or even more extreme actions.[29] Driven by increasing economic despair, a considerable number of Jewish men resorted to suicide in the 1930s. Konrad Kwiet and Helmut Eschwege in their 1984 pioneering study, and more recently Susanne Fischer and Christian Göschel, have analysed suicide among German Jews in Nazi Germany. They have demonstrated that during the course of the 1930s, many Jewish men committed suicide in cases that were directly related to the perceived degradation and emasculation in their work lives. When middle-class and assimilated German Jews saw themselves economically threatened, their businesses vandalized and boycotted, and their civil service jobs lost, the result was an estimated 300 to 400 suicides for April and May 1933 alone.[30]

Christian Göschel asserts that the events of 1933 and the aggressive push towards "Aryanizing" Jewish businesses, the growing financial problems within Jewish families, and the perceived humiliations of many Jews who had considered themselves patriotic Germans led to hundreds of suicides amongst German Jews in the prewar years. The loss of military masculinity (see chapter 1) and even indictments based on sexual transgression (see chapter 2) led some Jewish men to end their lives. But it was predominantly socio-economic fears that caused Jewish men to end their lives prematurely. Both Judge Dr Hans Bettmann, after being dismissed from court, and Professor Jacobsohn of Marburg, after being discharged from teaching, ended their lives.[31] The example of Moritz Sachs is particularly striking. Born in 1873, he had worked for a Berlin brewery for more than forty years and was even a member of the board of directors. In 1933, he was dismissed but was able to procure a significant annual pension of 7,200 marks, which allowed him to provide for his family. Eventually, however, the pension was reduced and after 1938 entirely discontinued. In the end, he was entirely dependent on the generous support of his two former secretaries, an unbearable degradation. He ended his life in 1940.[32]

German Jews who ended their lives prematurely had multiple reasons for doing so. Jewish men's loss of employment, however, was an important factor, particularly in the early years of the Third Reich. The material deterioration for many middle- and upper-class Jewish men does not sufficiently explain the decision to commit suicide. Instead, for men who had accumulated considerable economic, social, and cultural capital in the professions, their perceived loss of social standing was so emasculating that some decided to end their lives. Intersecting with gender, emasculation was intricately tied to concepts of class and age. Former professors, judges, lawyers, and other upper civil servants and businessmen who had devoted many years of their lives to their country's service (and who were often war veterans) perceived their humiliation as too painful to allow them to act otherwise.

Contrary to the hypothesis of a widespread Jewish emasculation, however, considerable evidence points to Jewish men's gradual adaptation to the economic restrictions imposed by the Nazis and their continued strong will to undertake the challenge not only to provide for the material needs of their families, but – equally importantly – to preserve their gendered identities as men. The following three sections will demonstrate how Jewish men struggled yet persevered in their double-edged endeavours by a) managing to remain in their accustomed professions, b) discovering alternative ways and niches to make an income, and c) even finding surprising meaning in forced labour.

People write memoirs, diaries, and letters to record what they find noteworthy. Typically, such records revolve around special events in one's life or in society in general. They represent cognitive ruptures in their lives, in a positive or negative sense, such as the election of Hitler in January 1933 that most memoirs refer to in some detail, or more personal issues, such as a death in the family. Continuities, on the other hand, are less frequently reflected on and recorded by authors in diaries and memoirs. Consequently, there is a relative lack of commentary in memoirs pertaining to the continued, uninterrupted socio-economic life of many German Jews between 1933 and 1938. Instead, such sources often start with a radical moment in the author's and his or her family's lives, such as *Kristallnacht* in November 1938. The preceding years are often either not discussed or abbreviated into a few paragraphs. For German Jews, the loss of employment and the ensuing sudden confrontation with existential insecurities and concerns for their future were causes of such major disjunctions from their previous lives.

At first and for the time being, life continued relatively unchanged for many Jewish families, despite the heightened prevalence of antisemitism in the press and media. Many Jews could remain in their professions. As mentioned above, almost half of Germany's Jews in employment in 1933 were self-employed and thus did not have to face dismissals. In their attempts to convince Germans to boycott Jewish businesses, the Nazis were also not (yet) widely successful. Though most Germans did begin to sever their social relations, if they had any, with Jewish friends and neighbours, this was a gradual process. For years, many German Jews felt they could adapt to the new and presumably not permanent conditions of Nazi Germany and maintain sufficient means to provide an income. For the historian, therefore, it is essential to comprehend some of the subtler yet important continuities that might not be directly addressed in the primary sources.

The neurologist Dr Hermann Pineas (b. 1892) recalled that he was excluded from the chamber of German health care providers (Krankenkassen), a membership that was required if he wanted to continue practising as a physician. His exclusion, however, happened in 1937, more than four years after the Nazis had come to power. It was the first time he had experienced work-related discrimination.[33] Up to that time, due to his war veteran privileges, his work life had remained relatively uninterrupted. In another example of "delayed" work-related discrimination, Wilhelm Buchheim (1887–1957), the principal of the Jewish Gymnasium in Dortmund, relayed a sense of normality in his diary. The only change in his job worth mentioning was that he and his Jewish colleagues had to swear an oath to the "crazy criminal Hitler." Other than that, he pursued his job with as much passion and devotion as ever prior to his dismissal in November 1938. He and his wife left Germany in 1939.[34] As real estate agent Joseph Adler (b. 1895) wrote in his 1939 memoir, "The political events, the brutal and cruel treatments from the Nazis did not touch us personally until Kristallnacht ... We always found a way to keep the office busy and the children in school."[35] As he further noted,

> In Germany, as a front soldier, I still had certain privileges. The children were in school, I had work and we thought we could squeeze through. I had the Iron Cross and the Front Fighter Orden (a war medal) from Hitler's government. In this regard, we were a little bit better off than the other Jews.[36]

For people like Pineas, Buchheim, and Adler, well into the mid- to late 1930s, life seemingly continued on a somewhat manageable trajectory that featured sustained and meaningful employment and a secure income.

For most German Jews, however, economic conditions took a turn for the worse after 1933, dominated by fears and anxieties related to maintaining a level of subsistence. Hermann Badt (1887–1957), the first

Jewish assessor in the state of Prussia and later a government minister, received a generic letter from the government on 5 July 1933 applying the new civil service law that was designed to remove Jews and the politically unwanted from government work. The letter required him to submit documentary proof of employment prior to 1914 or of participation in military combat during World War I. Such letters were sent to all civil servants, Jewish and non-Jewish, as a step to identify Jewish employees who were not war veterans. If the exemptions did not apply to the individual employee, he was required to submit proof of his grandparents' "Aryan" ancestry; in the case of a Jewish background, an employee would be dismissed. Badt had to submit all necessary paperwork within three weeks.[37] The Berlin-based teacher Fritz Friedländer (b. 1901) was given even less time – three days – to respond to a similar request.[38]

A comparably sudden intrusion into his life faced Erich Seligmann (1880–1954), the founder of the Jewish hospital in Berlin. He was denounced at work in 1933 for having made comments of an unpatriotic nature, and thus he was let go based on the civil service law's stipulation that permitted the dismissal of "untrustworthy" employees. In several desperate letters sent to the municipal office in Berlin, Seligmann tirelessly expressed how the denunciations had hurt him. He listed all his merits and accomplishments as a scholar, physician, and veteran of World War I. In a letter addressed to the city on 30 August 1933, he articulated his sense of national belonging, referring to his impeccable record of thirty years of service for the country, and his persistent refusal to engage in politics. He had always "felt national" during times of peace and war and had always done his duty with great devotion. In growing desperation, in ever more letters sent over the course of 1933, Seligmann increasingly spoke of the honours he had accumulated over the years. At one point, he referred to a badge he had received for participating in a militia whose task it had been to maintain law and order in Berlin in the chaotic months following the end of the war in 1918, and alluded to how he had fought Bolshevist-communist forces. A congratulatory birthday note from the mayor of Berlin was also part of his efforts to protest his impending dismissal.[39]

In the cases described above, it becomes evident that more and more Jewish men struggled to sustain their forms of employment that were so central to their male identities. The state acted relentlessly and systematically in getting rid of Jewish employees who did not qualify for an exemption. However, a finer reading of these sources also reveals that Jewish men did not simply give in and crumble to Nazi pressure. Far from passively despairing over what their futures might hold,

Jewish men passionately fought to remain in their positions for which they had striven for years. Adolf Asch's case exemplifies this. Though he was fired as a lawyer in early 1933, six weeks later the war veteran was successfully reinstated.[40]

Trying to benefit from war veteran privileges, many Jewish men consciously coupled their masculine work identities to their military masculinity. Jewish men made use of military masculinity not only to defend their sense of male honour and to exhibit steadfastness as men who had fought in battle but also to preserve another gender marker: their jobs. Strikingly, even a renowned physician like Seligmann, who had published numerous articles and books and who was a recognized medical expert in his field and beyond, felt the need to resort to evidence of military masculinity to defend his position defined by work. Military and bourgeois masculinities were mutually reinforcing and often simultaneously employed in specific contexts. Similar to Till van Rahden's concept of a "situational ethnicity,"[41] Jewish men and women modulated their gender identities in situational contexts. As instances of situational gender identities, military and bourgeois masculinity could overlap and be utilized in specific situations when statements about one's military service or work accomplishments seemed appropriate or even warranted. As war veterans, Seligmann and others claimed they had proven themselves as faithful, patriotic Germans and thus deserved to stay in their accustomed employment.

The case of the lawyer Ludwig Bendix (1877–1954) is particularly illuminating. He was arrested in 1933 for having taken on a client prior to 1933 who allegedly had been a communist. Upon his release from jail several months later, Bendix, a war veteran, still categorically refused to give emigration a serious thought, according to his son Reinhard, and immediately set about returning to his established profession, making a living as a legal counselor (*Rechtsberater*). In a letter to his son, Bendix justified his zeal for work:

> Disappointments and intimidations did not get me down ... I fought every inch of ground. I did not want to let myself be uprooted. My efforts to regain the basis of my professional existence inevitably meant an affirmative attitude toward the country despite the discriminatory measures of those in power.[42]

Upon his release, Bendix commissioned an announcement in the newspaper in which he proffered his services as a legal counselor (*Rechtsberater*), a new title that the Nazis imposed on former Jewish lawyers, who were allowed to counsel Jewish clients only. Fighting against being uprooted and not frightened by further disappointments, Bendix hardly appeared emasculated. On the contrary, though no longer a lawyer, he used all available means to stay in his accustomed profession, using this not just to make a living but, equally importantly, to uphold his gender identity. "To have acted otherwise would have meant to my father that he willingly repudiated his career."[43]

Bendix's efforts as a legal counselor soon attracted attention from his Gentile competitors. Again denounced, he was notified to appear before the police, where he was confronted with the circular he had distributed. The Berlin Bar Association had initiated criminal proceedings against him, accusing the counselor of unfair competition. Witnessing his father's struggle as a lawyer under the Nazis was a major formative experience of Reinhard's youth: "We had no way of comprehending how utterly devastated my father felt at this destruction of his world." Fending off the looming loss of a job and a subsequent erosion of their gender identity, even when successful at first, was no easy undertaking for Jewish men who, however, as the Bendix case proves, often did take up the fight and were successful in winning a temporary reprieve. For former civil servants such as Bendix, while remaining in their accustomed profession ensured economic subsistence, it was also a matter of pride. Jewish men's work was an essential part of their identities.

Jewish men's struggle to maintain their jobs and provide for their families significantly affected family life and the people involved as part of the family structure. It could even impact the architecture of social living itself, with the possible rearrangement of living quarters. Hans Hermann Kuttner recalled that when his father, a practising dentist, was forced to give up his office in the summer of 1938, he moved the office home. "I had to move out of my room, the children's room, so my father could have his doctor's office in the apartment."[44] Palpably, Jewish men's desperate attempts to sustain their professions and to make a living could have direct spatial implications for the rest of their families when living quarters became compressed and living and working spaces started to compete in the domestic sphere. Kuttner remembered that soon after his father's move, the patients stopped coming. Yet Kuttner's reaction is symptomatic of how Jewish men responded to their impending loss of employment. While it was an economic struggle to make a living, Jewish men like Kuttner *chose* to find ways to stay in their previous professions as a way of maintaining their accustomed lives and their identities. Looking for alternative work, possibly abroad, or acquiring new professional skills, was for Kuttner, Seligmann, and all others examined above not (yet) an option.

Over the course of several years, privileges that allowed Jewish civil servants to remain employed if they had fought in World War I or had been employed prior to 1914 were revoked. Jewish businessmen also faced increased pressure to liquidate or transfer their businesses. Contemplating new and different means of employment became, therefore, an increasingly pressing issue for many Jewish men. As Fritz Friedländer (1901–80), a left-wing journalist and teacher, blithely claimed, one had to get over all the antisemitic tirades in the press: "Well, one had to adapt to the new situation. Were the former Jewish lawyers and physicians not able to find employment in industry and commerce? With a strong will, one could do it."[45] Equally defiant, Rosenberg expressed fervour for action to his diary in April 1933:

> The work of eight years of hard labour is trampled down. We [my partners and I] had to let go of our nine employees. We are in the midst of liquidating our lives' work, and are full of bitterness and anger. But I am not helpless and I will make sure that the emotional foundation of my family will not get shattered, not making them subject to demoralization. I am full of energy to work and have accepted the fight over my fate.[46]

Though both examples remain vague in terms of how German Jews were actually supposed to circumvent the increasing economic restrictions that were imposed on them, it is striking that they nevertheless communicate an optimistic sense of eagerness for work.

Jewish men took matters into their own hands, not lacking initiative to find work. Konrad Latte (1922–2005) vividly recalled how his father, the owner of a textile store, fought to make a living for his family. After his father had been pushed out by his former business partners in the mid-1930s, "my father desperately tried to keep our family above water. As an itinerant salesman with heavy bags of merchandise, he wandered through the city of Breslau, coming home at night completely exhausted."[47] In his memoir, Hans Rosenthal (1925–87) recounted his father's struggle. As a senior associate for a bank, his father first faced demotion at work in 1935 and was finally let go in 1937. Rosenthal's father then tried to build a new career from scratch; he purchased a car, and hoped to make a living by soliciting merchandise in the outer districts of Berlin. This did not bring any improvement, however. The discrimination had eroded his father's "feeble composure and aggravated his health. He suffered tremendously by this defamation." A few months later, his father died.[48]

Unlike the two examples with an optimistic tone, Latte's and Rosenthal's observations of their fathers seem quite grim. Both men had desperately tried to provide for their families by adapting to the challenge. Seeking alternative forms of employment as salesmen, both men, as their children remember, suffered tremendously in trying to secure an economic existence. Clearly, for men attempting with limited financial means to start a new line of work and with adverse prospects for success in a hostile country, "getting over" their perilous situation was not as easy as Friedländer suggested in his memoir. However, Latte's and Rosenthal's memories can also be read as manifestos of a middle-class Jewish work ethic and a commitment to conform to the masculine role of being the breadwinner. Both fathers are portrayed as men who struggled to retain considerable agency over their and their families' lives, making it possible for them to survive, even if only provisionally.

While many Jewish men struggled even to get by, others resorted to illegal measures to make ends meet. Alfred Meyer (b. 1920) recollected that his father, only very late and with utmost reluctance, was ready to relocate a tiny part of his assets abroad, in violation of the law, to shield them from government taxation and confiscation. His father had been a notary, a Prussian official, and had "sworn an oath to regard the law as holy, [but in] later years, this seemingly safe nest egg was to grow by more than a few hundred marks." With the assets safely abroad, Alfred was able to leave Germany later on. A further concession to illegality by his father was to "get paid under the table for his services as attorney since registered earnings were taxed too heavily. That was called black money."[49]

While Meyer's story is tragic, as both his father and mother perished in the Holocaust, it is also illuminating, as it demonstrates how Jewish men tried through all available, even illegal, means to provide for their families and to ensure economic survival and continued existence for their dependants. Meyer's father certainly could not have foreseen the coming implementation of the Nazis' murderous intentions. His priority was, based on social custom and the gendered role expected of men, to provide for his children and wife.

Erich Bloch recounted that as a graphic artist in the advertising industry his licence was revoked, but that in order to make a living, he too continued with his work illegally.[50] Ernst Sachs (b. 1888) reminisced that after his business was "Aryanized" in late 1938, he continued to work illegally as a window cleaner.[51] The teacher Hans Schwarz illegally instructed students in English.[52] Clearly, the pressure to make an income for themselves and their dependants made some Jewish men cross moral and legal boundaries, resorting to illicit means as a last resort to generate the necessary funds needed for life. Such conduct, while it might have begun in 1933, intensified by the end of the decade and after the war began, when Nazi economic restrictions became even more severe.

Jewish men's provider role was tightly interwoven with the ever-more-pressing question of emigration. But as chapter 1 has shown, Jewish war veterans defended their military masculine identities, and as part of this reaction, for a long time rejected the idea of emigrating from the country for which they had patriotically fought and risked their lives. It can be further deduced that military masculinity was linked to work masculinity in the sense that Jewish men tried to preserve both and utilize both in order to perpetuate their masculine identities. Thus, it is no surprise that many Jewish men in the first half of the Third Reich refused to consider their family's emigration.

What contributed to men's reluctance to leave Germany was the fact that the bourgeois professions of civil servant, lawyer, notary, and teacher were not in demand or not readily transferable to practice in South and North America or Palestine. As Marion Kaplan has shown, women were at first more accepting of and open to the idea of changing their occupations and working in perhaps lower status professions abroad than were Jewish men, who found it degrading to have to switch to more manual and physically labour-intensive jobs. According to Kaplan,

> [because of] men's close identification with their occupations, they often felt trapped into staying. Women were familiar with the kinds of work, generally domestic ... Women seemed less status-conscious than men ... women did not experience perhaps the descent as intensely as men ... Men and women led relatively distinct lives and often interpreted daily events differently.[53]

Hilde Honnet-Sichel, whose husband had refused to eat due to the shame he felt as an unemployed man, said he was not open to considering the option of emigration and finding employment abroad: "One of the main reasons my husband did not want to emigrate was his job."[54] Somewhat condemningly, the physician Martin Gumpert (1897–1955) concluded in his 1950 autobiography that he had seen Jews knowingly run into the gas chambers because many could not overcome the prospect of giving up their work accomplishments:

> His mind is destroyed when he has to give up what he has accumulated over a lifetime of toil or even has gathered over generations of ancestors, the background of his prestige and his social standings.[55]

Gumpert juxtaposed, with some hindsight, his decision to leave Germany in 1933, following his ad hoc dismissal, with other Jews' reluctance. Gumpert interpreted this unwillingness by many German Jews to emigrate as being closely connected to men's material and social achievements based on their professions. As the historian Judith Gerson remarks,

> [t]he younger generation of Jewish men had not built up their hopes yet, developed honorable reputation and accumulated resources, all of which their fathers, uncles and grandfathers had secured through years of hard work and military service, offering ostensible protections to their elders and making it harder to leave.[56]

Yet more Jewish men than women did emigrate from Germany. The construction of masculinity varied greatly, depending on time and place and the individual himself, and to some Jewish men, attachment to military masculinity and their previous jobs did not constitute an insurmountable hurdle, particularly if their employment had not led to significant social status and prestige (e.g., in blue-collar occupations). For men, going abroad, whether by choice or necessity, was almost always tied to the concepts of gender and class. For Jewish men, keeping their masculine identities as providers was imperative. In a letter sent from Berlin in July 1940 to his son Bernhard (b. 1914) who already had found his way to Shanghai, Gerschon Leib Frum (1879–1943) asked his son for an affidavit from Shanghai and made unequivocal statements of how he still intended to work once he and his wife had arrived there. He would be no burden to anyone.[57] Evidently, the sixty-one-year-old Gerschon felt physically agile enough for a new start in Asia, willing to do any kind of work.

Others contemplated registering for retraining programs that Jewish organizations offered as steps to prepare and enhance their chances for emigration. The sixty-year-old businessman Salo Rosenthal (1879–1945) had accepted a retraining option in Berlin, and prior to his emigration agreed to learn the profession of tailoring with the hope of building a new life in South America. His credential (Zeugnis) from his apprenticeship read, in May 1939,

> Mr. Salo Rosenthal … learned in my house the tailoring of men's and women's apparel as well as stitching. Mr. Rosenthal has excelled through a high degree of motivation as well as his already existing skills and industrious demeanour. I can warmly recommend him as a committed and useful cutter. Mr. Rosenthal is capable of taking over any leading position. For his future, I wish him the best. B. Nathan.[58]

Interestingly, however, the options of starting an expedited apprenticeship program attracted slightly more female than male applicants. This gender imbalance, however, does not necessarily lead to a conclusion of gender role reversal that postulates that women were more prone to take on the challenges that the Nazis imposed on them while Jewish men remained inactive and potentially despondent. Rather, it suggests that many Jewish men, especially if older and well established in formerly higher-paying professions, were reluctant to move down on the ladder of work-related reputation and status. As Kaplan has shown, in 1933–4, of those seeking retraining, 51 per cent of women and only 26 per cent of men were over the age of thirty.[59] As most training programs focused on manual labour (farming, cooking, sewing), for upper-class Jewish men retraining was not an appealing option. For the time being, many preferred other options within Germany or hoped to establish themselves again in their preferred profession in another country once they received their visas to leave.

Finally, some Jewish men resorted to continuing their work, despite their dismissals, from home and often for no pay. Willy Cohn, a teacher in Breslau, found some relief in an article he had published in the *Hamburger Familienblatt* after his dismissal in 1933. It was "something very important to me," despite his growing financial concerns.[60] Writing an article on regional culture constituted a coping mechanism to maintain self-worth and honour. To Cohn, it resembled meaningful, self-defined work even if it resulted in no material rewards. As late as May 1941, he felt relief in finding refuge in his self-directed, intellectual work: "Yesterday morning I spent almost four happy hours dictating my memoirs ... when I am able to work, I forget everything that depresses me." At the end of September 1941, and only weeks prior to his and his family's deportation, he found more self-satisfaction when he wrote, "I had such a sense of happiness yesterday at having completed my work."[61] For Cohn, "having work to do" was a means to an end. It ensured a somewhat normal life, with his gender identity as a working man partially intact.

When he was cut off from society, no longer allowed to borrow books from the public library, the former professor Victor Klemperer continued with his professional calling as a scholar. His work ethic could not be shattered. Clinging to his work in fact helped Klemperer to overcome some of the hardships the Nazis had caused.[62] Maintaining an imagined presence in the world of academia as a scholar, Klemperer did not perceive himself as a nobody: "I have proven to myself once again that I can still produce. And once again I solemnly swear to myself to continue working in the face of every challenge."[63]

Writing scholarly books in his field of expertise, essays, and his diary and already conceptualizing a *postwar* scholarly monograph on the language of the Third Reich (which he subsequently published under the title *Lingua Tertii Imperii* in 1947), Klemperer achieved an impressive output. Such adapted and new types of meaningful work, typically performed in the private sphere, which these men turned into a new "space of creation,"[64] could serve as an essential tool for some Jewish men in salvaging a sense of manhood during a time of otherwise self-perceived uselessness. As men struggled to stay in positions of productive labour, even the loss of income could be partially compensated.

Forced labour in the Third Reich was degrading and dehumanizing for European Jews, POWs, and others. Forced labourers, used as the cheapest possible human resources to produce war materiel, were conscripted to compensate for a shortage of German workers, who were needed at the front. For German Jews, memoirs have further illustrated how hard forced labour was on their bodies and psyches, how disruptive to their personal and family lives, and how economically exploitive, given the extremely low wages they were paid. In one such recollection, Erich Hopp remembered how physically draining forced labour was for him. Using a third-person narrative voice, Hopp noted,

> Since 5 a.m., he is on his feet. For months now, he has been doing forced labour, shoveling soil and carrying coal, and when he comes home at 7.30 at night, [feeling] maltreated and demoralized, Charlotte's and his son's hearts bleed at his dreary appearance.[65]

Despite the state's attempt to reduce Jewish human beings to the entities required for maximum economic output, it is worth inquiring into how Jews came to process and make sense of their new situations.

Jewish forced labour during the war could ensure a temporary survival. When the first deportations from Germany began in late 1941, German Jews soon realized that these "resettlements" were in fact euphemisms for murder. For a while, it became a routine for German-Jewish female and male forced labourers to ask for deferment papers from their employers as a way of delaying or perhaps avoiding deportation altogether. Ludwig Neumann, for instance, who at first had been exempt from forced labour in 1940 due to a medical condition, felt major relief when he was finally conscripted.[66] Evidently, work, during the early phase of the Holocaust, held significant importance for both Jewish men and women. It could guarantee temporary survival for both.

Yet there is also substantial evidence that while working as forced labourers – regardless of how they envisioned their futures – some Jewish men discovered meaning in their work, apart from the potential for survival it could offer. Central to their masculine self-understandings, Jewish men as forced labourers did not think of themselves as useless as long they were needed for economic production. Even following the outbreak of World War II, these men still made serious efforts to remain employed and draw life-affirming meaning from their employment. Surprisingly, this could even include forced labour.

Erich Frey (b.1889), formerly employed in the banking industry, had to quit his job in February 1940 because of his deteriorating eyesight. In his 1942 diary addressed to his children abroad, he noted that

> After giving up my job, working only sporadically and realizing that at present there was no hope of emigrating to Palestine, I looked around for another occupation [which he found at the firm Blindenwerkstatt Otto Weidt in Berlin, an army-supplying factory that hired blind people]. I am still working there producing scouring brushes, scrubbers … I am very happy to have chosen this trade that allows me to earn some money … so that I won't become completely dependent on other people even under the most unfavorable circumstances.[67]

Frey's diary passionately elucidates how some Jewish men could conceive work as an identity- and meaning-giving element in their lives. At a time when Jews in Berlin and all over the continent were facing deportation to extermination camps in eastern Europe, the blind, fifty-year-old Erich Frey felt the urge to write to his children abroad that under no circumstances did he want to become a burden to anyone. Even more remarkable, in his diary entry, even if we consider the fact that he might have written his remarks in a filtered, overly positive tone aimed at sparing his children agony, Frey conveys a sense of contentment and independence, making it seem that he freely chose his profession when in actual fact all Jews under the age of sixty-five had to perform forced labour. Even if we concede that he was putting on a brave face in his writing, a sense of fulfilment emerges from the fact that he was employed and that his work was not a meaningless waste of time. For some Jewish middle-class men like Frey, up to the very end life had to orbit around the coordinates of a cultural and gender order that governed the roles of individuals and thereby produced meaning. For Jewish men, to be at work meant adhering to such gendered system

of coordinates; without work, an integral part of their identity would
have disintegrated.

Gad Beck remembered the pride his father took from his forced labour
assignment, working for the federal railways, replacing tiles. "He had
to perform very hard physical labor, but in fact he was very content.
He had an important task to do!"[68] As Cioma Schönhaus (1922–2015)
recalled in his memoir,

> Papa was a navvy at the time for a civil engineering firm. Fit and bronzed,
> he explained to me how proper workmen use a shovel: "First of all, you
> never just use your wrists. And then you must get the leverage right. That
> way, this work that was meant to shame us just ends up making me stron-
> ger. At any rate, I have never felt better."[69]

Though such memoirs should perhaps be taken with a grain of salt as
they were written often decades after the actual events and thus might
distort the actual physical pain and the existential anxieties that these
people and their relatives lived through, particularly in light of the terrible events yet to come for some of these writers, statements of pride
through referencing one's work are striking. Moreover, sources written
during the time emphasize this pattern of adaptation and gendered construction of meaning and purposefulness by Jewish men.

In an emotional farewell letter written by Yakob Langer's father on
23 November 1941, and addressed to his son who had emigrated, the
author recalled some of the major events since his son's departure.
Sensing that he might never see his son again as his deportation was
imminent (his wife had already died), the father annotated his recent
work assignment as a forced labourer at the city plant nursery:

> The work is diverse and not too exhausting. I must dig, load dirt and drive
> or carry it away … I am living the life of a day labourer … and I will gladly
> tolerate it until the end of the war. The good thing about the work is that
> it prevents me from thinking and makes me temporarily forget my fate.
> Oma, who now has the sole responsibility over the household, takes great
> care of me in a loving manner, cooks, tidies up, cleans and is occupied the
> entire day to make my life as comfortable as possible. This kind of work is
> surely suitable for her because it fills her life and surely gives her a sense
> of internal fulfilment.[70]

The work ethic and pride which German middle-class Jews grew up
with and were supposed to internalize are discernible. Finding some
sense and purpose in manual labour (instead of facing boredom and

a sense of uselessness at home), Yakob Langer's father not only drew some contentment from his work at the nursery; he also reproduced the established gender convention that divided masculinity and femininity according to different types of work in different spheres. Langer thought that the traditional work space for women was in the domestic sphere, whereas men, even as forced labourers in the Third Reich, could find some meaning in their engagement in (manual) labour outside the home.

In 1941, when regular mail was still maintained between Germany and neutral countries or places such as Shanghai, Norbert Neufeld (1913–43), who with his wife Vera and their son Denny (b. 1941) had remained in Germany, wrote a letter addressed to his parents-in-law, who had moved to Shanghai:

> I am very content with my work. I earn 1.25 marks but we have high deductions … At least it is better than everything else … I am working in one of the biggest uniform factories. It is only five minutes away from home.[71]

Perhaps written as a type of justification for not trying harder or sooner to emigrate with his in-laws, Neufeld takes astonishing pride in his work in one of the largest factories in the country. Working for a supplier of the Wehrmacht, the institution responsible for carrying out Germany's war, Neufeld, a Jewish man, found meaning in his employment. The letter serves as an indication that as long as he, the husband and father, could work, a Jewish existence seemed possible in Germany. The interconnection between the decision-making process pertaining to emigration and the gendered concept of male work and making a living is again evident.

Former professor Victor Klemperer, who had privately continued in his intellectual pursuits, noted some new-found pride in a radically different work environment as an unskilled, blue-collar forced labourer in a factory in Dresden in December 1943:

> Now for the last three weeks, I have been operating the simple no. 14 machine by myself. I produce document files for the army … 25,000 of superior paper are finished … How much ingenuity there is in a window envelope, such as banks use! The machine required for that is literally a machine town.[72]

Klemperer, who in his lifetime had taken few opportunities to engage in physical labour, found, though in unforeseen and unsolicited circumstances, a gratifying sense of purpose in his forced labour assignment.

He described it as almost an adventure in which he was placed into an unknown world of industrial processes with machines that he had previously never encountered but that he was now fascinated by. To him, forced labour was simultaneously hard on his fragile physique *and* inspiring.

Other similar sources from the time demonstrate how symbolically important remaining in work was for Jewish men. After the war had broken out and deportations had begun, International Red Cross letters with their twenty-five-word limits constituted the only means to communicate between separated family members. Many of these letters are written proof of how work continued its function of giving meaning to men's lives. In each of four such letters, sent on 17 September 1942, 4 December 1942, 4 January 1943, and 8 November 1943, the young Ernst Wachsner (b. 1919) wrote to his sister in the United States that he was healthy and working. In one he wrote, "Parents departed to unknown [destination] on my birthday. I am working and living well like before" (Figure 20).[73] In such letters, a perhaps shocking impression of normality pervades, likely because the authors of such letters hoped to evade censorship but also to avoid causing concern and fear among their relatives. Strikingly, though, the concept of work constituted a central facet in this pervasive illusion of normal Jewish life in wartime Germany.

When regular mail was suspended and civilians were restricted to Red Cross letter correspondence, Norbert Neufeld's wife, Vera Neufeld (1920–43), made it a routine to write about their son, Denny, and her husband's work:

13 June 1942,
Beloved Parents & Brother,
   We are healthy. Norbert is working. Denny is walking now. Write every month. Denny kisses your pictures. Comes after us. Many kisses Vera, Norbert, Denny.

26 October 1942,
Dear Parents & Brother,
   We are all heathy. Norbert is working. Since January, I have written monthly. Denny is walking; he is a smart, blond curly boy. Kisses Vera, Denny, Norbert.

5 January 1943,
   Everyone healthy. Norbert is working. Denny is getting big, smart, developing well. Comes after us. Says Oma, Opa. Showing him pictures, which he kisses. Kisses Vera, Norbert.

Deutsches Rotes Kreuz

Präsidium / Auslandsdienst
Berlin SW 61, Blücherplatz 2

15. SEP. 1942   397966

ANTRAG
an die *Agence Centrale des Prisonniers de Guerre, Genf*
— Internationales Komitee vom Roten Kreuz —
auf Nachrichtenvermittlung

REQUÊTE
de la Croix-Rouge Allemande, Présidence, Service Etranger
à l'Agence Centrale des Prisonniers de Guerre, Genève
— Comité International de la Croix-Rouge —
concernant la correspondance

1. Absender   Ernst Israel Wachsner
   Expéditeur Berlin W50 Schaperstr. 30

bittet, an
prie de bien vouloir faire parvenir à

Verwandtschaftsgrad: Bruder

2. Empfänger   Lotte Meyerhoff
   Destinataire   Jacksonville Fla. USA
                  2581 Park Str.

folgendes zu übermitteln / *ce qui suit:*

(Höchstzahl 25 Worte!)
(25 mots au plus!)   Eltern an meinem Geburtstag
unbekannt abgereist. Wohne, arbeite,
lebe unverändert gut. Freunde und
kleine Freundin sorgen rührend.
Mitteilen Rudolf. Trotzdem Kopf hoch!
                Schreibt Eurem Ernst.

(Datum / date) 13. 9. 42   (Unterschrift / Signature)

3. Empfänger antwortet umseitig   Ernst Israel Wachsner
   Destinataire répond au verso Jude, Kennwort Berlin
                                   Kennummer B 45 32 17

Figure 20. Red Cross letter from Ernst Wachsner in Berlin to his sister
Charlotte Meyerhoff in the United States, 1942.

In February 1943, the young family was deported to Auschwitz.

For Jewish men born in the late nineteenth or early twentieth century, work had become an integral part of their lives and their identities. Even during the Nazi regime and World War II, work was deemed so important to perform that life without it seemed illogical. Work provided a normalizing sense of life for both Jewish men and their families. With the husband at work, even forced work, as Eva Neufeld indicated in her letters, life continued to orbit on a seemingly stable and predictable trajectory that governed, among other coordinates, gender roles. A world in which these coordinates were invalidated was hard to conceive. As the father of Hans Oskar Löwenstein (b. 1926) soberly opined, because all German men were at the front, someone had to produce the armaments: "The Germans cannot be that stupid to kill all the cheap laborers."[74]

Conclusion

John Tosh has argued that work is one of the central foundations of masculinity. Yet a proper job and a viable household are highly vulnerable to the vicissitudes of the economic cycle: "Individual men might experience acute loss of masculine self-respect by being thrown out of work."[75] Unemployment, as James Messerschmidt concurs, undermines the patriarchal breadwinner/good provider masculinity.[76] In the Third Reich, it was more than just a few individual Jewish men who were "thrown out" of work. Through their economic attacks against all German Jews, the Nazis violently undermined hegemonic masculinity for Jewish men who had been participating in a capitalist system and had internalized the two ways in which work masculinity functioned. Work was considered an economic necessity; Jewish men performed work to acquire capital to provide for themselves and their families. Work, however, also gained cultural symbolic significance as a means to obtain status and respect and to legitimize the power that they exercised within their families and within society in general.

There is a need for a more pronounced differentiation and understanding of the concept of Jewish work masculinity in the Third Reich. It is logical to reason that Jewish men in the Third Reich increasingly faced the pressure to conform to gender expectations to be self-sufficient and provide for themselves and their families. These pressures became increasingly acute, especially for men of the upper-middle class who had made significant achievements in their work lives and who had linked their status to their professions. Their gender identities as respected men thus significantly intersected with their class consciousness. It was, strikingly, Jewish men of the higher classes who responded to their growing concerns and fears by drastically changing their demeanours, withdrawing into the private sphere, becoming desolate or passive men, and sometimes even resorting to suicide. Honnet-Sichel's memory of her husband's loss of appetite records one of the more classic signs of depression. This feeling of failure was aggravated by the state propaganda that not only praised the Nazi economic recovery and the creation of millions of jobs but also discursively put the "Aryan" male in a central position, with images of self-sufficient men who presided over their obedient children and loving housewives at home. While ordinary German families pursued economic improvement, Jewish men as the heads of their households were excluded. As Judith Gerson has argued,

> [E]mployment in the postwar memoirs of Jewish men points to an important understanding of dominant and subordinate masculinities. While in Germany, men's ability to provide for their families was a sign of their successful participation in hegemonic, patriarchal life, the significance of the loss of jobs and earnings ... signals another form of exclusion of German-Jewish men from participating in hegemonic masculinity.[77]

However, as this chapter also elucidates, Jewish emasculation through marginalization did not inevitably follow from Jewish men's cumulative pressures and losses in the field of employment. Instead, this chapter has demonstrated that, especially in the first few years of Hitler's regime, a considerable number of men took on proactive roles in defending their socio-economic positions *and* gender identities as working men. For several years, many Jewish men were successful in integrating their notions of military masculinity and their understandings of work masculinity. As war veterans, many benefited from the veteran exemptions that temporarily postponed their dismissals, even though the process of obtaining such exemptions must have been nerve-wracking and arduous. Some men managed to stay self-employed, either in their accustomed professions or, when by the late 1930s military exemptions no longer applied and more Jewish businesses were Aryanized, by carving out niches that promised to provide at least some income in Germany as salesmen, tutors, or black-marketeers. Their endeavours were highly performative, as they not only reflected a means to make an economic subsistence. Jewish men's behaviours were also an implicit acknowledgment of the social practice that pays respect to hard-working men. Thus, Jewish men's attempt to remain in work was to a large extent governed by social and cultural expectations that in turn had an impact on their gender identities.

The degrading process of struggling to remain employed often coincided with the reduction of standards of living, with smaller living quarters and other material losses, as well as adverse effects on men's psychological well-being. Yet, it would be inaccurate to speak of an overwhelmingly emasculating process. As long as men remained in work, they could frequently derive the essential meaning needed to preserve their gender identities as men. This could include even the unpaid yet meaningful work performed by former teachers and scholars such as Victor Klemperer and Willy Cohn, who found genuine satisfaction in their continued intellectual activity.

Finally, this chapter has shown that even forced labour under certain circumstances could support the maintainance of gender identities. As degrading and exploitive as forced labour was, for some Jewish men it provided a sense of purpose, a sense of being needed, and a sense of being useful and productive. While it might have camouflaged the looming fate for many to come, for the time being, as Eva Neufeld's letters indicate, it helped them and their dependants to maintain some sense of normal life with traditional gender conventions in place.

In short, even when Jewish men were deprived of the work that contributed to their sense of identity and through which they built cultural-social capital, it is misleading to prematurely conclude that when their familiar work was taken away, men felt they were no longer men. Even suicide, the last resort available to Jewish men who thought they had lost everything, does not signify emasculation. Some in fact chose suicide to avoid having the German state legally become the heir to all their possessions. Jews who "relocated" outside of the Reich – a euphemism for deportation – were deemed to have automatically agreed to confer their belongings on the state. Josef Juliusberger (b. 1871), a wealthy businessman, chose to circumvent exactly this type of Nazi robbery. In his suicide note and last will, he declared that it was against his honour to let the remains of the wealth that he had accumulated through honest and arduous work over the course of thirty-six years be confiscated.[78] Evidently, the material manifestations of male labour and the pride associated with it could even influence some Jewish men's decision to end their lives. We thus need to be careful in our conclusions about the motives and driving factors of Jewish men's behaviours. As in Juliusberger's case, it is more sensible to argue not that the author was emasculated but that to the end he retained some decision-making power over his life, his lifetime's achievements, and his gender identity.

Chapter Four

Double Burden? Jewish Men as Husbands and Fathers

Definitions and constructions of "the ideal man" are subject to the vicissitudes of time, and yet, as George Mosse has noted, certain features remain remarkably stable and resistant to change.[1] Notions of fatherhood and marriage are two such elements, the topics of this chapter. As the sociologist Steve Nock explains,

> The traditional model of marriage assumes a husband who supports his wife and children. Few acceptable alternatives exist for married men ... Historically, masculinity has implied three things about a man. He should be the father of his wife's children, he should be the provider for his wife and children, and he should protect the family. Accordingly, the male who refused to provide [for] or protect his family was not only a bad husband; he was somehow less than a man.[2]

Throughout the nineteenth century, the family took on a new importance in the discourse of European reformers, scientists, and other experts, who argued that only in the family could virtuous humans be raised. The family was elevated into a bastion of morality, a sacred institution that needed to be preserved and protected. With a new interest in the organization of the nation-state, the proper order of the sexes became a key issue in public debates and publications beginning around 1800. Ute Frevert has shown how such male-dominated discourses sought to define the proper role for women, whose natural place was assigned to the private sphere where they would take care of the household, the upbringing of children, and religious matters.[3] The public sphere has been discursively (though not necessarily practically) reserved for men to engage in work, politics, and male-exclusive institutions of socialization. With such separate yet complementary gender spheres embedded in the cultural framework in Europe, the focus of attention shifted by the end of the century to scientific and medical but also *völkisch* and racial discourses, expressing concern over birth rates and the health of the nation. Yet it was the Nazis who pushed the notion of ensuring Germans' survival by means of population growth. The politics of demographics and eugenics became legally intertwined in pursuit of imperialist-racialist grand schemes, with "Aryan" women being awarded medals for delivering Hitler's future soldiers.[4]

The process of establishing oneself as a respected man, Jewish or not, and moving beyond the state of adolescence was multi-faceted and typically included the cultivation of honour and reputation in different domains such as the military or the public sphere, in which men were supposed to find meaningful and financially rewarding employment. In a system that considered men the central figures, with wives and children as men's legal subordinates and dependants, men took on a growing number of pressing responsibilities. Yet men were expected not only to provide for their family – the growing struggle for Jews to conform to this role in the Third Reich was analysed in the previous chapter – but to perform the role of protector. A family's well-being rested not only on the satisfaction of material needs but also on their physical and emotional comfort and safety.

In nineteenth-century Jewish thought, the family stood at the heart of Jewish society.[5] Acculturated and emancipated, German-Jewish middle-class men took on ever more of the dominant and decision-making roles in their families and marriages, as did Gentile men. In Jewish as in Gentile families, the status of the *pater familias*, the patriarch, was considered a symbol, a sign that a man had reached full adulthood. Because the majority of German Jews had acculturated and accepted the associated norms and values of Gentile society, as heads of their households who successfully performed the provider and protector role, Jewish men were granted participation and acceptance in the public sphere of politics and civil affairs in the second half of the nineteenth century.[6] When, forty years later, the Nazi system undermined Jewish masculinity in the realms of military honour and employment, the Nazis also challenged Jewish men's roles as heads of households and their ability to perform their domestic protector and guardian roles, a change in Jewish everyday life to which, however, historians so far have paid little attention.

In her study on gender and the Holocaust, Dalia Ofer declares that "Jewish husbands and fathers lost the ability to function as heads of families."[7] Similarly, as Nechama Tec writes, in the conclusion of *Resilience and Courage: Men and Women and the Holocaust*,

[B]y barring Jewish men from the fulfillment of their traditional family obligations, the Germans had attacked their core masculine identification.

That is, the Germans made it impossible for Jewish men to fulfill the role of protector and placed almost impossible challenges in the fulfillment of that of breadwinner. When Jewish men found themselves unable to do what traditional society expected of them, they frequently became demoralized and depressed.[8]

Apart from such insights offered by Tec and others, historical studies of the family have so far included few men and paid little attention to masculinity. As Robert Moeller has argued, "We seem to have written fatherless history," and according to Anna-Madeleine Halkes-Carey, an image of Jewish fathers as passive, despondent, and depressed prevails: "As if fathers played no role."[9]

Building on the conclusion of my previous chapter that Jewish men assigned considerable significance to the practice of remaining in meaningful employment and that a remarkable number continued in their provider role, this chapter argues that monolithic depictions of Jewish men's experiences in the Third Reich must be reconsidered. To argue that Jewish men were emasculated because they were unable to provide for their families – a hypothesis I have partially refuted – and that *because of this* they could no longer perform the role of protector is an oversimplification that does not give proper credit to how Jewish men tried to persevere in doing their duty as fathers and husbands.

Masculine identities of Jewish men as husbands and fathers were subject to a transformation, with protector roles in the public sphere often reduced to a symbolic level. Yet, as part of this process, Jewish men remained far from passive in reacting to the contingencies of a Nazi dictatorship. By promoting their families' emigration efforts (though quite late and often by yielding to spousal pressure), Jewish men sought to keep up a semblance of the protector role. While such efforts became harder to realize over time, Jewish men compensated for their "inabilities" by taking on a new presence in the domestic sphere as emotional caretakers and thereby helping to alleviate some of the hardships experienced by their spouses and children. With their manhood questioned in the public sphere through the loss of military status, or through propaganda depicting them as sexual perverts, combined with the increasing struggle to meet income needs, Jewish men (and aspects of their gender identity) increasingly took on the role of the private, non-public man, the supportive and supported partner, family man, and fatherly mentor.

Jewish Husbands in the Third Reich

Paradoxically, despite a universally accepted definition of bourgeois masculinity in the nineteenth century, the key concept of men acting as protectors (unlike the concept of men as economic providers) was constructed in rather vague terms and never materialized into concrete patterns of expectations and generic behaviours. The concept remained confined to the world of cultural and literary discourses (if one thinks of medieval tales and love stories with princely knights rescuing noble women from evil). In reality, the gender construction of the male protector had few historical precedents. The nineteenth century was a relatively peaceful era in European history, and even some of the romanticized propaganda during World War I, which depicted men as the heroic defenders of fatherland and family, provided little practical guidance in relation to the actual display and behaviour of men as protectors of women and children. Men, thus, were not born as warrior-heroes who instinctively protected fatherland and family but as individuals who were exposed to cultural gender norms and values that defined what was considered normative masculinity. As imagined protectors, men had to first learn to internalize and enact such roles.[10] Thus, when in the 1930s German-Jewish men started to have concerns and anxieties about their dependants' lives and physical well-being under ever-increasing Nazi curtailments and restrictions, these men had few precedents they could rely on and use for orientation and guidance. The gendered norm of men protecting their wives and children remained a pressing yet vague element of masculinity.

In sources written at the time and in retrospect, Jewish men relied on a form of narrativity that was surprisingly self-reflexive and self-critical, in contradiction to some of the historiography that attributes to men, unlike women, a distortive tendency to portray themselves in positions of power and control, even under duress. Yet, some Jewish men "confessed" the growing anxieties they felt in their roles as protectors for their wives. Increasingly, Jewish men's adherence to the cultural image of the protector gradually eroded, though the actual circumstances, the time, and the place could vary. Particularly when the Nazis outlawed emigration in 1941 and German Jews became ever more subject to arbitrary, discriminatory restrictions, deprivations, and other laws, the emotional and physical health of Jewish men and women rapidly deteriorated. Though there was little hope and no concrete way to rectify their predicaments, Jewish men still felt responsible for their wives. In a diary-memoir that Adolf Guttentag (b. 1868) started to keep in 1942 for his overseas son, he wrote,

> 22 August 1942:
>   How I wish that Mutti looked a little better. Her pallor surely is related to her vascular spasm[s] which occur at every new worry and every frightening news … She sleeps well, if only she allowed herself more

rest! … While I am at home much of the time, helping Mutti as best I can, Mutti runs errands.

2 September 1942:
    Again and again, I am faced with the question, shall I or shall I not take Veronal[11] and end my life on the day I receive notice of our evacuation. My first concern is for Mutti; if she wanted it, I would do it immediately. But if she had hopes of seeing you again some time, it would, of course, be sad if I didn't make it, too.

10 October 1942:
    I have lived a happy life, long united with Mutti and I am eternally grateful to her, so my greatest worry is how to spare her these worrisome changes.[12]

Guttentag's diary excerpts offer a valuable insight into the author's emotional state during the final phase of German-Jewish existence prior to the implementation of the Holocaust. Palpably, the author is greatly concerned over his wife's well-being. As a former physician, he notes his wife's deteriorating condition, about which he seemingly cannot do anything apart from his compensatory performance as a houseman in the private sphere, helping "Mutti" as much as possible with strenuous household tasks. In a final selfless statement, he also consigned to his wife the decision-making power to end their lives through suicide. In his helpless state, all Guttentag could do, it seems, was to express pity for his wife, regret his impotence to remedy the situation, and implicitly acknowledge his failure to have spared his wife all the agony that she had not deserved. Guttentag and his wife ended their lives on 29 October 1942.

    Again, as gender constitutes itself relationally with men and women equally partaking, women's perceptions of Jewish men's struggles contributed to the erosion of the latter's protector role. Camilla Neumann, for instance, recalled in her postwar memoirs the moment when the deportation orders for her and her husband arrived in 1942. The Berlin couple contemplated committing suicide to spare themselves the inhuman treatment that they assumed was awaiting them. In this moment, according to the author, her husband, Ludwig, felt the need to apologize for his failure as a husband, for having messed up in his duty of protection. When both husband and wife were no longer shielded from deportation by their employer, he took full responsibility upon himself for not having tried to emigrate sooner:

[Ludwig] asked me for forgiveness because he had not dealt with the issue of emigration when it was still possible. I could not watch how he, in addition to all the other agonies, tortured himself with self-reproaches [*Selbstvorwürfe*]. Thus, I consoled him and told him that ... back then, it also had not been my full conviction [to emigrate]. I only said this to calm him down. Since 1939, when we had arguments over the question of emigration, there has never been any discord [*Mißton*] between us.[13]

In Neumann's memoir, the gender image of the husband as the supposed protector emerges next to the underlying gender structure according to which men had the final say in important family and marriage decisions. According to Neumann, she had been in favour of emigration from Germany for some time but was unable to prevail against her husband's reservations.[14] Though having lost on this issue she stayed by her husband's side and did not criticize her husband directly for his "mistake." Yet, in her memoir, she implied that because of her husband's hesitancy, he had failed in his protector role and instead put both at serious risk. When they were unable to adhere to or enforce the gender role, Jewish men could be perceived as helpless and unmanly. Another crucial piece of the gender mosaic that constituted Jewish men's identities was broken.[15]

The pretence of keeping up a gender order with prescribed roles of physically protecting their wives was paramount for German-Jewish men in coping with Nazi antisemitism, and they expressed such concrete concerns and feelings of responsibility more explicitly when for the first time they came in direct contact with Nazi violence. Julius Guggenheim (1883–1970) recalled in his 1940 memoir that both he and his wife had secured immigration documents for the United States when one day he was arrested for alleged departure tax fraud. During his maltreatment in several prisons in Berlin, all he was thinking about – according to his postwar recollection – was how to spare his wife from torture by the Nazis:

> After I still had not made a confession, because I had not committed any crime, I was told that my wife would be arrested. I would then surely make a confession. He [the Gestapo official] was making allegations of God knows what. I can only remember that I emphatically explained to him that he can cut me into pieces, but he should spare my innocent wife who would break over this.[16]

In Guggenheim's memoir, the author's relived concerns over his wife's safety are revealing, even more so since his wife was in fact not subjected to torture. The author acknowledges his powerlessness over their torturers and by implication the impossibility of protecting his wife, placing him in a serious state of concern.

   With the deterioration of the home front and the beginning of air raid attacks over Germany by the Allied forces, German Jews became subject to the direct effects of war. Jews were not spared from losing their shelter and lives in the war zone that Germany had become. Victor Klemperer, who was one of the last remaining Jews in the city of Dresden, reflected in his diary how he had experienced the infamous "firestorm" in February 1945. As an elderly and unfit man in deteriorating health, he could offer little physical protection to keep his wife safe during the bombardment. Yet Klemperer was in a state of constant worry about his wife, from whom he was separated in the chaos of the firestorm. In his diary, it seems almost incongruous that Klemperer should still accept his male role as protector in the face of obstacles that he was completely helpless to overcome. "Was Eva lost, had she been able to save herself? Had I thought too little about her?"[17] Even if his wife had stayed by his side during the bombing and they had not been separated, Klemperer would likely not have been able to offer her any additional protection and shelter. And yet, being unable to fulfil this gender norm, Klemperer was overridden by a sense of guilt. As the above examples demonstrate, Klemperer and Guggenheim were the products of their socio-cultural environments in which external pressures of gender-role conformity regarding proper husbandly behaviour were at work. Jewish men had a firm tradition of internalizing cultural gender norms that they eventually came to view as uncoerced and normal. But when the means to publicly perform them were restricted, Jewish masculinity was undermined and marginalized. As all the above cases demonstrate, Jewish men and women were fully aware of men's powerlessness and inability to care for their dependants.
   Even though there was little to do to physically embody and enact the male protector role for Jewish men in the Third Reich, there were symbolic means and gestures for Jewish husbands to maintain healthy marriages – most notably by providing comfort and a sense of happiness to their wives. Bourgeois standards not only distinguished a proper husband by the material rewards he brought to the table and the protection from outside adversities he afforded for his family. A good husband was a man who reciprocated, in a controlled and nuanced manner, the emotional comfort, love, and care he received from his wife.[18] According to Klaus-Michael Bogdal, bourgeois masculine identity had become bound to the ideal of the family man in the nineteenth century, with proximity and intimacy arising within the confines of the nuclear family.[19] Especially in Jewish orthodox religioisty, Jewish men were lauded if they practiced virtues and expressions of masculine tenderness, softness, and forgiveness.[20]

In the Third Reich, Jewish husbands continued to demonstrate affection in an attempt to make their wives' lives more comfortable. Even though material resources became scarce, Jewish husbands were able to symbolically if not materially perform chivalric behaviours, trying to make their wives feel loved and even spoiled on certain occasions. While this might seem trivial at first glance, it is important to examine such an *Alltagsgeschichte* (history of the everyday) of the emotional lives of German Jews, who by 1942 had lived through almost an entire decade of a Nazi dictatorship whose central tenet was the elimination of all things Jewish. Alf Lüdtke's pioneering scholarship has inspired scholars to unravel and scrutinize the meaning of mundane behaviours, behind which lie hidden choices that German Jews made and thus agency that they retained. Far from being passive victims who held no decision-making powers, German Jews, in this case men, were able to assign some meaning to their increasingly restricted lives according to a catalogue of norms and values to which they were accustomed.[21]

In their recent work, Aleida Assmann and Ines Detmers argue that historians have only recently discovered the role of emotions in the making and experiencing of history.[22] Such histories illuminate how emotions connect human beings to one another. Because emotions are founded upon reciprocity and create relationships, facilitating social bonding, they are integral to any study that examines German-Jewish life in the Third Reich.[23] In his memoir, Gad Beck recalled that while at work performing forced labour in 1940, his father

> one day brought my mother a gigantic bottle of French perfume. It was in bad taste but was quite a big deal. One of his foremen had sold it to him under the table.[24]

Beck's father's purchase of a such gift for his wife – something which under normal circumstances a teenage boy might not have taken note of in a diary or remembered decades later in a memoir – represents an instance that shows that the coordinates of a cultural gender order with men acting as chivalric gentlemen vis-à-vis women did not entirely vanish under the Nazi dictatorship. Living as outcasts and facing destitution, poverty, and an omnipresent violence, German Jews did not shatter their cultural norms and behaviours. Instead, expressions and gestures of love and care sustained and strengthened the social bonds between husband and wife. Emotions are exchanged reciprocally, and Jewish men, like their wives, participated in this system of maintaining, if not buttressing, family and marriage relationships in which emotions took a central role and which German Jews continued to rely on in their darkest hour. The perfume bottle was such a symbolic gesture of love by a Jewish husband who conformed to the cultural gender conventions that were considered normative for husbands. By keeping up with such traditions, German Jews not only preserved a vital sense of agency in an environment that tried to deprive them of that capacity but continued in their day-to-day lives with marriage conventions that provided a sense of normalizing stability and dignity. Though continuing with their "normal" lives was an exasperating endeavour, driven by despair and marked by setbacks, it yet points to an image opposite to that of the passive, despondent Jewish man. Revealing continuities, particularly when one would have expected otherwise, is as important a task as the historian's quest to uncover change.

On his wife's birthday, 12 July 1944, Victor Klemperer wrote, "Eva's birthday today. My hands quite empty again. Not even a flower."[25] On his wedding anniversary two weeks earlier, Klemperer had lamented, "Any kind of celebration is made impossible."[26] The fact that Klemperer wrote down these notes is revealing in itself. Klemperer's diary entries are indicative of the gender expectation of indulging one's wife on special occasions such as her birthday or a wedding anniversary. This norm did not change or become invalidated even under the most severe oppression and attacks against their livelihoods during the war. As Klemperer also noted, "The only novelty on this wedding anniversary: an air raid warning from quarter to nine to quarter to ten."[27] In a situation of mutual peril, Klemperer was mentally preserving his identity as a man by being a husband who, if not able to present his wife with a proper gift on her special day, then at least could critically reflect on his expected role and contemplate his perceived failure to adhere to these norms. The thought itself counted. Klemperer's reflections thus validate Nock's point that marriage needs to be viewed as a social institution that symbolizes more than just the act of marrying a woman; it was a system of rules defined by cultural assumptions.[28] Flowers on a wedding day or the purchase of perfume resemble standard conventions that Jewish men hoped to adhere to, and in the case of Beck's father, successfully did so.

The marriage of Camilla Neumann is a further example of how gestures – visible demonstrations of thinking about one other – could count for much. When both husband and wife were conscripted to forced labour in 1941, their marriage drastically changed. Because Germany's wartime economy was geared to full mobilization, Jewish forced workers (and others) were subjected to shift work, and Camilla and her husband, Ludwig, as it turned out, had to work shifts at different times. Camilla remembered that worse than accepting the double burden of doing housework and factory work was the fact that she and her husband could hardly see each other:

> When I worked a late shift, I would not see Ludwig from Sunday night to Saturday at noon, thus six days. But every night, there were a few endearing lines written by Ludwig on my night table, and of course, I would also leave him similar notes on his table. When he got up and left early in the morning, I was still asleep and when I returned from work at midnight, he was already asleep. Before I went to bed, I ate something and then prepared Ludwig's breakfast. Thus, I did not go to bed until 1:30 am and Ludwig got up at 4 am.[29]

For the Neumanns, and most other Jewish couples, their marriage relationships came under stress in the Third Reich. Not only the quality of time spent together was affected but the quantity as well. While husbands had typically worked outside the home and were absent for much of the day, this was perceived as a normal arrangement in the socio-economic and gender-cultural order of which German Jews were part. However, with married life violently turned upside down when both husband and wife were driven outside their homes for forced labour, there were few other ways to nurture their marriage other than to write doting notes to one another expressing care and love.

While it was imperative for Jewish husbands to perform if not the protector role then at least the role of comforter to their wives, preserving a healthy marriage was no one-sided project to which Jewish men contributed without also benefiting from it. Marriage improved Jewish men's lives. Carl Schwabe (1891–1967) recounted that during his struggle to keep his business alive in the 1930s, he could rely on his wife's support, without which he could not have endured all the pain.[30] In his diary, Paul Steiner noted in 1939 that he could forget, even if only temporarily, all the negatives in his life when he was with his girlfriend.[31] As Willy Cohn, whose existential concerns I have analysed in the previous chapter, wrote in his diary in 1933,

> Yesterday evening we [his wife Trudi and he] spoke frankly about a number of matters, the things that weigh heavily on me, and so it is now easier for me. I told Trudi how unbearable I find things and how helpless I often feel about the struggle to make a living.[32]

Two years later, on his wedding anniversary, he wrote:

> We married twelve years ago today, a dozen years that have not always been easy. But Trudi has stuck by me through thick and thin and raised

my children. For this I am deeply grateful and for everything that she has been to me. Hopefully we will be granted many more years to fight this battle for existence together … To celebrate the day, we plan to ride out a bit into the country.[33]

In diary excerpts such as these, a new level of emotionality in husband-wife relationships is discernible. References to their wives' emotional support deliver an understanding of married life and show how living in a serious relationship was of fundamental importance to both Jewish men and women. As "emotional men," Jewish husbands adapted to their new situations and were able to give support to and provide emotionally for their wives, while in turn, they increasingly relied on emotional support from their wives.

In a suicide note to his son Yakob Langer, who had previously emigrated to the United States, Yakob's father wrote as follows:

Essen, 23 November 1941
My Beloved Son,

…

When Mama's lifeless body was brought into the hospital room, following her death, I stayed with her for one and a half hours to say goodbye. How terrible these hours and days were … You know how happy our marriage has been, in what an intimately heartful and spiritual relationship we have lived together and how we have been adjusted to one another. Mama has been of such affectionateness in the last few months that I have repeatedly told her that she is wasting her entire love that she has felt for you and for me, now on me alone. Thus, we lived even more withdrawn in the last while. We were enough for one another and did not need anyone. In fact, we have not found anyone in Essen who was close to us and who meant much to us. All the more terrible now is the emptiness that I am feeling. I often consider myself superfluous … Following Mama's death, I have lost all motivation to emigrate because securing an existence all by myself in a foreign country with foreign people did not seem appealing to me at my age … Now I am closing this letter my beloved son and take farewell from you with a heavy heart. Have a good life and stay healthy … God bless you. I kiss you in faithful, fatherly love. Your Papa.[34]

Langer's affectionate letter is a rich historical source. It alludes not only to some of the themes that have been analysed by historians, most saliently the complex issue of Jewish emigration from Germany, but also and especially to the emotional world of Jewish men, in this case a Jewish husband who expressed his eternal gratitude to his wife who had just died. The letter also reflects an evaluation of the emotional stages Jews went through. Living withdrawn and isolated from society, the couple in fact seem to have strengthened their emotional bonds. In this letter, it becomes strikingly clear that marriage was an important social institution for both Jewish men and women. Jewish men who tried to perform roles of being proper husbands under the excruciating circumstances of the Third Reich palpably benefited from being in such mutual relationships. Langer makes no secret in his letter about the sense of happiness and contentment that he had gained from his marriage as long as it lasted during the Nazi era. Especially between 1933 and 1941, living together and supporting one another, emotionally if not materially, provided meaning to both partners more than ever. In the Third Reich, marriage grew to become an essential part of Jewish men's identities and a sensitive coping mechanism for survival. How Klemperer enjoyed the days when he could take out his wife in his car – mastery of which represented a symbol of masculinity in itself.[35] As Willy Cohn noted in October 1941,

> Today we have been married for eighteen years. The years have passed quickly. They have brought us joy and they have brought us sorrows. But such is married life, and Trudi has been a very good partner in marriage. We have brought up five children who will carry on for us when we are gone.[36]

Jewish Fathers

To be considered a man, it was not sufficient for German-Jewish men to have reached adulthood, learned a profession, and acquired the economic means to provide for themselves. To be respected, Jewish and non-Jewish men were also expected to settle down, get married, and have children. In the nineteenth century, as in earlier and later periods, fatherhood was essential to masculinity according to John Tosh, because "it so markedly contributed to a man's immediate social standing. It lent greater substance to his role as sustainer and protector of family dependants."[37]

So far, German-Jewish fathers have appeared at several crossroads. Many of the German-Jewish men who identified themselves as World War I veterans were fathers; Jewish men who struggled to retain their socio-economic positions and to provide for their families were, in many cases, fathers. But Jewish fathers have been the objects rather than subjects of this analysis so far, as men being remembered, interpreted, and observed by their wives and children. Jewish men as independent agents and their distinct experiences in relation to fatherhood in the Third Reich so far have not been the subject of detailed historical scrutiny.[38] Yet, as John Tosh puts it, it is necessary to pay more attention to the documentary evidence produced by fathers themselves.[39] Closely related to their roles as husbands, Jewish men as fathers tried to adhere to norms and expectations that were synchronic to that of husbands but that were at the same time distinct.[40] One aspect pertained to the protector role: as heads of their homes, Jewish men had internalized the cultural expectation that extended the protective grip over their spouses to their children.

The evidence suggests that some Jewish fathers in the mid-1930s were inclined to encourage their children to emigrate but stay in Germany themselves. This was for instance the case for families that had Zionist convictions and saw the building of a Jewish state in Palestine as an attractive option. Josef Zwienicki (b. 1892) requested from the Office for Economic Aid (*Zentralstelle für Wirtschaftshilfe*) of the Jewish Community in Bremen financial aid for his son's two-year *hachschara* (preparation), a Zionist program for Jewish youth to prepare for their emigration to Palestine.[41] Overall, however, it was quite uncommon for parents to separate and send their children abroad prior to the pogroms of 1938. Only when antisemitic discrimination and violence escalated in 1938 and Jewish men were arrested did many overcome their reluctance to emigrate and react to this unexpected eruption of violence by re-evaluating their families' and children's future. In a situation of acute desperation and men's physical absence from their homes in cases of arrest, numerous Jewish parents decided that because of the fathers' exposed vulnerability and insecure future, it was time for their children to get out of Germany.

As Marion Kaplan has pointed out, the question of emigration was gendered, with many Jewish men in the early years of the Third Reich being especially hesitant to give up their military honour and work achievements. When Jewish men considered emigration more seriously in the late 1930s, often acceding to their wives' pressure, many found themselves on a waiting list for obtaining visas to foreign countries. In such a situation, Jewish fathers, together with their wives or unilaterally, sometimes decided to expedite their children's emigration through various means, such as the *Kindertransporte* programs designed by foreign aid agencies to facilitate the immediate emigration of Jewish refugee children from Germany.

As the architect Otto Kollisch of Baden in Austria recorded in his memoir soon after *Kristallnacht*,

> I tried everything to get out of Germany. In the meantime, I registered
> my children for an action to England at the *Kultusgemeinde*, where they

promised me that at least the older boy, 6 years old, could go in January to England.[42]

Also in 1938, Hermann Pineas (b. 1892), a neurologist at the Jewish hospital in Berlin, registered his son with the Youth Aliyah (Hebrew for immigration) Program, founded in 1933, that sponsored and organized the emigration of Jewish youth to Palestine. Pineas was racked with guilt after signing his son up for this project, as the program was based on hard manual labour and an agricultural lifestyle in Palestine, a "trade" in which his son had shown no interest at all.[43] Yet, in this situation of perceived increasing danger to the family's existence, Pineas deemed his son's safety more important than his possible future profession. Born to a non-Jewish mother but raised Jewish (and considered Jewish by the government), Hans Alfred Rosenthal (b. 1924) remembered that when his father returned from a concentration camp months after *Kristallnacht*, his father and his uncle both immediately left for Shanghai, likely anticipating more violence against them and other Jewish men. As his father deemed the tropical weather and unsanitary conditions in Asia not suitable for his wife and child, however, prior to his own departure he registered his son for a *hachschara* program.[44] It was his way of making sure his child was safe while also taking care of himself.

With children leaving first and parents staying behind in Germany, the latter were not spared continued anxiety. For fathers, being separated from their children was painful, as they were no longer able to perform the protector role, though ambiguous in the first place. As Erich Frey recalled in his diary in 1941,

> Our worries began immediately after your departure, Miriam. We believed you were already in Palestine and then the war started. The Palestine Office informed us only that your group was well but had not landed yet in Haifa.[45]

Parents suffering from separation from their children was one thing, but the ensuing concerns following the separation, as Frey's diary entry demonstrates, were another. Their inability to intervene on behalf of their children's safety was troubling for many Jewish parents and especially for fathers who had adhered to an image of the shielding protector but who were now reduced to a state of powerlessness and inactivity.

In cases when Jewish parents left Germany without their children, and even if these had long reached adulthood, it was not only women who expressed emotional concern. Jewish fathers as the supposed guardians could still display serious concerns over their children's well-being. The fifty-eight-year-old Salomon Riemer (b. 1880), after having settled in Palestine together with his wife in 1936, sent the following letter to his sister-in-law, who lived either in Britain or North America:

Tel Aviv, 1 October 1938
My dear, faithful Sister-in-law,
    Herr Max Slaten was so kind as to forward your address to me. We have not written to each other in over three decades, and I was very pleased to hear that you are still alive. Hopefully you are healthy and doing well. In eight days, I will be married for twenty-eight years and eight days after that I will turn fifty-eight years old. I have three children. One son is twenty-seven and in Berlin. His name is Werner. The second's name is Herbert, twenty-six; he is married and lives in Antwerp. Then I have a little girl, who is eighteen and a half. For two and a half years, my wife and I have been living in Palestine. I am subsisting from the sale of coffee, cacao and tea … It is hard but I am managing to provide [*Lebensunterhalt aufbringen*] … I would be immensely grateful if you could help us regarding my oldest son. Palestine is currently not allowing anyone to enter. Germany is a hell and Jews are being persecuted innocently. They are not allowed to live, are not allowed to work, and if things continue the way they are, Jews will vanish due to starvation. My wife Minna and I are very much concerned for our boy and don't know, due to all this excitement and trouble, what to do. Believe me, Dear Pauline, when Werner sends us a letter, our hearts tremble and we have sleepless nights. Perhaps you can give us some advice and get into touch with people who can do something … An immediate solution is required if the boy is not to perish (*untergehen*) in Berlin … Heartfelt greetings from your loving brother-in-law Salomon.[46]

Riemer's letter provides valuable insights into the emotional state of Jewish parents, and especially Jewish fathers, for a number of reasons. First, in a somewhat expected, generic manner, Riemer refers to his profession and the source of income as a display of bourgeois masculinity. His status as income-maker and head of a household is codified. Second, Riemer emphatically echoes his understanding of the male protector role. Though his wife is equally worried about her son (and possibly more directly related by blood to the addressee of the letter), it was the father's task to draft the letter and make sure that his children were physically safe and sound. Though his son was well into adulthood, and despite the considerable geographic distance that lay between father and "child" and despite having no practical solutions at hand, Riemer still felt responsible for his son's well-being.

Starting in 1933, Jewish fathers had to confront the predicament of somehow fulfilling the protector role in Nazi Germany while facing an uncertain future. Even though many German Jews were able to escape Nazi Germany prior to the Holocaust, many did remain. For Jewish fathers who were not able to send their children abroad first, being a guardian thus turned into a challenge. On the day of *Kristallnacht*, 10 November 1938, the Wiesbaden merchant and war veteran Hans Berger saw the burning synagogue in his hometown when he decided to drive to his children's school to assess their safety. Even as Jewish men were being arrested *en masse*, Berger found the time to make the arrangements that day for his children to be picked up and safely returned to their home.[47] It was his way of fulfilling his role as a father. Siegmund Weltlinger (1886–1974), founding member and first Jewish president of the Society for Christian-Jewish Cooperation in Berlin in 1949, recalled that in 1938, "I brought my daughter to piano lessons in the afternoon because I thought it was not safe for her to go alone."[48] The safety concerns were based on a gendered tradition that made Jewish fathers take an active role in the family by trying to maintain a level of comfort and security for their children.

Apart from expressions of concern and seeking immigration, there was little that Jewish fathers could do to protect their families in the Third Reich, a striking example of the undermining of their fatherhood roles and marginalization of masculinity. The war veteran Joseph Adler (b. 1895), in a reflection written only weeks after the pogroms, recalled that when a non-Jewish acquaintance of his offered to take his children temporarily to her place for them to be safe, Adler grudgingly accepted. As a father, he had realized his limited options:

> And if they come to pick me up and shoot me tomorrow morning – What can I do about it? Shall I flee tonight, leaving everything behind, without a passport, without possessions, and dependent upon the charity of strangers? And is it all possible with a wife and two children to cross the border on the black market?[49]

Adler's disillusionment and despair over being the decision maker and head of the family is striking. Sending his own children away in such an extraordinary situation was perceived as a final option, yet no less embarrassing. Berger's and Adler's reactions demonstrate that safety was a major concern for Jewish parents, both mothers and fathers.

Jewish mothers were no less concerned than their husbands and no less active in trying to bring their children into safety.[50] But as part of a gendered cultural catalogue of norms and expectations, Jewish men were severely affected by the pressure to perform the expected protector role. Though there were several means that Jewish fathers could, under certain circumstances, make use of, such as relocating their children out of Germany or to parts of Germany that were deemed safer, on the whole the means to conform to and display their gendered behaviour of being the protector were increasingly limited. As a result, Jewish fathers experienced their loss of patriarchal power not simply as Jews but as Jewish men.

Jewish fathers' roles in the Third Reich were transformed, in addition to the curtailment of the protector role, in other ways that paralleled the situations of Jewish men as husbands. With rising unemployment, Jewish men took on a new and increasingly visible presence in the domestic sphere. As was pointed out earlier, Jewish masculinities developed unevenly, with some Jewish men adopting depressive behaviours and even committing suicide, while for others their new lives opened new doors. Being at home had an impact not only on Jewish men's self-understanding as former breadwinners or husbands but also on family life, leading fathers and children to spend more time together and to build a new intimacy of trust.

So far, historians have paid little attention to reciprocal relationships that existed between fathers and their children and the exchange of signs of love and affection between both.[51] The construct of the authoritative/absent father has been recently questioned by historians, who have revealed in their studies that historians too often have uncritically conflated cultural norms and social realities.[52] John LaRossa thus argues for the distinction between the *culture* and *conduct* of fatherhood. The first refers to norms, values, beliefs, and expressive symbols that fathers were expected to follow and the attitudes and sentiments people had towards fathers; the second connotes routine practices by fathers in "trying to act fatherly."[53] While historians have often focused on cultures of fatherhood that might have prescribed proper fatherly behaviours as being emotionally reserved and strict, the *conduct* of fatherhood has received less attention. Yet much evidence suggests that German fathers, Jewish and non-Jewish, demonstrated interest in and affection for their children in the late nineteenth and early twentieth centuries. Even in the Third Reich, as Amy Beth Carney has demonstrated in her study of fatherhood among SS soldiers, the Nazi state encouraged fathers to show affection and actively support mothers in infant care by changing diapers or pushing a stroller, in soldierly uniform, with no repercussions in terms of undermining their masculinity and soldierly dignity.[54]

Similarly, an abundance of evidence shows that Jewish men openly acknowledged their affection for their children and expressed it in writing, even if only in private spaces such as diaries. Starting in the nineteenth century, many Jewish fathers strove to be involved in the raising of children; contemporary Jewish educators and ideologues certainly advised them to do so, and traditional rabbinical advice had long praised what were considered feminine virtues and behaviours as part of Jewish masculinity.[55] And even though, in the nineteenth century, notions of military masculinity gradually undermined the relevance and importance of the "feminine" side of Jewish men, in the private sphere the model of the affectionate, tender father was common, and as the following discussion will demonstrate, could seamlessly co-exist with more "masculine" qualities under Nazi oppression or, paradoxically, even be strengthened.

In the Third Reich, Jewish fathers spent more time at home and were thus in closer contact with their children.[56] This was a significant departure from established practices. Baader points out that in the late nineteenth century Jewish men spent more time outside the home, conforming to ruling middle-class standards of conduct:

> [Jewish] contemporaries elevated motherhood and raised doubts about fathers' aptitudes for deeply bonding with the children ... Men ... who had to divide their time and their energy between public and domestic duties were "occupied too much and too fully outside of the [domestic] sanctuary" to provide full moral and religious guidance to their children.[57]

It was not until 1933 that many Jewish fathers were abruptly faced with a surplus of free time, which they used to stay at home and thus come into closer contact with their children. While "Aryan" men (and to some degree women) were supposed to spend increasing amounts of time outside the home in various Nazi organizations, for Jewish parents, and unemployed men especially, it was the opposite. Unlike their Gentile counterparts, Jewish men withdrew into the quiet, private sphere. Alfred Meyer (b. 1920) dryly recalled that his father, an attorney by profession, prior to 1933 had spent little time with him and his brothers growing up:

Only in the Third Reich did he spend more time [with us] because his job as an attorney resulted in more free time. He devoted much attention to his children's education, including learning languages.[58]

With their newly available time, Jewish fathers could spend this time with their children in a variety of ways. They would walk with their children to the city park, or as Willy Cohn recorded in his diary, alleviate their wives' work pressure by bringing their children to kindergarten.[59] In 1941, he noted:

Yesterday went for a walk in the sun with Tamara [his daughter, b. 1938] and bought something at the automat. This is the only happiness I can provide the children, going with them to the automat ... the only one that currently has sweets. The children of today have become very modest in their wants.[60]

The increased periods of time fathers spent with their children meant an increase in intimacy, trust, and friendship. On a walk with his other daughter in March 1940, Cohn noted,

Went for a walk in the afternoon with Susanne [b. 1932]. When I walk alone with her, she talks more openly. She told me that she often cries at night thinking about her brothers and sister.[61]

Fritz Goldberg (b. 1923) recalled how his father in the 1930s took him to nearby public baths following the closure of the city pool for Jews in his hometown of Altenburg. In his car, Goldberg senior would drive his son into smaller towns where no Jews lived and thus no similar antisemitic prohibitions had yet been implemented.[62] It is one of the paradoxes of the social history of Jewish life in the Third Reich that while adult Jews were becoming more desperate, some children in fact remembered parts of their childhood in the Third Reich in a rather positive light, as quality time spent with the *entire* family.

While increased and unprecedented socialization with children could transform Jewish fathers into private persons who could better extend their love and trust to their children, these men also continued in their bourgeois endeavour to further their children's development through education, a central and defining element of the German-Jewish middle class.[63] Furthering their children's education was striking proof not only of how Jewish fathers remained active agents, seeking to engage in "productive labour," but also of how they envisioned a future existence in Germany or abroad, thus making it imperative for their children to be better prepared for the post-Nazi era. Together with his children, Alfred Schwerin studied English and Spanish.[64] Victor Klemperer observed how several Jewish male acquaintances had started teaching their children:

> Aris said he is teaching his two children, the eldest is nine, himself, so that afterward, they would immediately be able to enter a secondary school. Likewise, Eisenmann senior told me that he teaches his nine-year old Lisel himself. The ban on schooling is a dreadful disgrace. The Jews are simply supposed to sink down into a state of illiteracy. But the Nazis will not achieve that.[65]

Even absent children received fatherly advice and solemn reminders to take their studies seriously. Jewish fathers as much as mothers engaged in long-distance parenting during the years of the Holocaust, regardless of age.[66] In many letters sent in 1939 to his son Erich, who had emigrated to the United States, the fifty-seven-year-old lawyer Albert Rose (b. 1882) reminded his son to stay focused.

> Dear Erich,
>   You write that you are going to be in Berkeley by the end of May. When does the next semester begin there? Do not waste any time because you have no time to waste. In particular, do not go to New York. You can achieve more in Berkeley than in New York ... Your ambition should be to start and finish your studies in Berkeley as soon as possible, and I am of the opinion that you cannot get to Berkeley fast enough. Who knows what is going to happen in the meantime ... If I were you, I would pull all strings to get to Berkeley as fast as possible. Think about it again ... In the meantime, learn English, English and again English.[67]

In a letter that soon followed the first one, on 14 February 1939, Rose demandingly inquired,

> Are you learning English? Have you received the geography book about the United States and the technical lexicon? I am also going to send you an English-American dictionary which will certainly be of help to you.[68]

Other fathers started teaching their children as a way of fighting boredom while also making some money on the side and maintaining a sense of usefulness.[69] As these examples demonstrate, Jewish fathers' unemployment could have a positive side-effect, in a paradoxical way, resulting from their new free time that they could spend with their offspring. Children provided them with an amusing pastime but also relayed to them an emotional sense of belonging and, more importantly, a sense of purpose. Jewish masculinity in the Third Reich could evolve into the role of the entertaining and mentor father, a reciprocal relationship that benefited both father and child.

Yet, dependencies in this father-child relationship also began to shift. Though both father and children benefited from each other's support, it was Jewish fathers who became increasingly dependent on their children for their own psychological and physical well-being. As the former lawyer Kurt Rosenberg (1900–77) pointed out in his diary,

> I belong to the kind of people who are suffering from tiredness that appears when the path in front of you melts away. The feeling of safety of your own home and the harmony with wives and children are the only and decisive counterweights.[70]

To some fathers, like Rosenberg, their children heightened a will to persevere, to make it through the Nazi years and avoid ending their lives prematurely. As Willy Cohn noted in his diary on 5 May 1933, "What I would really like to do is just give it up, if I didn't have a modicum of a sense of responsibility and weren't thinking of my family."[71] Max Krakauer (1888–1965), who with his wife went illegally underground in 1942, defying Nazi deportation orders, had to change hiding places numerous times, being reliant on the goodwill of strangers. He remembered how tired and despondent both he and his wife had become after being transferred from one place to another. "Did this all still make sense? The thought of our only daughter in England pulled us up."[72] Instead of one-dimensionally performing the role of the supporter, Jewish fathers thus also found an existential source of sustenance in their children. Even absent children could conjure up a stronger will to live in their fathers. Thinking of seeing their children again could constitute a life-inspiring survival strategy. In his diary-memoir written in 1939 after he had recently followed his two daughters to the United States, Max Cohnreich (1882–1949) expressed gratitude to his children for helping him overcome his perceived failures:

> Rutchen and Evchen, beside my wife, were and are giving me the fundamental reason for liking my life. My pride in my daughters, resulting from their success, equals my love for them, but surpasses its importance for my very existence. It is this pride that was and still is my greatest stimulus for every action or effort. It is this pride that on the one hand lets me forget the defeats of my own life and on the other hand, convinces me

that at least one goal of my striving has been reached, the happiness of my children.[73]

In a similar vein, the single parent Alfred Schwerin (b. 1892) was quite moved when he saw a letter of gratitude from his daughter, whom Schwerin had managed to send to France in 1939 with the help of a children's refugee organization. On her last day at home, his daughter wrote the following letter:

> Dear Papa,
>   I thank you for everything you have done for me and hope that you are going to be all right while I am gone. You shall long live under this roof. I wish you all the best. Many heartfelt greetings and kisses from your Ellen.[74]

Schwerin recalled that when he saw the letter, he kissed his sleeping child and took the letter. "It weighed more than gold and jewels," he recalled in his 1944 memoir.[75] Both father and child were reunited in Switzerland following the father's illegal border crossing. It was such signs of affection, at times openly expressed and acknowledged between father and child and at other times relegated to the private realm of diaries and retrospective memoirs, that helped Jewish fathers (and children) to better endure times of hardship. Children's love for their parents could constitute an important counterweight and inspiration to these men.

As has been pointed out, Jewish fathers in their self-perceived provider and protector roles primarily pursued their children's well-being. Not being able to fulfil this principle of fatherhood was a painful experience and constituted a challenge to Jewish hegemonic masculinity. Particularly because of reduced incomes with fewer financial means available, Jewish parents were increasingly unable to provide material resources for their children as they had done previously. Special treats as signs of parental love became rare. Hans Winterfeldt remembered how as a young boy he had wished for a bicycle. His father's business, a general store in a small town in Brandenburg, was doing so poorly that his father was unable to purchase the bike. His father had even contacted the manufacturer directly, hoping for a reduced price, but even this, Hans recalled, was too much for his father, who felt deeply sorry.[76] Similarly unable to purchase any gifts for his children, the former teacher Willy Cohn confessed to his diary, "I am short on money ... It is very difficult for a father when he is unable to do what he would like to do."[77] Marie Jalowicz (1922–98) remembered her father's desperation during the war: "Again and again, he told me that he wanted to offer me a nice life. But he could not do anything. Again and again, I tried to tell him that I did not care for this."[78] Bourgeois concepts of work masculinity and notions of Jewish fatherhood patently overlapped. Bereft of incomes, Jewish providers could also not entirely fulfil their fatherly roles.

The inability of Jewish fathers to provide material happiness and their ensuing pain as emasculated fathers, however, was minor compared to the pain fathers together with their wives experienced when they had to separate from their children. Already in late 1935, the physician Hertha Nathorff bluntly noted in her diary, "Poor parents ... How terrible these transports are ... From now on, their lives will consist of waiting for letters from their children."[79]

From a Jewish father's perspective, while the loss of the provider and protector role might have been humiliating and painful, his separation from his children was certainly the most excruciating blow.[80] Numerous accounts encapsulate the pain of fathers at their forced separation from their children. Grete Rosenzweig recalls the tears that ran down her husband's cheek when they dropped off their daughter at the train station for her departure to England. "It was the only time I ever saw him cry."[81] Otto Kollisch, too, remembered the day of his children's *Kindertransport*:

> For our children, the leaving was rather fun, because of all the other children, and we were kind of happy about that, that the children did not feel any psychological pain. We also pulled ourselves extremely together when we said good-bye, so that they couldn't tell our sad hearts. When the train pulled out of the hall, hardly anyone could withhold their tears ... We drove home depressed. Once we arrived here, we really could feel the absence of the children because of the sudden stillness, and tears came down my wife's and my cheeks.[82]

Kollisch's excerpt is intriguing as it evinces how *both* mother and father experienced their painful separation from their children. While references to women in tears and crying might not surprise or challenge cultural gender norms (but in fact reinforce images of feminine emotionality), overt expressions of agony by Jewish men such as Kollisch's do. Such instances deviate, as LaRossa has argued, from the culture of fatherhood that foresaw a type of tough masculinity, according to which men were to act unwaveringly and withstand any adversity without shedding a tear. As this study demonstrates, the conduct of Jewish fatherhood paints a different picture.

One of the most revealing sources that underlines the pain Jewish men endured as fathers is Willy Cohn's diary (figures 21 and 22). Over the course of several years, he expressed his suffering at being forcibly separated from his children:

18 April 1933: Wölfl [his eldest son, b. 1915] is gone now. It was a very difficult farewell. But a father is not eager to commit to paper or express how he feels at such a moment.

6 October 1933: Trudi went to see Sophie Kaim, who leads the Youth Aliyah; we got the forms. I decided quickly and filled out the forms. Registering can be withdrawn at any time but it keeps the door open. I would find separation from this son very difficult as well, but in these times, we must not be egoistic but think only of the future of our children.

31 December 1933: This year … For me personally, it was very painful to separate from my eldest son.

7 August 1934: My separation from Wölfl weighs heavily on me, as does the shrinking prospect of me seeing him again in the foreseeable future. This feeling overwhelms me at night in particular. But none of this is of any help and we must simply endure it.

9 November 1934: We received news from the Jewish youth assistance society that Ernst's group will probably leave in December. And so the time draws ever nearer when the pain of separation will be upon me. Nonetheless, I know that the boy will be set free and have a future ahead of him. As a father one may not be selfish in any way.

8 December 1934: It is always wonderful to see the pleasure in the children's eyes … I was fearful after Wölfl left. It is now almost three-quarters of a year since he has been gone, and unfortunately, I will be unable to meet him in St Gallen at Christmas. I won't have the money together.

18 December1934: I decided to travel to St Gallen after all since they granted me the necessary foreign currency. Felix Perle was good enough to lend 200 marks to finance the trip. I hope that I will be able to repay him over the course of January from receipts from my lecture tour. Exactly how much that will bring in I cannot tell at the moment. Nonetheless, a person must be willing to incur risk to see his child again.

30 November 1936: I have a great desire to see my children.

12 December 1937: Wölfl and Ernst haven't celebrated my birthday here for quite a few years, but I am grateful to G'd that they are doing well so far.

24 November 1938: Efforts to find a place for Ruth and Susanne in Switzerland … We agreed immediately … What our hearts will endure if

Figure 21. Photograph of Willy Cohn, 1937.

Figure 22. Photographs of Willy Cohn's daughters, 1939.

we must send our children away is something best not talked about. But that is not the point. The main thing is that the children be safe in case these things repeat, which could quickly happen again! The children look forward to the prospect.

4 March 1939: Susannchen is seven years old today. The child is my heart's consolation and my sunshine. I cannot imagine ever separating from her.

16 September 1939: Ruth's train will be leaving in fifteen minutes, Trudi took Susannchen with her to the train station. I stayed at home so as not to leave Tamara alone. It is hard to say what a person feels at such moments. It is as if everything has frozen up. Nonetheless, I must reconcile myself because it is in my child's best interest. The tragedy of our times is that we must send her on her way completely alone much too early, but hopefully it is best for her.

Footnote by the diaries' editor: Ruth later wrote that her father stayed home because he would have found saying goodbye at the train station unbearable.

25 December 1940: We gave Hanukah presents to Susanne and Tamara in the afternoon … [They] were very happy which makes all the work that we have done the whole year through worth it, just to see the happiness in our children's eyes.[83]

Cohn's affection for his children is salient, and it is likely that he did not limit his love to the realm of the diary but treated his children lovingly in person. Cohn's diary illustrates how torn fathers were when they had to separate from their children and how dependent they had become on their children's well-being for their own well-being. Weltlinger poignantly summed up how excruciating it was to depart from his children as follows:

> What it means for parents to separate from their children – often in the most tender age – for an unknown period, perhaps for always, anyone can understand. When I returned from the concentration camp, I had to separate from my children. They departed, aged 15 and 17 with 10 Marks in their pockets into foreign lands. Only many years later did we hear from one another, after they had thought us to be long dead. The heart-breaking scenes at the departures of children from their parents at the train stations are the most terrible thing I have ever experienced. Most children never saw their parents again.[84]

Physically separating from their children in the late 1930s, as the above examples demonstrate, was a painful experience for both Jewish mothers and fathers. Perhaps even more excruciating was the final farewell to their children. During the war, Jewish parents, whose children often had left for overseas, sent their last (Red Cross) letters, made final diary entries that directly addressed their children, and sometimes wrote suicide notes, also addressed to their children. These writings reflected an awareness that they would never see their children again. In such situations, with ambivalent emotions of anger, love, despair, and calmness, Jewish fathers could not help but provide some final advice to the children. The former lawyer Gustav Meyer (b. 1884), in his farewell letter prior to his and his wife's deportation to Theresienstadt in March 1943, wrote as follows to his three sons:

> Let the picture of your parents, which you have taken with you in your spirit into foreign lands, be an example for the organization of your own family lives. Do think often about us when you are unsure how to handle this or that problem! Keep tight among you the brotherly ties and help one another ... We are thinking about you day and night and are keeping you in our memories as good, industrious [tüchtig] and affectionate children ... Be dearly kissed from your Father.[85]

Yakob Langer's father, in his suicide note to his son, included several addresses of people his son could contact to ask for help once the war was over.[86] Erich Frey in his diary, addressing his overseas children, also included a number of names and addresses in case they ever needed help. These people were "very much obligated to me," he stated. He also included tax information about his assets, prudently foreseeing legal issues of restitution in the postwar era.[87] Besides giving sombre advice and reaching out to support their children via acquaintances, they also commonly used their diaries or letters as a medium to give an emotional farewell that carried a final element of fatherly loving advice, as exemplified in this letter from Erich Frey:

> Dear Beloved Children,
>   … Perhaps we may no longer be alive and that is not improbable in view of the happenings of the last year. Do not be sad then. Read calmly through this report, which I kept as factual and sober as possible and tell yourselves: thank God they have finished enduring. But you can believe us that we are attached to you with every fibre of our hearts and that we have only one wish for you: may you be healthy and happy. As far as we are concerned, our only wish is to see you again and to talk to at least one of you. We thus will be reassured that you are well and can look forward to a future that will be more beautiful and radiant than anything Jewry has ever experienced, even in its prime.[88]

The final instruction not to mourn was, of course, hardly meant. Still, the fatherly hope to spare their children from future agony was certainly genuine.

Conclusion

The challenges of losing status and respect in society as well as the means of income were all aggravated by the fact that Jewish men felt responsible not only for themselves but also for their wives and children, facing pressures to conform to traditional gender roles that defined men, regardless of class, age, or ethnicity, as breadwinners for and protectors of their families.[89] James Bachner (b. 1922) recalled how emotionally unsettling the increasing constraints in 1938 had become for his father:

> After we had boarded the train … Papa couldn't contain himself and started crying like a child. We hugged each other lovingly and eventually, he regained his composure. Everything he had worked for all those years was gone. All his plans for our future had evaporated into thin air. Our family was torn apart and the immediate future depended upon finding

refuge … with our [relatives] so that Mutti and Fred [his brother] could follow us.[90]

Based on the postulated hypothesis that Jewish men in the Holocaust became despondent and unable to protect their families,[91] this chapter has sought to analyse in detail how Jewish men's protector roles deteriorated yet did not fully dissolve, and how, through multiple means, Jewish men sustained their masculine identities as husbands and fathers in Nazi Germany. Providing practical and symbolic protection, communicating affection and tenderness, as well as offering guidance and mentoring advice were central elements of this identity construction, from which Jewish husbands and fathers also reciprocally benefited.

In their attempts to cope with the variety of Nazi challenges, German-Jewish men relied on gender conventions such as the protector role. Men's reliance on gender norms reflected in the plurality of masculinities that Jewish men used to construct their masculine identities. Some Jewish men, for instance, combined work masculinity and the protector role and moved to different parts of Germany or abroad seeking to fulfil both roles. Military masculinity also guided the coping strategies of some men in their roles as guardians and heads of households. Some, such as Alfred Schwerin, tried to create a feeling of security at home for their families through performing the role of the military hero. With a great dose of hindsight, Schwerin remembered in his memoir that around 1938 he had anticipated a major *Aktion* against Germany's Jews and thus was mentally prepared. Even more, he wanted to prepare his nine-year-old daughter for future adversities. As he recalled telling her,

> Should I ever get arrested and sent to Dachau, do not be afraid and do not get frightened by anyone. You know I have participated in the world war. I have also told you many times that I had always been in the first line of combat and that even though I had been injured several times and contracted typhoid in Russia, I never had the feeling that something bad could happen to me. Conversely, I felt the confidence that I would return to my home [*Heimat*] healthy and safely. This feeling did not betray me. Listen then closely: Should I get arrested and transferred to Dachau, stay calm and wait. As confident as I had been in 1914–1918 that I would return home, as strongly I declare to you today that I will also endure Dachau and return to you.[92]

Schwerin's memory attests to the gendered character memories can take.[93] Jewish men's narrative recollections of taking a heroic role served a purpose that went beyond the events in question, one that might have helped the authors at the time of writing to regain authority and status that they had lost but that the memoirists did not fully disclose in their writing. It seems puzzling that Schwerin could have precisely predicted a nation-wide pogrom that caught most other German Jews by surprise on 9 November 1938, and that he even could foresee the place of his internment, as he was indeed later sent to Dachau. His memoir, though imbued with hindsight, is still insightful as it integrates the author's military identity and his identity as the protecting father, cumulatively constituting Jewish masculinity.

Again, age is a crucial factor to be considered in this context, as Jewish fathers who were also World War I veterans often felt safer from Nazi insults. They had survived the war, they reasoned, so they would endure Hitler's dictatorship as well. Perhaps naively, these men radiated their belief in safety within their home and among their families. As war veterans, many felt prepared for Nazi attacks and thought they could project their mental strength and sense of preparedness onto their families. Many did not even envision that Nazi insults could be directed at deserving war veterans. Military masculinity and concepts of the male protector were intertwined.

Though Jewish men could rely on other types of masculinity, as this chapter has argued, some Jewish men's identities as husbands and fathers altered. Cut off from the public sphere, some Jewish men started to cherish norms of traditional Jewish culture by coming to re-appreciate or newly appreciate models of domesticity, marriage, and the family, especially if they had a certain class background, having previously come to esteem education. As mentor-educators, they could now personally pass on the bourgeois ideal of being well-educated.[94] Though men might have varied in the degree to which they built relations of trust, care, and support with their children and spouses – and it was not only after the Nazis had come to power that Jewish men started to become emotional subjects and to display affection towards their families – considerable evidence suggests that after 1933 Jewish men became more "domesticated," taking on a new presence at home and interacting with the rest of the family, while women, as Marion Kaplan has shown, took on increasing responsibilities in the public sphere.

In addition to acting as the *providers* of protection, guidance, and emotional care, especially through a new level of intimate interaction with their children at home or abroad, Jewish men were also the *recipients* of important emotional support that made their lives more bearable but also dependent. Men gained a sense of relief as children provided a distraction from the harsh realities they were facing. Children gave meaning and purpose to the lives of Jewish parents, motivating them to work to ensure their children's well-being as well as strengthening their own will to persevere and survive. Children, in other words, were fundamentally important for the emotional and psychological health of Jewish men in the Third Reich. Even though their roles as fathers changed and the means to perform the protector role (albeit ambiguous in the first place) became more restricted, they were not deprived of fatherhood. By maintaining fatherhood, Jewish men could retain an important element of their masculinity. The affection and guidance but also the pain and agony that Jewish fathers inscribed in their diaries – perhaps only meant for posterity – and in letters addressed to their children – often far away – are thus emblematic of how they understood their masculine roles as fathers and husbands.[95] Nazism, in short, was not successful in undermining German Jews' dignity and sense of self-worth. German-Jewish men succeeded in preserving identities as husbands and fathers, a notion that historiography needs to take more note of.[96]

And what about Jewish sons? Observing how their role-model fathers and other men had accepted their responsibilities as men and not given up, neither surrendering to passive behaviour nor abandoning their families, Jewish sons, internalized and grew into the roles and expectations their fathers had adhered to for years. Over the course of the Third Reich, witnessing their often elderly parents suffer and decline emotionally and economically, adolescent Jewish sons came to a reckoning of their increased responsibility in helping out the family. This included precisely the same roles that Jewish fathers and husbands had exemplified through their own lives of being the protector, caregiver, and mentor. Arthur Katz-Kamer (b. 1910) did not leave Nazi Germany, since he could not imagine leaving his parents behind in such a calamitous situation.[97] He felt his parents needed him. Others who did leave Germany, hoping to first establish themselves economically and then have their parents follow later, did so reluctantly and often with feelings of guilt. The war veteran Joseph Adler (b. 1895) recalled how hard it was to leave his mother behind. The department store owner Carl Schwabe, the Berlin-based journalist Alexander Szanto (1899–1972), and the economist Dr Alfred Wolf (1898–1981) expressed similar feelings of guilt.[98] On the other hand, adult sons who did stay behind, voluntarily or not, offered important support to their elderly parents. Isaak Behar (1923–2011) felt major relief when he and his father were assigned forced labour assignments with the same firm. At work, Isaak could make sure his elderly father was safe, and if his father could not keep up with the hard and fast-paced work, the son could help and protect him from his cruel supervisor.[99] As Cioma Schönhaus (1922–2015) recalled when his father was arrested and sent to a concentration camp in 1938,

> Eleven o'clock passed and Papa did not come back ... We walked across Alexanderplatz ... Mama was biting her lip. Tears were rolling down her face. I gave her my arm and she took it. I was the man of the family now.[100]

Chapter Five

Outside the *KZ*: Jewish Masculinities and the Rise of Nazi Violence

The following two chapters analyse the forms of violence and brutality that Nazi terror inflicted on Jewish men in the prewar years and demonstrate how such violence had an impact on Jewish masculine identities and gender relations. The chapters bring to light a new understanding of the bias of Nazi antisemitic violence *prior* to the actual Holocaust, with Jewish men as the primary victims. Chapters 5 and 6, thus, go against a historiography that solely focuses on racist ideology as the driving force of Nazi antisemitism and instead argue that German-Jewish men were targeted gender-specifically and victimized in prewar Nazi Germany not simply as Jews but as Jewish men. In turn, Jewish men as "endangered men" reacted in gendered ways and developed gender-specific coping mechanisms to avoid violations of their bodies and psyches. Thus, while in chapter 2 the focus has been on Nazi attacks in discursive forms used for propaganda purposes, the following two chapters look at physical attacks and its effects on Jewish men. Whereas chapter 6 focuses on Jewish men and their gendered experiences inside prewar Nazi concentration camps, this chapter examines forms of gendered violence and reactions outside the camps, in the private and public spheres, including German Jews' homes, workplaces, and public places of socialization.

Based on the widespread dissemination of antisemitic propaganda by the Nazi state throughout the 1930s, Jewish men in the prewar years were not just discursively emasculated in print media or motion pictures. Gendered Nazi propaganda could have a direct and immediate physical impact on Jewish masculinities. Based on the racial notion of a distinct Jewish physicality and demeanour, Jewish men corresponding to aforementioned features in the early to mid-1930s were singled out and victimized by the Nazis. By the late 1930s – prior to the decision to annihilate the entirety of European Jewry – antisemitic violence had evolved and increasingly targeted all Jewish men, regardless of their looks or economic backgrounds.

Adam Jones has charted how feminist scholarship has centred on the roots of male violence against women resulting in a "feminist-dominated analysis that designated males as the agents of the over-whelming majority of violent acts against women."[1] The result has been a large corpus of scholarship on gender and genocide that looks at victims of violence but uses gender synonymously for women. Important works on women and the Holocaust, such as those by Gisela Bock, Judith Baumel, Rochelle Saidel, and others, have significantly contributed to a deeper understanding of (Jewish) women's experience of dehumanization, sexual exploitation, and murder under the Nazi regime.[2] Yet, in such studies there is a lingering sense that men's victimization warrants no further scrutiny and can be taken for granted. The editor of *Gender and Catastrophe* (1997), Ronit Lentin, has argued that "the concentration camp was an ultimate expression of the extreme masculinity and misogyny that undergirded Nazi ideology in that both Aryan and non-Aryan women were targeted on the basis of their biological destiny."[3] Referencing the Nazi concentration camps and the practice of forced sterilizations in the Third Reich as salient examples of Nazi misogynist oppression, Lentin argues for an understanding of women's oppression by the Nazis. Such genocidal projects, the author asserts,

> rested on the eugenic conviction of German racial superiority [that] ine-vitably discriminated against women as child-bearers ... Elderly Jewish women (and men), useless to the Nazis, were sentenced to death. Women of childbearing age, although useful as workers, posed a menace because they could bear Jewish children and ensure the continuity of Jewish life.[4]

The research efforts and scholarship of historians who have adhered to a feminist understanding of gender have substantially added to a more sophisticated understanding of the myriad ways in which Jews in the Holocaust were persecuted and have come to process their victimization. However, excerpts such as the ones presented above tend to conflate the terms "gender" and "female." Such studies undermine gendered aspects of male suffering and male processing of violence. Lentin's use of brackets in the above quotation to include men who were also sentenced to death underlines this. Moreover, as chapter 2 has demonstrated, Jewish men were as important to the continued existence of the Jewish "race" as were childbearing women, and the previous discussion of Jewish race male "defilers" buttresses the central position that Jewish men, as potential impregnators of "Aryan" women, had in such discourses. Finally, it is questionable whether the

Nazi concentration camp was the ultimate expression of misogyny. Nazi concentration camps were first erected in 1933 and not, as the sheer number of studies on the Holocaust sometimes suggests, with the outbreak of World War II. With the beginning of the Third Reich in 1933, for years men – Jewish and non-Jewish – constituted the overwhelming number of prisoners who were tortured and often murdered, while, as Kim Wünschmann has argued, in the early years of the Third Reich, women were spared brutal forms of abuse as they did not reflect the male-gendered Jewish enemy stereotypes,[5] a process Nikolaus Wachsmann refers to as a "gender-determined delay in the use of terror."[6]

To be fair, some existing historiography has emphasized men's unique vulnerability in the pre-Holocaust period. Focusing on Jewish women, Sybil Milton and Joan Ringelheim were among the first to note, even if only tangentially, that Jewish men were the primary targets of the Nazis: "They were certainly the first Jewish victims of forced labor and in the beginning, the primary targets of the *Einsatzgruppen*."[7] Claudia Koonz also asserted that "women suffered far less from violent attacks than Jewish men until the deportations began in 1941. Before, the Gestapo, SA, police and angry mobs on the street assaulted only men."[8] Finally, as Marion Kaplan emphasized,

> [Nazi] racism was not gender-neutral. In imagery and practice, the Nazi government and most Germans treated Jewish women differently from Jewish men. Nazi propaganda castigated Jewish men as cheats and traitors, depicting them as greedy bankers and pimps. The Nazis persecuted Jewish men early on, culminating with their arrests during the November pogrom. With rare exceptions, Nazi policy before the deportations bowed to taboos against physically abusing women in the public.[9]

Such balanced findings by (feminist) historians of Jewish men's distinctly precarious situation in the pre-Holocaust years are a significant contribution to gender scholarship. Yet insights into men's vulnerable positions remain isolated and underemphasized. With a focus on women's history, the scholarship of the 1990s did not pursue deeper and nuanced distinctions with regard to the kind of violence men faced, and more importantly, what the consequences of such violence were for men and masculinity.[10] The objective of the following two chapters, then, is not to challenge feminist scholarship. Instead, it is to complement that literature with a work in which men, in this case Jewish men, as gendered beings prominently feature both as victims of violence and as agents of gendered responses.

As a starting point, a study of the effects of antisemitic propaganda and how it could be translated into violence against certain types of men proves helpful in conceptualizing early violence against German Jews. Chapter 2 has illustrated that racial-sexual antisemitic discourses targeted Jewish men and depicted them as sexual perverts, rapists, and race defilers, stigmatizing them as perpetrators of the most heinous crime in Nazi ideology. In turn, some Jewish men adapted to such discourses by conceptualizing themselves as "endangered men," withdrawing more into the private sphere or shying away from interacting with unfamiliar women in the public sphere. Antisemitic propaganda, however, was not limited to sexualized discourses but incorporated other themes that were political and economic in nature. Even in nonsexualized propaganda, Nazi antisemitism essentially relied on similar physiognomic features (e.g., nose, lips, hair) that portrayed the Jew as male and made *him*, "the Jew," easily recognizable.[11] There is a clear relationship between Nazi imagery of the 1930s and the violence that German-Jewish men faced.[12] The stereotyping of "the Jew" using male bodily features was not restricted to some radical Nazi ideologues working for a censored press but, as the photograph of the carnival parade demonstrates (Figure 23), was socially accepted and perpetuated. From this shared image of the enemy, it was one more step to target and assault German Jews physically.

As chapter 2 has illustrated, it was not only the visibility and recognizability of Jewishness, defined by Jewish maleness, that could lead to direct violence. A crucial association of Jewishness with criminality was forged. Jewish men were depicted as racial-sexual, economic, or political threats, ranging from race defilers to exploitative capitalist-profiteers or Judeo-Bolshevist conspirators. Ringelheim thus rightly argues that legitimation for targeting Jewish men was plentiful in antisemitic and racist propaganda: "They were already identified as dangerous."[13]

With the Jew being markedly identifiable as a Jewish man and being associated with notions of criminality, street violence against Jews became more frequent. Already in 1934, the German-Jewish émigré organization *Comité des Délégations Juives* published evidence of violent outbursts against Jews "on the street." Conceding that most of these attacks were politically motivated, the *Comité* argued, however, that given the pervasiveness of anti-Jewish propaganda, it would have been astonishing if some antisemites had not started to inflict violence on German Jews.[14] Violence, in other words, arrived in a predictable pattern that was synchronized with propaganda.

The young Hermann Pressmann (b. 1914), son of a wealthy entrepreneur in Berlin, noted several instances of violence in his diary entries during the first weeks of Hitler's regime:

Figure 23. A carnival procession in Cologne, 1934. This photograph shows antisemitic behaviour by Germans that was intended to ridicule Jews, depicted here as Jewish men, and urge Jews to leave Germany and emigrate to Palestine.

5 March 1933: Today is the elections for the new Reichstag … Earlier in the big traffic circle I saw two Nazis and their victim carried away on a stretcher. Maybe he was injured, maybe he was dead. I considered how dangerous it was even to walk along the streets, as I was doing. I thought to myself that I was lucky to be walking away, when I saw another victim being carried.

23 March 1933: In the streets are troublemakers and anti-Semites. You must let them have their peace without fighting or talking back … my own mind tells me to consider getting out of Germany while I am [still] alive.

22 April 1933: Yesterday … I was alone with the salesman. A large man drunk, or pretending to be drunk, entered our store. His name was Heine. He was one of the men involved in the hold up against my father a short time ago. He said he wanted money to buy a beer. He refused to leave empty-handed. The salesman tried to keep peace by suggesting I give him money … [Then] he came … to me for a leather jacket. He threatened to beat me to death unless I complied. I locked myself in our private office. He threatened to jump through the plate glass. When I unlocked the office, he punched my chin. I could not call the police. Last time they told me Jews were not entitled to police protection. Heine wanted to go to the back room and beat me. When he went into the back room, I ran outside. More of his buddies were out there. It was like going from the frying pan to the fire. I took a taxi and reported the incident to the police. I begged them to send [someone] to my father's store …

> By that time my parents were back in the store. Heine was still carrying
> on ... My parents bribed Heine to leave with a summer coat.[15]

Encounters such as these triggered in the junior Pressmann the decision to emigrate. "I would like to get out of this country as soon as
possible ... Germany is growing more dangerous"[16] Having settled in
Belgium a few months later, Pressmann resisted his parents' relentless
attempts to persuade him to return to Berlin. In his diary, he noted,
"I explained my position about Nazi arrests of visitors returning to Germany. Many of those in protective custody never returned alive."[17]

Pressmann's diary is instructive. In the first two diary entries, Pressmann did not make an explicit statement that the SA men were after
Jewish men only. However, he stated that he was lucky to walk away
unscathed and that it was too dangerous to talk back to these people.
In other words, Pressmann contemplated a possible scenario in which
he could fall victim to such street brutality. Because he had not been
engaged in politics, however, he should have had no reason to fear the
Nazi mob, unless he also considered his position as a Jewish man in
his early twenties whose looks corresponded to the Nazi stereotypes.
From the diarist's writing, it is unclear to what degree he perceived
his outward appearance to be a risk factor. Pressmann's diary entries
become more comprehensible when photographs of him are added to
the discussion of gendered imagery (Figure 24).

Pressman's outward resemblance to the Nazi stereotype of "the Jew"
is unmistakable, especially the caricature in the top-left of figure 25
that shares with the author black, slightly receding, frizzy hair, horn-
rimmed glasses, and protruding ears. The twenty-year-old bachelor was
clearly afraid of the Nazi violence that he had witnessed on the streets
and personally experienced in the first weeks of the Hitler regime. He
was so frightened and overwhelmed by it that he haphazardly, while
still dependent on his parents, decided to leave his family and home.
Though his case is not representative, as most German Jews in 1933 did
not escape from Germany and also did not fall victim to direct physical violence by antisemites, Pressmann convincingly demonstrates
that German Jews had become fair game in Nazi Germany, subject to
arbitrary violence at the hands of anyone who harboured antisemitic
resentment often without intervention by the state and the police. His
diary entries further suggest that violence was directed against men,
and though it remains speculation, it is likely that because of his close
resemblance to the pervasive and gendered propaganda images that
the Nazis constructed of the archetypical Jew, Pressmann in the first
months of the Hitler regime felt threatened.

Figure 24. Photograph of Hermann Pressmann (seated, far right) and family, c. 1930.

If Pressmann's diary is not explicit enough in regard to how a "Jewish-looking" man might have felt unsafe, other accounts are. Linking Nazi violence to antisemitic propaganda that showcased a distinct Jewish male physiognomy, the Berlin physician Hertha Nathorff (1895–1993) recorded an entry in her diary on 10 January 1934 about a male patient who had been beaten bloody on the street because people had thought he looked Jewish.[18] The physician and author Martin Gumpert (b. 1897) of Berlin, who managed to emigrate from Germany in 1936, recalled the following event that had occurred probably sometime in 1935:

> Hordes of young men emerged in the street. No doubt, they were camouflaged SA men. The night prior, a new, antisemitic movie had premiered in one of the major movie theatres … Windows were smashed and a train of people formed to search for Jews. Someone was carrying a distorted caricature of an old Jew with bloodshot eyes and wiry hair that was hanging down wild … A young man with a pince-nez on his nose was in panic running to the other side of the street, and a howling mob was running after him. A much larger group stood on the sidewalk and watched. The people were all silent. The expressions in their faces oscillated between curious enjoyment and repulsion. I stood next to these people and felt safe because they could not recognize in me the Jew, who was perpetually shown to them in the nefarious caricatures … *Der Stürmer* was displayed in showcases on the street … It was distributed in schools.[19]

Figure 25. An antisemitic caricature in *Der Stürmer*, titled "The Jewish Body," 1938. Clearly, the caricaturist relied on physiognomic features of Jewish men as representations of Jews in general.

Like Pressmann's excerpt, Gumpert's recollection is telling. First, the memoir illustrates that a large enough minority of German citizens – not only SA men in this case – succeeded in carrying out violent acts against German Jews in the early years of the Third Reich (while a larger group was standing by and observing the scene). More importantly, however, the episode indicates that antisemitic propaganda could directly lead to antisemitic violence. It clearly demonstrates that propaganda alone could be sufficient to inspire violent acts against Jewish men. Even more strikingly, no criminal act had to be formulated and no criminal evidence was needed to turn the Jewish-looking male with the pince-nez into a villain. His Jewish male appearance sufficed. Conclusively, it can be argued that it was not just a general manifestation of antisemitism in Nazi Germany that theoretically targeted all

Jews, not even all Jewish males, that led to violence in this case. Only through the male's identification by the angry mob as Jewish did he become the target of a hunt. Whether he actually was Jewish or not remains, ironically, unknown.

On the other hand, it would be misleading to argue that violence directed against German Jews in the prewar years was limited to Jewish-looking males. Violence simmered for years, with occasional eruptions, as in the days of the anti-Jewish boycotts in April 1933, or, of course, during *Kristallnacht* in November 1938. In these and other instances, Jews confronted forms of violence regardless of their outward appearance. Undoubtedly, other identifiers were also utilized to brand and persecute Jews.

Through communal and personal relations, German Jews' Jewish identity was generally known to Germans. Living within and on good terms with a Gentile society for decades, particularly in smaller towns where communal interactions were more customary, one knew if one's neighbour was Jewish or made his purchases in a Jewish store. Gerta Pfeffer (b. 1912) recalled that in the early months of the Third Reich, anyone could denounce or arrest a Jew. A well-known lawyer, Dr Werner, a highly decorated war veteran,[20] was in these tumultuous days arrested and murdered by the Nazis. Only after a few weeks of "letting off steam," according to Pfeffer, did some order return, and even though one could read about a reward for finding Dr Werner's murderer, no one was ever arrested.[21] Remembering the anti-Jewish boycott on 1 April 1933, Hermann Tuggelin (b. 1908) said,

> I went to the store because I did not want to leave [my] mother alone there. I was reading a newspaper, [when] SA thugs entered the business. "Today we can settle scores with the Jewish pigs." I did not fall for the provocation. In this moment, I received a terrible punch below my left eye. The blood splashed. I fell to the floor … The SA men fell over me, beating me. I do not know how long I was beaten … I was brought to the Jewish hospital. Afterwards, I did not walk to my mother. I did not want to jeopardize her.[22]

For Paul Barnay (b. 1884), an actor in Breslau, life dramatically changed on 10 March 1933. At his front door, he was arrested and told by two SA men to come with them to the police station. However, Barnay was driven to a nearby forest, and after walking for a few minutes, he was told to undress himself and do fifty push-ups. "Then punches pattered on me, whereupon I hit with my fist one of the guys in his face, making him fall into the bush." Barnay was then more brutally beaten. After this, the SA men drove away.

> I was lying naked and bleeding alone in the forest. From my neck to my knees, there was no uninjured part. Through my underpants, I felt a soft matter. Was it an injury? It was not a wound, and this angered and hurt me the most. Due to the kicks into my abdomen, I had emptied myself and now I was lying in blood and my feces. A bunch of blood and dirt. I was ashamed more than I was hurt.[23]

The three abridged examples of early violence inflicted upon German Jews are particularly revealing as there still remains a tendency, because of the (understandable) focus on the mass murder of European Jews during the Holocaust, to brush over the prewar years of Nazi rule when German Jews, men in particular, had become victims of physical violence. Moreover, while antisemitic propaganda was well supplied with claims of alleged Jewish misdeeds and criminal behaviour, the actual violence that was inflicted on Jews (and others) was downplayed or denied in the media.[24] Antisemitic violence occurred within a semi-public sphere, surrounded by a cloud of silence. Often, there was not even the pretence of a connection between the choice of victim and the application of antisemitic violence.[25] Jewish men like Barnay, it seems, were randomly and arbitrarily selected and victimized; not even theft seems to have been the main motive for the two SA men. It is thus crucial to realize that while antisemitic propaganda and its imagery of an alleged Jewish appearance could lead to direct violence against some men or to criminal investigations and convictions, as in the case of alleged Jewish race defilers, with the German law enforcement and courts being involved, others in the early years of the Third Reich were affected by more arbitrary circumstances.

By 1938, antisemitic violence had become more widespread. The forms of discrimination and humiliation that both German-Jewish men and women faced during *Kristallnacht* in the night of 9 November were numerous and cannot be all listed here, but they included forcing men to play soccer with Torah scrolls; coating men with tar, attaching them to an oxen-wagon, and forcing men to pull it through town; coercing men to walk barefoot over broken glass;[26] making men stand at attention for ten or more hours in the cold;[27] and shooting men without any ambulance coming for help.[28] Torture in jail, prior to imprisonment in a concentration camp, included beatings, being forced to beat another prisoner, military drill exercises such as push-ups and squads, being forced to open one's mouth for Nazis to spit in, or to use the toilet on command,[29] engage in boxing matches against another prisoner, or pull and root out another prisoner's hair and beard, and more.[30]

The question, thus, is how Jewish men internalized the notion of an alleged Jewish physicality in antisemitic propaganda and how they adapted to it in their day-to-day experiences. A great many accounts illustrate that German Jews in the 1930s were quite aware of the rise in antisemitic imagery in Nazified papers, even if these readers were not always, or hardly at all, subjected to direct physical assault. Martin Gumpert's description of a Jewish man with horn-rimmed glasses anxiously taking flight from an angry mob is instructive as the author, a Jewish man, explicitly distinguished himself from the persecuted individual due to the serendipitous fact that the bystanders did not identify him as a Jew. For Gumpert, it was relatively safe to witness the assault. Had he thought otherwise, assessing himself to be at risk, his behaviour and reaction to the situation might have been dramatically different, likely a rapid escape.

Gumpert's case is instructive to the historian as it also strengthens the argument that Nazi propaganda had a significant impact on the self-understanding of German Jews, some of whom came to react to and identify themselves as mirror images of the vilified caricatured Jew in the media; while others internalized yet rejected such impositions and dissociated themselves from antisemitism based on appearance, as in Gumpert's case. Even then, however, a direct influence of such propaganda on the individual is discernible. It is crucial to realize that even men like Gumpert, who seemingly changed little in their approach to life and who were not directly confronted with verbal and physical violence, had internalized the prevailing discourses of Nazi antisemitism. For some Jewish men, thus, their gender identities as men were increasingly contingent on Nazi constructions. The businessman Siegmund Weltlinger (1886–1974) delineated his behaviour during *Kristallnacht*:

On Monday 10 November, I was warned already early in the morning by phone not to leave the house because Jews were being arrested on the street and on public transportation. But this seemed unlikely to me and moreover, I did not have to fear being physically recognized as a Jew. Thus, I drove into the city and saw everything ... a terrible sight. Most stores had no windows left.[31]

The businessman Adolf Riesenfeld (1884–1977) of Vienna also recalled that he was able to witness the events of *Kristallnacht* on the street without having to fear any attacks on him *as he also was not Jewish in appearance.*[32]

Unlike Weltlinger and Riesenfeld, however, other Jewish men in the Third Reich became increasingly wary about appearing in public and adjusted their behaviours accordingly. Walter Besser (b. 1911) remembered how his social life changed in the 1930s as a direct result of Nazi propaganda:

> I have never tried to go to the movie theatre. Doing so was risky. Blonde Jews did not stand out. But anyone who looked a bit more Jewish, as I did, could not dare. The Jewish appearance was of course a cliché. There were many people who looked more Jewish than a Jew. But a slightly curved nose and a different walk [*Gang*] due to flat feet, black hair, and dark eyes were characteristic.[33]

Besser illustrates how Nazi propaganda attempts to visually mark Jews could have a profound effect on Jewish men and women. While some men felt safer *because* they did not conform to the antisemitic clichés, others felt less secure and were more self-aware *because of* their looks and the possibility that they could get into compromising situations. Gerhard Bry (b. 1911), professor of economics, interpreted his appearance as making it too risky for him to go to work: "It was dangerous for Jews to show their faces at the school, and my face looked sufficiently [stereo]typical to make matters worse."[34]

The process of negotiating one's identity based on antisemitic body stereotypes was complex and not a male-exclusive experience. Women too internalized Nazi discourses on antisemitic imagery, evaluating Jewish men's resemblance or dissimilarities to the propagated images. In oral interviews as late as the 1990s, German-Jewish survivors occasionally still reflected on how they had adapted to the Nazi way of visually conceptualizing "the Jew." In a letter, Monika Joseph interpreted her late husband's survival in Nazi Germany as the serendipitous result of his appearance, which did not correspond to the then prevailing clichés about the complexion of Jewish men. About her husband, she wrote:

> He was grown tall: 182 cm.
> He had light blue-grey eyes.
> He was always elegantly and neatly dressed (*gepflegt*), even in his darkest days.[35]

Strikingly, sixty years after the events, the author continued to perpetuate a Nazi-instigated discourse of a distinct Jewish physicality and still emphasized that her husband, in contradiction to the stereotype, was a tall, blue-eyed handsome man who took care of his appearance, all features that previously had been codified as un-Jewish. Such references suggest that German Jews, men and women alike, had taken the Nazi discrimination based on physiognomic markers to the innermost core of their identities, with lasting implications. The stereotypical Jew was a benchmark that German Jews now had to live with, whether they accepted or resisted this fascist iconography.

Statements that German Jews lived in fear in Nazi Germany might seem trivially obvious. However, without retrospective notions of the Holocaust, it is notable that for many years, the fears that German Jews developed, besides existential-economic ones (chapter 2), were predominantly of physical harm and were by and on behalf of husbands, sons, and other male relatives. Hertha Nathorff confessed in her diary in 1935 how anxious she was every time her husband, a physician, left the house:

> Late at night, he [my husband] gets called and every time, I am afraid, especially when it is new patients. They often lure physicians into a trap, and rob or beat them.[36]

Already on 1 May 1933 Willy Cohn (1888–1941) was scribbling down his fears of the Nazi regime in his diary: "Woke up at 3 in the morning, bathed in sweat. I dreamed that I was in protective custody."[37] Both Cohn, an upright citizen, father of four, and a teacher by profession, and Nathorff's husband, a respected physician, had legitimate reasons for being fearful. The Nazi takeover in early 1933 triggered an atmosphere of fear among German Jews, and witnessing the ensuing street brutalities, arrests, denunciations, and verbal harassment made Jewish men and women feel that they, and particularly the men, could also be among the numerous victims of Hitler's regime.

Strikingly, the reconfiguration of Jewish men into "endangered men" in response to their fears was a process in which men and women equally participated. Jewish women were fully aware of the disproportionate danger to which men were exposed. Jewish women, in their anxiety for the males in their lives, participated in the emotional and social life of German Jewry that perceived men to be at greater risk. As Kurt Rosenberg (1900–77) noted in his diary, his wife was very concerned for him when the doorbell rang one evening in April 1933. It was a courier, but his wife immediately thought of the SA.[38]

Following a temporary relaxation of violence after 1933, physical fears could and did simmer down during the mid-1930s, but they blazed up again in 1938. Walter Tausk (1890–1941), a merchant of Breslau, wrote about the renewal of tensions in his diary:

> For months, I have been tortured by enduring sleep deprivation during the day … At night, I wake up three to four times, being in all kinds of anxious states. In the daytime, anxiety, plus sudden rising heat rushes and headaches.[39]

For Tausk, the issue of fear was not so much a matter of potentially being brutalized by Nazi thugs sometime in the future; instead, the anticipation of such a scenario caused serious mental distress with severe effects on his body. Alexander Szanto (1899–1972), a journalist who had been interrogated by the Gestapo several times, recalled that in 1938 he still had not become accustomed to the dread that rushed through his bones when he thought about being taken away from his bed at night.[40] Having watched the invasion of his friend's home by the SA, Adolf Riesenfeld started to fear his own arrest in the spring of 1938. As a result, he always carried cyanide pills, then a common chemical used to commit suicide.[41] These excerpts show that the actual violence inflicted by the Nazis on the street or in people's homes was not necessarily always the primary cause of fear. It was the nerve-wracking anticipation, the uncertainty, the not-knowing if and when the arrest, deportation, and maltreatment would occur that turned out to be so menacing to Jewish men and their families. On 20 November 1938, ten days after the *Kristallnacht* pogroms, Willy Cohn recounted his unceasing state of anxiety:

> After dinner, I took a walk with Trudi for the first time since Friday a week ago and breathed fresh air for the first time. It did me good! A person feels like a criminal walking along empty and ill-lit alleys, hoping to avoid people who might ask, "How come you aren't in the camp?"[42]

Though 1938 marked a high point in terms of prewar violence and the mass deportation of Jewish men into concentration camps (chapter 6), fears by and directed at Jewish men did not dissipate in the following two years. After the war had broken out, but before German Jews learned about the extermination camps in Poland, families, and Jewish wives especially, continued to be concerned for the safety of their husbands and other male relatives. Elizabeth Freund (1898–1982) recalled how fearful she was for her husband:

> On a Saturday night, around quarter to ten, the door rings. Good Heavens! Who can it be so late and unannounced? It cannot be Jewish acquaintances

because they are not allowed to be outside after 8 o'clock. It can only be a house search. The doorbell rings a second time! What shall we do? They are going to take my husband – but where should he hide in this small apartment? Nothing helps, we must open.[43]

In such cases, fear was not a gendered reaction. Men and women both developed and shared fears in Nazi Germany. Yet, fear over physical safety could be pronounced in gendered terms, and typically was about Jewish men. In their sporadic attacks, SA men attacked Jewish men but ignored women.[44]

While fears could take on a gendered layer, the reactions to these fears are no less important to consider. Jewish-looking or not, German Jews resorted to gendered reactions in situations that they perceived as perilous in two interrelated ways: by escaping and by hiding. Stories about Jewish men who resorted to hiding and escaping date back to early 1933, in the weeks following the Nazi takeover. Hermann Pressmann (see above) decided immediately to leave Germany after his incident with a drunkard in his father's shop. Martin Hausner, following an altercation at work, also escaped from Germany, fearing a co-worker and his SA colleagues.[45] Julius Goldstein (b. 1914) of Dortmund recalled that after he was insulted in a pub by vulgar language ("Are swine allowed in here now?") by an SA man in mid-1933, he picked up an ashtray with which to hit the SA thug. He fled the pub and, shortly after, Germany.[46] Joseph Dünner (1908–78), a medical student and author of critical articles on fascism, feared for his safety after the Nazis took power. First, he found accommodation at a physician friend's residence. On 1 April he illegally crossed the Swiss border near Basel.[47] Hermann Zimmermann (b. 1925) was still a teenager when local Nazi boys began harassing him on the street. One day, his older brother, who accompanied him from school, decided to fist-fight with the SA. Zimmermann's brother shortly afterward decided to flee from Germany, illegally crossing the German-Belgian border.[48]

   In these early cases of escaping from Germany, the individuals typically had a specific reason to predict adverse treatment by the Nazis. Men who were active in political or journalistic work or who had chosen to stand their ground and fight back against Nazi assaulters prudently interpreted their safety to be at imminent risk. Defying Nazi intimidation and deciding to physically resist could represent a short-term victory – as a Nazi threat might have been temporarily diverted and Jewish (military) masculinity enacted by brave and courageous behaviour – but it was soon superseded by long-term concerns and fears over the conflict's consequences, with escape remaining the best option.

After the German takeover of Austria in the spring of 1938, Austrian Jews who had been known to be politically active were on the hunting lists of the Nazis. Paul Martin Neurath (1911–2001) recalled that in March 1938, when the Nazis were after him, he first hid at his aunt's place in Vienna. Then he decided to make his way to Czechoslovakia on foot. After some days of sleeping under the open sky, he got denounced by a farmer near a village where had hoped to purchase some food, and after a brief pursuit over some cornfields by the police, he was arrested and sent to Buchenwald.[49] In the summer of 1938, first in Austria and then all over Germany, the Nazis started rounding up Jewish and non-Jewish individuals with minor criminal pasts, beggars, and the unemployed.[50] Hans Reichmann (1900–64) remembered the numerous crying wives who came to see him in his function as counselor at the *Reichsvertretung der Juden* (Reich Federation of Jews) in the summer of 1938, desperately begging him to help their men.[51] At this time, with growing fears among German Jews, more resorted to hide-and-escape strategies, even those who had no record of criminal offences. In his diary, the Austrian Paul Steiner (1913–96) confessed in June 1938 that he only dared to go out in the dark, and for a maximum of fifteen minutes, "to catch at least some fresh air."[52]

For the majority of German Jews, the ninth to the eleventh of November 1938 marked a sudden turning point in their experience of Nazi antisemitism. Following the assassination of a diplomat in Paris a few days earlier, the Nazis staged a violent nationwide pogrom during the night of 9 November. In addition to the material destruction of their buildings and property, German Jews were brutally invaded in their homes, typically during the night, and verbally and physically assaulted in ways that led to the death of more than 90 Jewish men alone. In the following days, more than 30,000 Jewish men were arrested and sent to the concentration camps of Buchenwald, Dachau, and Sachsenhausen where hundreds more died in the following months.

News of Jewish men's arrest in these November days spread swiftly, and many Jews, both men and women, were encouraged to hide. James Bachner (b. 1922) and his father evaded arrest by escape:

Papa and I were fugitives and afraid of getting caught by the police and taken to a concentration camp. Going back to our home was not an option, and hiding in Berlin was out of the question too … and we didn't have a chance obtaining a visitor visa to escape to Amsterdam. Smuggling ourselves across any border was also hopeless as they were tightly guarded. The only option we had was to try to get into Poland.[53]

In the weeks and months following *Kristallnacht*, the Jewish Central Information Office (JCIO) in Amsterdam, headed by Alfred Wiener (1885–1964), collected witness testimonies and reports by Jews about their experiences of 9 November and after. In numerous accounts, German-Jewish men recalled their decision to hide in order to escape Nazi arrest and likely mistreatment. As one anonymous author recalled,

> Mother was restless. I was not supposed to stay inside the apartment. Therefore, for a while, I was driving the car through the city and witnessed how the destruction of the Jewish residences was fully in place. Eventually, I parked because I no longer felt safe in the car.[54]

Another account read,

> During these days when Jewish men one after another were taken out of bed early in the morning and dragged to KZs, our former maid Marie, a Catholic from Pomerania, took my father to her place where he spent several nights. SA men appeared multiple times in our apartment to take my father. At my aunt's, who had a two-bedroom apartment in Berlin, a total of six male relatives, my cousin included, lived there during the period of the pogroms. Others resided in the Grünewald forest, in spite of the November cold.[55]

A third report sent to the JCIO recalled that

> In Berlin it was possible to hide and between 10 and 20 November, thousands of Jewish men lived an existence similar to hunted game [*gehetztes Wild*]. Some were on the go day and night, using public transportation. Many spent their nights at different places, often in the homes of already arrested Jews, often with Aryans, some of whom were quite supportive. Eleven Jewish men stayed in a villa of an Aryan merchant, some who did not even know the proprietor but were told about him by friends. In a tiny cigar shop, owned by an Aryan, that was about nine square metres in size, two Jews spent fourteen consecutive nights there on chairs.[56]

The outcomes of hide-or-escape strategies varied and depended on situational factors like geography, but also luck. Leo Langnas (b. 1895) was able to escape from his arresters who came to his home when he faced detention in November 1938.[57] Ernst Eisenmayer (b. 1920), an experienced mountain climber, escaped over the Austrian Alps into Switzerland, from where, however, he was sent back and eventually imprisoned in Dachau.[58] Louis Srulowitz (b. 1922) had to try three times to escape into Belgium.[59] Klaus Loewald (b. 1920) and his father, Hans-Georg, on the other hand, escaped arrest in their hometown by going on a trip throughout Germany, staying in different cities. As they were not Jewish-looking, they figured there was minor risk in facing arrest. Yet they changed their location every few days, just to be safe.[60]

Hiding and escape, as illustrated, were gender-specific reactions by Jewish men who faced arrest, deportation, and victimization. Both strategies were pragmatic and spontaneous choices and augmented their new status as "endangered men." Men who had been accustomed to the provider and protector roles for years felt forced to jettison these gender conventions and flee from their homes, seeking refuge elsewhere.

Yet, in contrast to the accounts describing men's flight, there is equally significant and voluminous evidence that illustrates men's contradictory behaviours and understandings of masculinity. While many Jewish men, as the primary targets of Nazi violence during the 1930s and especially in 1938, reacted by removing themselves from their homes and workplaces, where they could easily be arrested, and placed themselves as a form of emergency measure in locations of hiding, other Jewish men either interpreted the looming danger differently or consciously decided not to run away.

Hertha Nathorff, after learning about the mass arrests on 10 November, called her husband, who was at work, urging him not to come home that night. He did so anyway.[61] Siegmund Weltlinger's son came running toward him on his walk home, warning his father that a Gestapo man was waiting at home. Weltlinger went home anyway, where he was arrested.[62] While these excerpts do not explicitly relay an impression of men's use of courageous military masculinity, it is likely that both men contemplated their likely arrest, weighed all other options and their obligations toward their spouses and children, and concluded it to be best to turn themselves in. Hugo Burkhardt (1899–1971) recalled similar thoughts when he faced arrest in early 1933. If he did not comply, perhaps his relatives would face retaliation and even arrest. He also turned himself in.[63] Otto Kollisch did not escape but in fact successfully negotiated with the SS to postpone his arrest on the grounds that he was a veteran and the single parent of two children.[64] Other accounts are even more explicit and demonstrate how men in situations of danger consciously applied gendered behaviours and norms that were linked to hegemonic models of military masculinity, including steadfastness, bravery, and courage. Many of these men were war veterans, and as in the war, they reasoned that they could not run away from danger. Alfred Schwerin (b. 1892) recalled in his memoirs that he did not want to act cowardly. After he had brought his daughter to school on the morning of 10 November and realized what was happening, he debated with himself:

> Should I dodge ...? This thought crossed my mind only for a few seconds. I abruptly made an entirely different decision. To direct threats, everyone reacts differently ... It went against my inner conviction to take flight [*in die Büsche schlagen*] and with a mixture of anger and stubborn defiance, I ran right into the danger.[65]

For the ones who did not shy away from a possible altercation with the Nazis, notions of military masculinity to cope with the aggressors were central. Otto Kollisch could defy his arrest as he was a father, but perhaps more important to the intruders was his military record:

> [My objection] that I was honoured with several distinctions as a combat fighter and had once risked my life for four years for this country ... calmed them down and they dropped the arrest and threatened that they would come for me in six weeks if by that time I should still be around.[66]

Facing arrest, other men also referred to their wartime accomplishments. The neurologist Hermann Pineas (b. 1892) convinced his arresters of his war injury with the fortunate outcome of no arrest.[67] Adolf Riesenfeld (1884–1977) was at a friend's when the SA marched into his place in March 1938, shortly after the annexation of Austria. When the SA hordes were searching the apartment for hidden communist literature and weapons and instead discovered a badge of military honour, the SA man in charge inquired about it and demanded proof that he had fought in the war. After a few minutes, Riesenfeld's friend was able to find the certification of honourable service that had been issued by Hitler. As a result, the leader asked his men to stand in military formation and salute to the comrade, after which the platoon marched out of his apartment.[68] Finally, the civil servant and local politician Franz Memelsdorff (1889–1958) put on his World War I medals upon his arrest to be sent to Dachau:

> I was greatly excited. I had participated in the war, had been a lieutenant for three years, had fought at Verdun, at the Somme, in Flanders, at the Chemin de Dames, in Russia and the Balkans, had been injured – but arrested I had never been in my life ... I was wearing the Iron Cross First and Second Class, the Front Fighter Badge [*Frontkämpferabzeichen*], the Badge of Injured Soldiers [*Verwundetenabzeichen*], etc.[69]

Patently, military masculinity was of vital significance to some Jewish men in such unexpected moments of personal violation, particularly the ones who identified as war veterans. In rare cases, it helped them to avoid being arrested. More often, however, it helped them maintain a sense of stoicism, dignity, and masculinity. From a literary perspective, it also helped them to reconstruct themselves in their memoirs as real men.[70] As military men who had witnessed and participated in a brutal war many years earlier, these men sustained a sense of self-worth. As hardened, toughened men, they were not to be intimidated by young Nazi thugs who, in their minds, knew nothing about military matters. Some, like Joseph Adler (b. 1895), even dared to verbally challenge the Nazi intruders when facing arrest. Adler asked the arresting officer if he had fought in the war and what his experience had been like:

> And then it turned out that during the years that I fought in the hell of Verdun, in the first trenches as an advanced artillery observer at the "Hoeh 304," he had a job way back from the front. Of course, it is much simpler and surer to attack innocent citizens than to lie in the furthest front trenches. I made this very clear to him. I made no bones about it.[71]

Undoubtedly, some recollections of *Kristallnacht* are distorted by a retrospective over-representation of military masculinity and must be taken with a grain of salt. In the examples above, often the narrators who had experienced *Kristallnacht* recalled their 1938 experiences years later. Boasting about their heroic behaviour when confronting Nazi invaders in their homes can be the product of a post-traumatic process in which men reassigned themselves agency and masculine identity that they had lost, or thought they had lost, under the Nazis. It is quite possible that many men did not act quite as courageously as they reported in their memoirs and that in fact their reactions might have differed little from those of men who decided to hide or flee. For others yet, their arrest was perceived as a shameful, emasculating event. Ernst Hochsinger, for instance, noted that

> I do not want to submit myself to the role of the prisoner; I do not want to be dependent on the orders by others in the presence of my wife; I am ashamed of having to wait for instructions from a stranger that I must follow.[72]

Men's accounts of courage and defiance in situations when they should have feared for their lives imply that military norms of standing one's ground and defending one's "castle" certainly might have influenced the behaviour of some Jewish men. Acting in a soldierly fashion while facing gangs of military-like men in uniform helped Jewish men in this moment *and* in their postwar reconstructed memoirs to sustain their sense of masculinity. In such situations of masculinized power exhibited by the Nazis, some Jewish men reacted by putting themselves on an equal footing. Former soldiers faced present-day soldiers, negotiating relationships of power and masculinity. In some of these cases, Jewish men were successful in generating respect, based on their past military sacrifices. Even in power negotiations that ended unsuccessfully for Jewish men, their strategies for preserving masculinity and keeping a clear conscience and the knowledge that they had resisted bravely and faced the danger "like men" were integral for them. The act of donning their war medals on their way to the concentration camps underscores this.

On the other hand, Jewish men who had decided to escape and hide did not necessarily emasculate themselves. In their postwar memoirs, admissions of guilt and wrongdoing are virtually absent. Whether boasting of oneself as a manly man was a common literary technique or an actual gendered behaviour at the time, evidence for the opposite is much rarer. Few regret their decision to go into hiding – something society, under normal circumstances, might have labelled as an unmanly demeanour. What man likes to appear cowardly in his own memoir?

Conclusion

Jewish men were gender-specifically targeted and victimized in the private sphere at home and in social-public spaces, starting in 1933 and escalating in late 1938. Their reactions varied according to standards and norms of masculinity. As with the ambiguously prescribed behaviour of protecting one's family and home, there was no universal template for courageous behaviour that Jewish men were supposed to follow. Attacks against them based on their religious-racial *and* gender identities were unprecedented, and most men had no guiding principles or frames of reference they could draw on. Most men realized that they were simply powerless in such situations as singled-out individuals. Being victimized, therefore, was not a sign of Jewish emasculation but simply an inevitable manifestation of being "endangered." Jewish men between 1933 and 1941, like Jews all over Europe during the Holocaust, had few if any means to resist. In realizing this, preferring to run away or hide was in fact a sensible survival strategy that no one within the Jewish communities then or in the postwar era condemned.

Chapter Six

Inside the *KZ*: Jewish Masculinities in Prewar Nazi Concentration Camps

Between 1933 and 1939, approximately 40,000 Jews were held in concentration camps, with the vast majority being men.[1] An estimated 2,000 to 3,000 Jewish men died during this time as a result of violence, either inside the camps or from consequences of their imprisonment.[2] Such numbers led Jane Caplan to conclude that it took several years, until the end of 1937, before women's camps "even began to diverge from the existing instructions and norms of women's custody and even longer before the treatment of women inmates approached the standard brutality long applied to men."[3] Despite such gender-biased statistics, however, historians have made relatively few attempts to examine (Jewish) men as a distinct category of victims, unlike feminist historians who have importantly enriched the scholarship of women's victimization under Nazi rule.[4]

This chapter will delineate some forms of violence that Jewish men faced in Germany's prewar concentration camps and will discuss the effects that concentration camp imprisonment had on individual Jewish men, their gender identities, and their gender relations with their families outside the *KZ*. Acknowledging Gisela Bock's caution, the guiding principle of this chapter is not to create a hierarchy of suffering, drawing judgmental comparisons between male and female suffering,[5] but to use gender methodology to enrich the metaphor "different horrors, same hell"[6] with more substance and meaning.

Immediately with the construction of concentration camps in early 1933, Jewish men became subject to arrest and incarceration. While in the first few months and years of the Third Reich Jewish men were often arrested due to their previous engagement in leftist politics, journalism, and law, as Nikolaus Wachsmann has explained, Jewish men were treated inside the camps as Jewish prisoners, subjected to additional abuse and violence by members of the SA/SS, who had a free hand to live out their antisemitism.[7] Over the course of the 1930s, men of Jewish origin were arrested on different pretexts (such as race defilement; see chapter 2) or as a means to compel them to transfer their properties and businesses to the state or individual Nazi authorities.[8] Finally, commencing in the summer of 1938, the Nazis drafted an impromptu policy intended to push for expedited Jewish emigration through intimidation, arrest, and brutalization. By first deporting Jewish men and then brutalizing them in sealed-off camps, the Nazis hoped to force larger numbers of German Jews to intensify their attempts to move abroad. The Nazis thus used "protective custody" – a Nazi euphemism for imprisonment in a concentration camp – in arbitrary ways to exclude Jews from the people's community.[9]

Witness accounts elucidate the suffering that Jewish men in German concentration camps prior to 1939 endured. Many accounts, in fact, recount how violence and torture started immediately following arrest, even before arrival in the camp. In the early years of the Third Reich, it was a degrading custom to march or drive the arrested men through town on their way to the concentration camps (or train stations), in order to showcase them in public and inflict further humiliation on these formerly respected, integrated working professionals (Figure 26).[10] In his account, Peter Wallner provides a grisly description of the beatings and humiliations he and his peers suffered in a train while in transit to Dachau,[11] and the rabbi Emil Schorsch (1899–1982) remembered that even before arriving in Buchenwald, many Jewish men were singled out by the SS and beaten with sticks, "making the prisoners scream like wild animals."[12]

In the camps, men fared even worse than outside the camps. Beatings, arbitrary and brutal punishments for all kinds of minor or alleged infractions, and murder, typically under pretence of having been shot "while trying to escape,"[13] were customary. Forced labour in unsafe conditions in places like stone quarries was so physically demanding that it resulted in the immediate deterioration of prisoners' mental and physical health and a rampant increase in sickness (e.g., pneumonia and heart failure) and premature death.[14] Inadequate nutrition and scandalous sanitary conditions aggravated the prisoners' lot.[15]

More specifically, common forms of physical oppression in camps included, as a Dachau prisoner reported, the incessant punitive drills that included running, jumping, rolling, and crawling in the mud for hours; or the blatant opposite, standing still at attention, sometimes for more than ten hours. In all their forms of torture, the SS disregarded the prisoners' age and physical condition. Older men had to perform like younger men; sick men with fever had to report for work like anyone

Figure 26. Photograph depicting the public shaming of Ludwig Marum and others socialist leaders and their deportation from Karlsruhe to the concentration camp Kislau, May 1933.

else. Unequipped with proper clothing, the prisoners were exposed to agonizing heat or freezing temperatures, with heat strokes and frostbite being common. Herbert Luft (1907–92) of Essen recalled that when a prisoner escaped from Buchenwald in 1938, all 16,000 inmates had to stand at attention for hours (Figure 27).

> Our stomach reminds us that it must be lunch time ... but we are still standing in line at attention like a wall of stone. Silently, we await our fate ... It is afternoon, the sun goes down and it is night. Three shifts of SS *Verfügungstruppen* [guards] have changed, but we haven't moved an inch ... Again, it is midnight. We are victims of a game, a vile game called "How to murder legally!" Many of our comrades lie freezing in the snow, slowly dying. The guards are sleepy, bored, and tired of beating their prisoners. It is hard to visualize what it means to be on your feet at rigid attention for 24 hours, hands straight down, without being allowed to move even a quarter of an inch. An inexorable cold in these high mountains adds to our suffering. We lose perceptive power and feel only

Figure 27. Photograph of newly arrived Jewish male prisoners, with shaven heads, standing at attention in their civilian clothes during a roll call in the Buchenwald concentration camp, following the events of Kristallnacht in November 1938.

an ice-cold emptiness inside. Our body is so paralysed that we could not move were we ordered to do so ... In heaven's name, there is a limit to what a man can stand – a limit to the value of life. Tonight, we are waiting for an end to it all. In our minds, nothing remains but the wish, "Let's have it over with." In the early dawn our resistance is at the breaking point. It seems no one can possibly survive. The SS officers, drunk in their canteen, make bets on how long human beings can stand this mortal game ... It ends at 11 pm when the prisoners get caught.[16]

In a similar vein, Kurt Juster from Hamburg recalled of his time in Sachsenhausen that worse than the incessant physical punishments was the nineteen-hour-long standing exercise.[17] Another man's account of Sachsenhausen testified that in order to resist the frigid temperatures, prisoners used towels and newspapers around their bodies, until this too was forbidden.[18] Louis Gumpert, war veteran and business owner, who fell victim to the June pogroms of 1938 and was interned in Buchenwald from mid-June to the end of August, recalled that the thirst in the camps was unbearable. He estimated that 150 to 180 people died during his summer stay in Buchenwald.[19] Nighttime in the camps was no less painful. It was strictly forbidden to use the outhouse at night, an anguish to the many who suffered from diarrhea due to the contaminated drinking water.

The gendered significance is that Jewish men's victimization constituted a bodily experience that had a profound impact on their masculine identity. As the dominant model of masculinity in Nazi Germany was defined by athletic, strong, "Aryan" bodies that were trained and hardened to weather any storm in order to fight Germany's adversaries, the Jewish experience stood diametrically opposed to this ideal. The body image of the weak, dirty, and diseased male was associated not only with images of unmanly men but specifically with Jewish emasculated men. Clearly, body and gender are intricately interconnected as cultural systems of meaning, and a healthy body represents authority; a dismembered, unhealthy body broadcasts powerlessness and questions masculinity.[20] A distorted, unhealthy male body is deemed to be incapable of fulfilling the tasks that define manhood: procreation, protection, and provision through labour. Furthermore, the body was also assigned moral character traits.[21] A healthy body was equated with proper moral traits and manners – such as courage, steadfastness, and discipline – while the unhealthy body, which the Nazis first discursively constructed in their propaganda and then tried to translate into reality in their camps, was equated with alienating and perilous traits. Because Jews allegedly had lax, flabby bodies that they did not use to manufacture things, their minds were described as those of manipulative and lazy cowards. In their euphemistic language, the Nazis tried to "repair" these Jewish deficiencies with their re-education camps [Erziehungslager]. Instead of masculinizing Jewish men, however, by violating and maltreating their bodies (and psyches), often leading to outright murder, the Nazis, if anything, dehumanized and emasculated them.

In addition to the bodily suffering Jewish men had to endure in the camps, various verbal and symbolic forms of torture were inflicted on Jewish men. In many contemporary reports, witnesses recalled how they had become puppets of SS despotism and capriciousness. Jewish men had to dance and sing in front of their torturers. Sporting events were organized where prisoners had to do frog-jumping in a kneeling position or go "bicycling," a term used to describe running up and down stairs until the "contestant" fainted. When a prisoner asked for water, he could be forced to lick the spit of his torturers. Cleaning outhouses was also usually "reserved" for Jewish inmates, who had to use their bare hands or toothbrushes.[22] Max Tabaschnik (b. 1893) recalled how he once had to eat pork and another time salty bread that caused an insurmountable thirst. Hans Reichmann (1900–64) recounted common verbal abuse:

> We had to stand in formation. Once in a while you would receive a slap in the face, but the derision hurt me deeper. "What is your profession? ... Have you ever worked? We will teach you, you dirt-bags. Here you will learn what work means, you pig."[23]

For Reichmann, a functionary for the Jewish Centralverein, as for many other Jewish men, his profession was a central part of his gender identity. Being ridiculed in the primitive language (in this case with a Bavarian accent) of his tormentor, who was much younger and was clearly uneducated, was for Reichmann a painful experience. Not only did Jewish men face serious existential challenges resulting from their loss of work, but as prisoners in concentration camps, they were treated as lazy and thus unmanly men who apparently had never learned the real meaning of work, defined as physically demanding labour. As concentration camps were euphemistically called education camps, Jewish men who in reality had reached a high standard of masculinity as defined by work achievements and successful provisioning for their families were degraded to the status of pupils who seemingly needed rigid supervision in athletic training and moral education. As the defining markers of masculinity in German society were shifting – from bourgeois values such as humanistic *Bildung* and economic wealth to physical fitness and military-like behaviour – Jewish men in concentration camps were effectively emasculated. While the SS performed an exhibitionist hyper-masculinity in front of their prisoners, Jewish men were reduced to childlike, dependent figures who required fatherly training. The verbal and physical forms of violence Jewish men were subjected to were meant to harden them. Teaching them to become fit and able to endure physical hardship, the SS directly challenged the definitions of Jewish masculinity, and in cases when "Aryan" and Jewish masculinities overlapped, such as in a shared adherence to military masculinity, the Nazis simply questioned or negated Jewish veterans' past military service and spiritual belonging to the community of former soldiers.

Forms of verbal disrespect and subjection to harsh treatment manifested in different ways. The German-language address *Du* was deliberately used by the SS instead of *Sie*, the customary polite form to address a stranger.[24] The Berlin-born civil servant Franz Memelsdorff (1889–1958) remembered how in the shower rooms, with ice cold water running over their bodies, they were ridiculed by the guards as dirty pigs who had never seen a shower before, a stereotypical reference to the antisemitic discourse of a Jewish lack of hygiene. Another common verbal insult was the Nazi reference to Jews as fat pigs, connoting a luxurious, ostentatious lifestyle that all Jews supposedly indulged in. "You gorged pigs, you will lose your fat here and then your clothes will fit you."[25] Though Memelsdorff suffered from the ceaseless beatings and exposure to the cold weather (he had lost a toe), the cultural mockery, the symbolic forms of discrimination, and indirect violence were equally if not more degrading to him, especially the incessant lack of hygiene they were exposed to:

> Our clothes were old and patched … At first, we had to wear them for two weeks, only then were they changed. It was an unimaginable mess. Because we had to keep them on also at night, and many of us could not wash ourselves properly, the clothes stank terribly.[26]

The Nazis, in their attempts to dehumanize German Jews, deliberately tried to deprive Jewish male inmates in concentration camps of their identities as humans and thereby also as men. The strategy of making them feel like and live the life of animals in unsanitary conditions reflected the propaganda imagery that had been previously established and that had depicted Jews as an ominous, racial threat to the purity and health of the nation. The discourse of race defilement, as discussed in chapter 2, heavily relied on such cultural constructs of Jewish dirtiness. In concentration camps, the Nazis embedded a validation of their beliefs, creating real-life examples of Jews living in filthy conditions who were ostensibly too inept to clean up after themselves. Instead of improving sanitary conditions in the camp, the camp authorities had prisoners shave their hair to prevent the spread of lice and other parasites.[27] Prior to doing so, however, and taking matters to the extreme, the staff of the *Der Stürmer* and other journals photographed the filthy, unkempt men as living proof of how Jews were untrustworthy characters with diseased bodies.[28]

The experience of being deported to and incarcerated in a camp and subsequently treated as a criminal was undoubtedly psychologically and physically injurious. Living in an environment of omnipresent violence and inhumane conditions made many men despair. Carl Schwabe (1891–1967) recalled a typical night in his barracks:

> The nights were terrible. Hysterics suffered from seizures. One guy was screaming he was going to get killed, another was preaching a sermon.

A third was talking about electric waves. In between, more screaming, crying …[29]

Another contemporary account wrote about a case of mental disturbance:

An elderly gentleman screamed suddenly, "Jews help me! They are coming after me." He couldn't stay on his pallet and started walking around, intermittently screaming, "They are after my life." Eventually, one of the older prisoners dealt with him. "You shut up now, or I'll slap you." "But they are after me." Another warning followed, and when the old guy again screamed, he was punched in his face so that he stumbled over several men sleeping on the floor, falling against the oven, which he almost toppled, but behind which he immediately hid. He started to scream again right away that they were after his life … Then four men beat his head non-stop for about a minute, which turned his head into a blue-black mass that made it impossible to distinguish nose from eye. The old guy was half-conscious and of course silent. There was a sense of contentment in the barrack. "We have brought many to silence who refused. We have our own methods. If it is inevitable, then one has to bite the dust instead of 1,000 or 2,000 having to suffer." After about half an hour the old man recovered inasmuch as he started to scream, "Let me live," whereas the same as before happened. The old guy was of incredible resilience and endured this procedure a few times … but it could not have lasted much longer.[30]

Survivor testimonies illustrate how violence and degradation were experienced differently by every individual. One report recalled that in the camp, first the weakest, and then the second weakest perished. "Of course, most deaths occurred among the old people."[31] As another witness wrote,

The older, less mobile prisoners were subjected to particular cruelties. From old people who typically had made something of themselves as businessmen, civil servants, academics, and intellectuals, more was expected than from young, healthy eighteen-year-olds in the most regimented army in the world.[32]

Prisoner victimization occurred not always for the same reasons but could vary dramatically. The SS used stereotypical markers of Jewishness to single out their victims. The SS picked on Jewish-looking, overweight, and wealthy men as the representation of the archetypical Jew, defined by physical (typically facial) features. As the same witness recalled, "Being an intellectual was a particular stigma. The wearers of glasses were especially mistreated."[33] Alfred Schwerin recalled that upon arrival in Dachau, a fellow who had previously been imprisoned warned that the SS could not stand prisoners with glasses and advised him to take them off.[34] As another witness recalled,

> The overweight, the clumsy and especially the Jewish-looking ones had to suffer the most. Our tormentors seemingly knew the Jew only from *Der Stürmer* and *Das Schwarze Korps*, whose jargon they perpetually used and whose words they carefully tried to translate into deeds. They lunged at anyone who reminded them of these magazines.[35]

Another marker the SS used was Jewish men's military records. As Christopher Dillon has argued, the SS in fact regarded Jewish men with military records "as a subversive threat to SS soldierly masculinity," and that in turn provoked a reaction: "Strategies of emasculation and subjugation were developed to delegitimize models of masculinity among Jewish men."[36] In their attempt to emasculate Jewish men, the Nazis often met Jewish protestations of military service with sarcastic incredulity and outraged violence. As one witness remembered,

> Especially the former front-fighters and veterans among the Jewish prisoners are the targets of hatred. They do not want to believe that Jews too fulfilled their duty in Germany's hardest time, during the war … They particularly hate those Jews who had been decorated for their bravery facing the enemy. They tear off their Iron Crosses and Badges of War Injury upon entering the camps, trample on them, and verbally abuse and mistreat them [the men]. These primitive tormentors in their black SS uniforms do not realize that they are simultaneously defiling German military honour.[37]

What makes all these horrendous stories of individual suffering so important is that, although hundreds if not more died in Germany's prewar concentration camps, thousands of Jewish men returned after a few weeks or months to their "normal" lives with their wives and families. Violence, thus, had a profound effect on men's survival strategies and their coping mechanisms in the camps as well as the tropes of communication between men and their families.

The terror that Jewish men in concentration camps were exposed to took place in a micro-environment in which power relations and different conceptions of masculinity came head-to-head. While in the domestic and public sphere, Jewish masculinity was constructed (though not exclusively) in relation to femininity, in Nazi concentration camps, the manifestations and meanings of Jewish masculinity crystallized in a relational context to "Aryan" masculinity. According to Jane Caplan, there was virtually an unbridgeable gulf between the de-masculinization of the inmates and the hyper-masculinization of their SS guards.[38] As prisoners, Jewish men identified themselves in relation to the behaviours and performance of the SS guards, including their unrestricted use of violence.[39] For Jewish men, developing effective coping mechanisms incorporated observation, internalization, and rejection of the divergent masculinity of the SS that Jewish men, though disempowered, came to see as inferior.

The Nazi state was a *Männerbund*, a homosocial association of males, in which *Kampfgemeinschaft* (community of fighting) was celebrated and according to which men were to acquire a tough, soldierly demeanour.[40] German soldiers and the SS in particular were trained in a type of self-control manifested in the suppression of emotions and other inhibitions in carrying out their tasks.[41] Camp guards were regularly drilled, and as Christopher Dillon argues, those who failed to conform to the standards of a militarized life and thus failed the ultimate test of manhood were held up to scorn and feminized as "crying little girls" and "sissies."[42] Nazi homophobia and misogynistic sexism were two sides of the same coin.

> The Nazi school of violence was calculatedly harsh, designed to foster aggression and to overcome recruits' inhibitions about using violence against others. It was expected that guards would cascade their wounded pride onto the prisoners. The inmates in turn were emasculated by the perpetrators, one component of the S.S. claim to ... "absolute power" in the concentration camps. The chasm between the hyper-masculine status of the guards and the emasculation of the prisoners forms an under-researched aspect of the encoding of domination in the camps.[43]

Filling in this gap of under-researched masculinity, this chapter contends that although Jewish men were targeted in Nazi concentration camps, SS masculinity and Jewish masculinity were in a co-dependent, tense relationship, and by projecting their own masculinity vis-à-vis that of the SS, Jewish men found ways to preserve their gender identity.

Strikingly, in memoirs by former concentration camp prisoners, Jewish men habitually rejected and criticized the masculinity that SS men, often still adolescents, exhibited. Inflicting violence on helpless individuals did not exemplify the type of courage that Jewish men ascribed to military masculinity. Jewish men questioned the Nazi torturers' membership in an honourable, spiritual association of male soldiers and veterans, and reviled them as low-class, uneducated ruffians who in their barbaric actions were led by animalistic instincts. A religious authority, Rabbi Dr Nussbaum, who was interned in Sachsenhausen, expressed similar condemnations of SS masculinity, describing the perpetrators as men who are "trained in all kinds of Nazi elite military schools ... In my opinion [they] are never suited for war but for cowardly mistreatments of the defenseless."[44]

With SS guards depicted as unsoldierly cowards whose only "merit" was in directing their violent aggression against helpless men, it is hardly surprising that in turn, Jewish men resorted to a palette of contrasting behaviours that they associated with humanistic, civic virtues and honourable military masculinity. As in the public sphere when their honour and reputation as righteous citizens and former veterans were questioned (chapter 1), in concentration camps Jewish men actively referred to their wartime sacrifices for the country and their adherence to what they considered honourable military masculinity. Their references to the war and their soldierly behaviour in Nazi prison camps therefore constituted an idiosyncratically and gendered coping mechanism that helped Jewish men to preserve their dignity in an environment that tried to deprive them of it. It helped them to distinguish themselves from the pseudo-military habitus, as Wünschmann enunciated it, that Jewish men saw as a cheap imitation of honourable soldierly behaviour.[45] Jewish men sought to save the masculine integrity that they had earned in the military by interpreting the camp experience in the models and vocabulary of the trenches. It was a trial of manhood.[46] The construction and cultivation of Jewish masculinity in camps in Nazi Germany was thus contingent on the rival conceptions of masculinity of the SS. In their reports and memoirs, Jewish men resorted to means of "doing gender," attempts to reclaim their sense of manliness by discrediting the false masculinity of the Nazis and reappraising their own.[47]

Jewish men who had learned military drill in Wilhelmine barracks and had participated in the war made two related yet distinct uses of military masculinity as a coping mechanism. On the one hand, many memoirists claim that their previous military experience in the war made them better suited to endure physical hardship, such as the military drills and the daily mustering on the *Appellplatz*. Military masculinity had hardened Jewish men and their bodies. On the other hand, military masculinity was used as a spiritual code of behaviour, a guidebook of principles that helped Jewish men better tolerate and process the indignities inflicted on them. References to steadfast behaviour of toughened men acting stoically in perilous situations were used – as part of coping mechanisms in the camp *and* as memory constructions afterward – to affirm those who were seemingly powerless, emasculated, and degraded as true men. Military prisoner behaviour, in other words, was of fundamental importance in the context of gender identity.[48]

After realizing that he and other men were being deported to Dachau by train, Alfred Schwerin recalled that

> Keeping your composure [*Haltung*] was the best thing to do. Don't let them see into you [*Nur nichts anmerken lassen!*]. And everyone kept up their composures, these poor, tortured, and hounded people. Muted and stiff, they were sitting there, gritting their teeth.[49]

Once inside the *KZ*, militarized behaviour was key to having a chance of survival, as Schwerin observed:

> A *Scharführer* [section-leader] read out our names, and we tried now, as well as later on, to exhibit a military composure [*militärische Haltung zur Schau stellen*] because we reckoned that only by being soldierly-stiff [*das Stramm-Soldatische*] could we keep the tempers of our new rulers in a smooth balance.[50]

A military attitude and composure, as Schwerin suggested, was a paradigmatic response pattern by many Jewish men who in their uncertainty relied on past behaviours and the cultural norms that they had learned and that had helped them endure situations of adversity in World War I. Furthermore, as astute observers of SS behaviour, many male prisoners realized that acting in a military way was what was expected of them. In fact, Jewish men's resorting to military masculinity can be partially interpreted as an expected adaptation to Nazi behaviour, despite the Nazis' belittling of Jewish men's war contribution.[51] Through a stoical outward appearance and bodily composure, the Jewish veteran performed the role of a rock that could not be uprooted by arbitrary Nazi assaults. Rabbi Schorsch remembered how he, as a veteran, could quite easily bear the imprisonment in the city jail before his deportation to Buchenwald.[52] Harvey Newtown (b. 1920) in his 1995 memoir described how he endured physical pain in Buchenwald. After an SS guard had hurt him,

> I stood at attention and submitted to it [*ließ es über mich ergehen*]. After a while, it was no more fun for the guard and he let go of me. I do not want to imagine what could have happened if I had shown any signs of pain, because it would have been a provocation for the SS to inflict more pain on me.[53]

In another report, written shortly after his release, a witness wrote,

> There was much confusion due to conflicting orders. If someone made a mistake, he was hit with a wooden bar or baton. If the one concerned was a soldier, then he clicked his heels and shut up. Then everything was fine. But if he did not stand to attention, or tried in an unsoldierly manner to explain the misunderstanding or apologize, more slashes with the bar followed, and it was up to fate or the mood of the torturer if the slashes were stronger or a bit weaker ...[54]

Evidently, military masculinity helped Jewish men adapt to the expectations of camp life and yield a more enduring, bearable experience in the camp. As former soldiers, many knew how to adapt to military authorities and institutions. Tacitly tolerating the pain that was inflicted on them, without showing signs of weakness, was part of this gendered demeanour. As veterans, they had been accustomed to a gendered code of behaviour according to which a soldierly man was not to crumble in the presence of his enemy. As the second example suggests, the military-like adaption to the SS monopoly of violence by conforming to the rules of the SS could lead to being less exposed to violence, whereas diametrically opposed forms of behaviour, such as explaining, arguing with, or apologizing to their superiors, generated more violence. This shift in values and behaviour was situationally contingent and is central to comprehending men's experience in the camps. Not "standing their ground" in a sense of communication and negotiation, as Jewish men had done before – such as during the April 1933 boycott when Jewish men had disseminated leaflets that outlined their military records or talked to passersby on the street – was now the right, masculine thing to do. In the camps, it was strict military obedience and discipline that were regarded as prudent means by which to survive. In short, Jewish men who had previously participated in militarized environments in barracks, military training, and war felt better prepared in their behavioural adaptations to endure their time in concentration camps than those who had not.

An adherence to military masculinity did not require past participation in a war, however. The internalization of military values such
as physical discipline, obedience, robustness, stoicism, and steadfastness sufficed. Younger men who had not been trained in the military
could still have observed and copied the practice of military masculinity by older role model comrades. Harry Ross recalled how he had
grown up with a military-style father at home. He and his brother had
to wear boots, even at home. As as result, during his arrest, he fared
better than everyone else with weak feet. As discipline, hardness, and
perseverance were also characteristics that resonated in the world of
sports, athletes of younger age later remembered that they too fared
relatively well during their imprisonments. Max Heimann recalled that
in Dachau he was able to bear the physical torments because he was
an athlete.[55] Ross's athletic body also helped him to carry on his back
bricks and bags of cement and salt of up to 112 pounds. A member in
a Jewish sports club of the veterans' organization *RjF*, he recalled that,
"I was so glad that I did sports as a young man."[56]

Another crucial element of military masculinity, in addition to the
mental and physical level of preparedness of individual Jewish men,
was the sense of belonging amid shared endurance. Most witness
accounts refer to fellow prisoner inmates as comrades. The experience
of comradeship in the camps was constructed as a parallel to Jewish
men's military past that similarly had created a spirit of soldierly community. Male bonding in 1920s veterans' organizations, *Freikorps* units,
and other associations constituted a male-exclusive sphere of belonging. Continuing to live this spirit in Nazi camps was a gendered form
of behaviour that helped Jewish men better cope with their fate. As
they had together endured hardship in the trenches of World War I,
they again felt a sense of safety in the presence of congenial brethren.[57]
As one witness recalled, in the camp he belonged to the world's largest Jewish paramilitary formation. "The massiveness [*Massenhaftigkeit*]
certainly gave everyone a sense of security, a sense of togetherness
[*Zusammengehörigkeit*]."[58]

The commonly experienced sense of comradeship and the performance of military masculinity did not deteriorate over time. Though
continuously exposed to violence, torment, and harsh weather conditions, men upheld what they considered to be masculine hardiness and
military acts of behaviour to the very end. Karl Guggenheim (b. 1879)
amusingly remembered the day of his and his comrades' release:

> Suddenly a command was issued from the middle of the crowd: "March
> in formation" – and a battle-ready Jewish company of veterans marched in

impeccable parade cadence through the gates of the concentration camp –
leaving behind there the shocked and dumbfounded faces of the camp
guards and the barely concealed smiles of the camp inmates. Even the
noble knight Götz von Berlichingen could not have bid a more suitable
farewell.[59]

How central the new military zeitgeist had become in Nazi Germany
became evident when Jewish war veterans – despite being subjected
to occasional additional mockery in the camps – were the first to be
released, starting a few weeks after their imprisonment in November
1938, likely a call made by Hermann Göring, second in the state hierarchy, also a veteran and celebrated war hero. To document their war
service, many of the Jewish men arrested had had the foresight to take
with them their military service badges (*Frontkämpferabzeichen*) that had
been awarded to them a few years earlier by Hitler's government. Others wrote with much urgency to their wives to mail them their military
papers.[60] For Jewish men, it was a sign of confirmation that adhering
to military behaviour and standards would eventually pay off. While
other men had to wait several more months for their release, the men
best prepared to endure camp life were the first to be let go.

Despite the utility and the benefits of personifying a military masculine identity in the camps (and before) that was widely shared among
male veteran inmates, the camp experience was a horrendous, excruciating ordeal that every inmate experienced differently. While many
Jewish men could resort to military masculinity when undergoing
the hardships of camp life, other men who either had had no prior
experience of regimented military culture or who could not identify
with things military had, without a doubt, a much harder time. Alfred
Schwerin recalled that he had never seen so many men cry.[61] Jewish
gender experience and the negotiation of identities in the camps, thus,
needs to be understood not only along a bipolar canvas of Aryan versus
Jewish masculinity and in terms of single, unilateral response strategies such as military masculinity. Rather, Jewish masculinity in concentration camps must further differentiate the different groups of Jewish
male prisoners. Different gendered experiences and response strategies
such as military masculinity could make a positive difference, but other
manifestations of manhood, such as the concepts of fatherhood and
marriage, were also of crucial importance.

Though the preservation of a military gender identity was an essential coping mechanism for many Jewish men, it was not the only one.
An analysis of Jewish men in concentration camps and their relations
to the outside world reveals that they further sustained their gender

identities by continuing to perform, or at least trying to perform, roles as the heads of and providers for their families as well as the roles of husbands and fathers.

Marion Kaplan has shown how Jewish women in the Third Reich undertook rescue efforts in trying to get their husbands out of imprisonment and sending them abroad first, with the rest of the family following at a later date.[62] Wives and other family members played an invaluable role, especially in the context of emigration. Historians agree that the November 1938 arrest of thousands of men was meant to encourage Jewish emigration efforts. Hans Reichmann recalled that in the camps "most of us … had only one thought: to emigrate in order to get out of here."[63] Often, Jewish men were only released as a result of their wives' or mothers' relentless negotiations with the Nazi bureaucracy and their compliance in obtaining visas that permitted their husbands' emigration.[64]

Though insights into women's roles are important in shedding light not only on women's emotional turmoil following their husbands' and sons' arrests but also on their active involvement in saving their husbands, men's voices need to be more closely studied. Through an analysis of letter exchanges between Jewish men in concentration camps and their families outside, two general patterns of behaviour are noticeable. On the one hand, Jewish men in their notes to their wives and children continued to provide advice and care to their families; and on the other hand, they received important support from their families. A focus on the often-neglected prewar years demonstrates that German-Jewish men were remarkably resilient and successful in performing their roles as heads of their families.

First, in the correspondence between Jewish men and their families as well as in memoirs and witness accounts, it is noticeable that Jewish men – despite being the direct recipients of Nazi violence – thought about and worried about their families' well-being. Frederick Weil (b. 1877), imprisoned in Buchenwald in 1938, remembered how at night he was constantly thinking about his wife and children.[65] As the rabbi Max Abraham, who was severely mistreated, wrote in an early account,

> I did not think I would get out of here alive … I no longer feared death. Only the thought of my bride caused some tormenting concern in me … She was without any protection.[66]

Abraham likely would not have been able to extend physical protection to his wife, shielding her from possible Nazi assault if he was released, but it is striking that he, the imprisoned, still responded emotionally in his supposed protector role. Concerns for one's family could also be directed to elderly parents and other relatives for whom young men felt responsible. Otto Schenkelbach (1914–85), imprisoned in 1938, strongly advised his father to get out of Germany while it was still possible. Though *he* was the subject of imprisonment and possible serious mistreatment, it was he who forwarded safety advice. In a letter from Dachau from late September 1938, Schenkelbach wrote,

> I have received your letters ... You cannot prevent me from worrying about you. For this reason, I am grateful that you write in such detail and spare me many questions. I am healthy and have my hopes for you ... Papa, do not remain as the last one in Vienna. Do not be considerate of me. It will be a great pleasure to get the news that none of you have remained in Vienna.[67]

More common than concerns over their families' safety, however, were existential economic fears by Jewish men who quickly realized that without their incomes, their families would face serious problems. The dental technician Max Tabaschnik (b. 1893) recalled that not only did he have to pay six marks a day for the duration of his arrest, but that he was also no longer making any income. But "wife and children must live."[68] Herbert Löwy, arrested in November 1938, even interpreted his inability to provide for his family as deeply shameful.[69] As Jewish men, often the primary breadwinners, were cut off from earning an income, financial concerns turned into serious problems. As one way out of this dilemma, as Reinhard Bendix recalled, the Bendix family cashed in their life insurance, a measure to which his father, due to the interruption in fulfilling the provider role, agreed.[70]

To counter pending financial and other problems, and to compensate for being in a helpless state, Jewish men offered advice to their families, trying to instil a sense of calm, an important facet of masculinity. Men's letters written to their families generally contained words of emotional encouragement and reassurance. Seldom were there any hidden references to torture detailing men's suffering and pain. As signs of life, such letters were meant to convey a sense of well-being by Jewish men with the intention of reassuring their families.[71] Though Jewish men harboured fears and concerns for their families, they generally did not relay such signs of concern. As the politician Ludwig Marum (1885–1934) wrote to his family, "Don't be afraid."[72] Oskar Richter wrote in his postcards and letters from Dachau between 18 November 1938 and early January 1939 that he was well and his family should not be concerned. "Be strong and brave. This separation will pass."[73]

From a more practical perspective, in their letters men performed masculinity by exhibiting a functional sense of objectivity, persevering in their roles as protectors and mentors despite their forced absence from home. In the form of instructions and advice, Jewish men provided information to their wives on how to handle various situations without them. Günther Rosenthal (b.1904), for instance, cautioned his wife to properly declare her taxes and not confuse the tax categories.[74] The author and activist Felix Fechenbach (1894–1933), already arrested in 1933, advised his wife not to be a burden to her relatives, where she and their two children were staying for the time being. He advised her to look for more affordable living quarters. Fechenbach further instructed his wife not to spend any money on him but only on the family. Fechenbach felt relief when he learned that his wife had taken on a job in a kindergarten, addressing her as a "brave guy" (*Du bist doch ein tapferer Kerl*). Yet his ardent wish remained the same: "My deepest wish is to again provide for all of you."[75]

The political activist and writer Erich Mühsam (1878–1934) in early 1933 wrote to his wife, "One can start afresh at the age of 55."[76] Ludwig Marum exhibited similar optimism and a zest for work. To his wife in a letter on 29 March 1933, Marum wrote,

> You, I, and the children, we will box ourselves through this … If one day I no longer can work as a lawyer, I will find something else. I also don't think yet that you should give up our apartment.[77]

In a letter sent at the end of May, he reiterated, "I have the courage to live on and as before to take care of us and the children. Once I am free, I will again provide for us [*unser Brot verdienen*]."[78] Yet, despite his eagerness to fulfil his gender role as male provider and head of his family, Marum had to acknowledge that the family suffered from his inability to make an income, and as a result, he eventually agreed to have his wife auction off furniture and other belongings that they had accumulated in more than twenty years of marriage and finally conceded to his family that moving into a different apartment to save money was necessary.[79] These instances prove that though men like Marum were cut off from work and absent from their families, they retained considerable influence and decision-making authority over their families.

In addition to giving emotional and economic advice that typically focused on monetary issues or suggestions for expediting emigration, Jewish men tried to further fulfil roles as fathers. They kept their children, especially the younger ones, protected from knowing about their father's imprisonment. Fechenbach, in a letter to his wife, speculated that their children would not for much longer believe the fairy tale of his being away looking for work.[80] More important for Jewish fathers, however, even while they were incarcerated in concentration camps, was to get their children out of Germany. Especially after the sudden arrests in 1938, it was an urgent matter for Jewish fathers and their wives to move children to foreign lands that promised more safety. Though their wives had easier means to apply for emigration and register their children with aid programs, Jewish fathers did not remain idle. In letters to foreign aid organizations, Jewish men begged for support to take their children out of the country. In one such letter addressed to a refugee organization for children in Amsterdam (*Kinderkommittee*), the author wrote,

> I do not know if this letter will reach you. I have sacrificed my last chattels for the delivery [of this letter] … My name is A., am living in M. I have a wife and six children aged three to fourteen. I am Jewish and stateless. Please save us! It is urgent.[81]

The widower Hirsch Schulmann (b. 1893) explained in a letter of 15 January 1939 sent from Dachau to his daughter Sonja (b. 1927) how he had been preoccupied with his daughter's emigration. He had signed a power of attorney from the orphanage that would enable her participation in a *Kindertransport*.[82]

Finally, while severely restricted in their attempts to sustain their gender roles as providers and protectors, Jewish men were still keen on preserving their emotional relationships in their letters to their loved ones and making their lives more tolerable. In numerous letters, Fechenbach wrote how he dearly missed his family. "I miss the children a lot and my longing for you is growing with the enduring separation."[83] He regretted not seeing his children grow up and, to partially compensate for this, being a gifted writer, he composed poems and lullabies on special occasions for his young children: for his daughter, a song about a rooster and the chicken; for his son, a song about a *Wau-Wau* (dog). In a 1933 letter sent directly to his son on his birthday, Fechenbach wrote,

> My dear Kurtl,
>   This time, unfortunately, I cannot be with you on your birthday. But I am thinking a lot about my small chap who by now has become a big boy. For your birthday, I wish you all the best. Be good, stay healthy, and please your mum a lot.[84]

In a similar expression of affection, Marum, on his wife's birthday, 2 May 1933, wrote the following letter:

Beloved,

I have never imagined that I would send you a love letter censored by the [*KZ*] director ... But it cannot harm. The censor might as well read that I love you deeply from my heart. We have been living together now for twenty-four years ... Our marriage has some years been hard; we are both stubborn and sensitive. But I could not imagine a life without you ... I thank you today for the present of your love. When our love began, I was a wild, naïve [*tumb*] student, you a romantic girl. Some shedding [*Häutung*] we had to endure since. But only in these years have we matured and learned to understand what love means. Community [*Lebensgemeinschaft*], goodness, endurance, and reciprocal help and bonding ... and the will always to come back to one another, the will to be one, and the feeling to be one until our hopefully distant death ... For this love, I thank you today on your birthday. I thank you today especially for our three children. I am so dearly fond of them [*lieb haben*] ... I embrace [*umfasse*] them with the same love as you do ...[85]

In a comparable situation, Julius Einstein wrote from a German prison in August 1941 in a letter to his two children in the United States who were awaiting their mother's arrival:

My dear dears [*Meine lieben Lieben*],

I am healthy, thank God, as well. The food is good. It is plentiful and tasty ... I hope to soon get released. In the meantime, I ask you not worry about me. Our dearly loved mother, [and you] dear Ruth, you both have given me so much love and goodness in my life that the memory of the happiest time of my life keeps me healthy and content ... Your loving [*menschenliebender*] Father.[86]

Jewish men could, as these examples indicate, use emotion as a tool to try to ensure a sense of relief within their families and their homes. Sending open expressions of affection helped Jewish men crucially in their endeavour to preserve their gender identity as caring, affectionate men, characteristics that had been traditionally praised and linked to domestic masculinity in Jewish religious culture.

While as "givers" Jewish men could provide practical and symbolic support, Jewish men also benefited from the sustained relationships to their families. Most significantly, being in touch with their families could trigger an inspirational, invigorating will to live and to endure the various hardships and camp deprivations. As was pointed out earlier, Jewish men, removed from their place of domestic authority, were often concerned about their families' well-being. Every sign of life from their families, thus, was meaningful to these men, as it meant that they could indirectly continue performing the roles of husbands and fathers. Knowing about their families' well-being, Jewish men had one less reason to be worried in camp. Hans Reichmann recalled in his memoir how during his imprisonment he repeatedly read his wife's letter and how he kept it tied to his rags, next to his handkerchief and a piece of bread. As a comrade of his prudently put it, "We must conserve ourselves for our wives, we must bear up [*durchhalten*] for our families."[87]

Surviving a Nazi concentration camp through familial mental support did not make men's transition back into normal life following their release a simple matter. Instead, Jewish men's return, recorded in their memoirs as well as by their family members, represented an upsetting and traumatizing ordeal for the entire family. With injured and disfigured bodies and traumatized psyches, Jewish men experienced their post-camp experience as a time when their masculinity was out of balance.

Many Jewish men remembered their deep embarrassment about their physical appearance upon their release. Either because of their dirty clothes and scruffy, dishevelled appearance as a result of being denied access to sanitary facilities or because of physical disfigurement such as a shaved head and visible injuries, Jewish men's return home was an emotionally unsettling event. It was gender-specific, as their violated physical appearance was unique to men and visibly demarcated them from men and women in mainstream society. Siegfried Oppenheimer recalled how at the train station on his way home, people pityingly looked at him and his comrades. Having reached his hometown, he walked on side streets only. "In the clothes I was wearing, I did not want to be seen by anyone I knew. And I had not washed myself in five weeks."[88] Alfred Schwerin even recalled that he and his fellow inmates had to travel by train in sealed-off wagons with shut windows to prevent the public from coming into contact with the ex-inmates, who were clearly aware of their special status.[89] Having arrived home, it was a "strange feeling that accompanied us on this first walk through the streets. A sense of uncertainty befell us. We imagined that every passerby had to turn around and look at us."[90]

For observers and families, the appearance of returning Jewish men was a shock, and this in turn enhanced Jewish men's feeling of being ostracized and emasculated, of belonging to a different group defined by the Nazis' notion of race and gender. As Inge Deutschkron (b. 1922) vividly remembered, "How these men looked! Their heads shaved

bald. Some had significantly lost weight, others were entirely disfigured from the beatings."[91] When through high-up connections the well-
known Jewish journalist Bella Fromm (1890–1972) was able to get an
acquaintance out of Buchenwald in 1937, she could not help but note
in her diary:

> There, I finally saw Dr. Kraft ... He was very emaciated, trembled con-
> tinuously and could hardly rise from his chair. I had to fight to keep the
> tears back when I saw this poor wreck of a human being.[92]

With the general public reacting so dishearteningly, for Jewish men's
families it was even more troubling. Carl Schwabe recalled that upon
his arrival at home, his maid, on opening the front door, screamed;
his wife was overwhelmed by tears and smiles; and his son said, "Oh,
Papa, look at you. You look like you are fifty-three." Schwabe agreed:
"I looked indeed quite different."[93] Hans Kuttner thought of his father
upon his return as a bald baby.[94] Ernst Hausmann (b. 1929), nine years
old at the time, remembered that his uncle returned with frostbite on
his extremities.[95] The daughter of Leon Szalet (1892–1958) described her
impression of seeing her father after he was released from Sachsenhausen in May 1940:

> What I saw was a human ruin, the wreck of a man, with a head which
> resembled a skull of a dead person covered with skin and a protruding
> nose. It was difficult to recognize the man in this distorted human body
> that was my father. If there had not been his eyes, I would not have reco-
> gnized him.[96]

After visiting his father in the camp in 1933, the ten-year-old Werner
Tabaschnik recalled that,

> After a while, the door opened and a man was standing there. I looked at
> him and said nothing because I did not think it was our father. This man
> was terribly thin und trembling. I felt sorry for him ... then I started to cry.
> My father was standing there, trembling, and did not dare to look at us.[97]

On the other hand, the father, Max Tabaschnik, experienced the family
reunion in this way:

> My wife did not recognize me. My child did not recognize me. After the
> SA man said, "Here he is" ... The boy started crying heavily. The SA man

was embarrassed about this and took the boy on his lap. He reassured my
wife that I would be transferred to a hospital on the same day.[98]

As plenty of these memoirs and contemporary sources evince, Jewish men's status had dramatically changed through their absence and
victimization in concentration camps. Jewish men were aware of their
changed position in society and at home. They experienced tremendous shame upon their return to the community and, more significantly, to their homes, where spouses and children might feel shocked
at the condition of their returned heads of household, seeing them as
disfigured strangers. While Jewish men had proven themselves able to
endure hardship, discrimination, and violence by the display of military masculinity *within* the camps, their reintegration into civilian life
was, at first, an emasculating process highlighted by shame and feelings of embarrassment.[99]

Getting back to a normal life proved difficult for many men,
though every individual fared differently. Prior to their release, Jewish inmates were explicitly warned not to talk to anyone about their
time in the camps and were further obliged to sign declarations that
they had not been mistreated in the camps.[100] Otherwise, they would
be rearrested. Their families, however, wanted their husbands and
fathers to talk about their experiences in places that seemed so hor-
rifyingly foreign. As Ingeborg Hecht (b. 1921) recalled, "We wanted
him to speak."[101] But with or without the Nazi threat to keep silent,
most survivors preferred not to talk about their haunting experiences.
As Marion Kaplan has asserted, threatened with worse punishment
if they told anyone of their suffering in the camps, many Jewish men
were too terrified to tell their families.[102] Either in order to suppress
their psychic trauma, or simply because they were threatened and
forbidden to talk, many never spoke about their time; out of shame,
others took years to talk or write about it.[103] For men, talking about
their inhumane treatment, their powerlessness, and their victimization would not have constructively helped to reestablish their position within their families and society as men of authority. As Rabbi
Emil Schorsch remembered,

> When we were getting released, an SS officer was standing in front of us
> who in a toxic voice warned us: "When you are abroad and talk about Ger-
> many and your arrest, we will catch you, wherever you are!" These were
> his approximate words, but the tone of his voice remained in my memory
> forever. I had not even told my wife about the concentration camp until
> we got to America.[104]

In addition to enduring their distorted, maltreated bodies, Jewish men relived psychological traumas at home. Emil Schorsch recalled his excessive thirst after his release, something his wife never could understand.[105] Siegmund Weltlinger thought he was freezing every night, despite the excessive heat in his bedroom. Hertha Nathorff recalled in her diary an episode when a friend begged her for help. The friend's husband, a sixty-year-old, educated, affluent, and well-respected businessman, had been having crying and screaming episodes ever since his release from Dachau. Several times, he had tried to jump out of a window in front of his wife.

> He cannot stand it any longer in the country of murderers and thieves. Hand-wringing, my friend conjured him to be silent ... I know they had beaten and maltreated him in the KZ. Others have told me. He too returned home sick and his life destroyed. He too is a victim of the Third Reich.[106]

Jewish men's ensuing pain could be communicated in other indirect ways. Many were fearful of renewed arrest. Others feared new violence on the street and further beatings. Still others, such as Siegmund Weltlinger, were haunted by terrible nightmares.[107] Alfred Schwerin, after being released from Dachau, remembered how tense and nervous Jewish life had become in Germany. When an unsuccessful assassination attempt was made on Hitler in September 1939, he contemplated his next move together with his female co-workers:

> I was standing at the door, thinking what to do. Under no circumstances staying here! ... because last year, too, the mob invaded this place, breaking everything. They probably would come here first again. "Should I go home and warn my father and my two brothers so that they can go hide with their Christian friends?" Miss Horendrekaler [sic?] asked me almost crying. "That should be the best," I answered. "I am also going to ride my bike to Mannheim to warn my husband," said Mrs Herz, running frantically down the stairs.[108]

As the previous passage has illustrated, men's unique predicament continued after the *Kristallnacht* pogroms of 1938. German Jews based their behaviour on men's previous experience of arrest. Jewish women again feared for their male relatives' safety, and once again hiding was chosen as the best means to circumvent another storm of arrests. As many Jewish men had already experienced what it meant to be imprisoned in a concentration camp, the ensuing fear and horrifying vision of again undergoing such an experience was a constant burden in Jewish men's lives in the late 1930s, a gender-idiosyncratic reality. When Walter Besser's brother was released from Dachau in 1936, after three years of confinement, including brutal mistreatment, and temporary solitary confinement in darkness, Walter (b. 1911) remembered how frightened his brother acted afterward:

> He spoke very little about Dachau ... When we went out on the street, he constantly looked behind himself, and when he entered a train, he always had to make sure that he was not being followed.[109]

The Polish-born tailor Moritz Mandelkern described his adolescent son's (b. 1922) return from Sachsenhausen in August 1940 as a blessed day for him and his wife.

> But sometimes, it was strange. When he saw a soldier, on the way to the synagogue, he would jump to attention ... He was so different. He might have been away five years instead of nine months ... Often when he talked the two of us just looked at him and wondered if this was our child. Often, he was silent, not at all like a boy of sixteen. He never spoke about his time in Sachsenhausen.[110]

Both examples strongly suggest that living in fear of renewed arrest by the Nazis and future violence was a haunting and gender-specific phenomenon in the lives of many Jewish men in the years preceding the Holocaust. Some men's demeanour had dramatically changed and overtly differed from the masculine ideal of appearing physically strong and confident at home and in the public.

As the most radical expression of their haunted and violated psyches and their inability to process and cope with their traumas, some Jewish men could not handle their predicament and resorted to suicide. Oskar Hirschfeld described a seventy-year-old fellow prisoner in Dachau who had lost his eyesight in the camp due to splintered glasses that had penetrated his eyes and who shot himself shortly after his release.[111] Hans Reichmann summed it up when he wrote,

> Some cannot endure the feelings of the regained freedom and break down in their memories of the experiences of Sachsenhausen. Comrade Gassmann, lawyer in Gleiwitz, in a state of mental destruction ended his life.[112]

All these post-release behaviours show that, for some men, an emasculating process commenced and came to full fruition *following* their release during their painful attempts at reintegration. Through fear,

Jewish men acted in ways that stood in stark contrast to what military masculinity simultaneously celebrated in non-Jewish society. While the fearless "Aryan" soldier would soon get his opportunity to prove his physical and mental prowess in Hitler's war, Jewish men in German society and within their homes had become powerless men who in addition to their deep economic anxieties about trying to fulfil the breadwinner role also had to deal with their violated bodies and the fear that they could no longer perform the protector role, as in their eyes they were not even able to protect themselves.

Conclusion

In the Third Reich prior to the Holocaust, as this chapter has demonstrated, much of the physical antisemitic violence weighed specifically on Jewish men. This violence was processed in gendered terms by Jewish men, their wives, their children, and Jewish society in general. As Dalia Ofer and Lenore Weitzman have rightly pointed out in the context of the Holocaust,

> Many families decided that it was safer for the women to go out in the streets ... Thus, family strategies for daily life, from who should wait in line for bread to who should go to the Nazi authorities – were forged in response to the perception and anticipation of how the Germans would treat men and women ... There was an initial focus on Jewish men for arrest and incarceration in both Western and Eastern Europe ... It was much more likely for men to be beaten, arrested and imprisoned ... more likely to be executed.[113]

This chapter shifted focus away from the years of the Holocaust to demonstrate that Nazi violence in discernible patterns was not different from what Ofer and Weitzman astutely described in the context of occupied wartime Europe. As Alan Steinweis has argued, antisemitic violence in the prewar Third Reich was much more common than is often assumed.[114] Starting with Hitler's takeover in 1933, Jewish men fell victim to a range of attacks that were executed by local perpetrators, in their homes, on the street, and in enclosed, isolated environments such as concentration camps. It is clear that primarily men were affected by the primitive and raw forms of physical violence in the first half of the Third Reich, when moral and cultural codes of sparing women and children were still in place. As previously shown, this violence could manifest itself as a corollary to the antisemitic propaganda and imagery focused on Jewish physicality. Few reports allude to gender-specific forms of torture that targeted Jewish men and their sexualities; yet the unilateral violence – incessant beatings, for instance – that Jewish men faced in the prewar years had an emasculating effect – as Jewish men were cast into situations in which they were powerless.

Jane Caplan has argued that monolithically depicting Nazi concentration camps as gendered male spaces is perilously close to saying that they had no gendered identity at all.[115] Concordantly, this chapter focuses on gender *relations* by not simply recapitulating the violence inflicted on men in the camps. Instead, by returning to the concept of military masculinity, this chapter shows how Jewish men adapted to their environments by carefully observing their tormentors and their displays of aggressive masculinity and how they subsequently adjusted their own demeanour in performative ways. Adhering to military norms, Jewish men were reminded of the 1914–18 period and soon realized that exhibiting the military-like composure that they had learned previously in a different setting could mean the difference between life and death.

Furthermore, again invoking military masculinity, Jewish men distinguished themselves from other male prisoners by effectively utilizing a repertoire of masculine values and behaviours, such as exhibiting (to their perpetrators and other prisoners) discipline, hardiness, steadfastness, and obedience. In a highly militarized, exclusively male context, Jewish men's adaptation of and resort to military behaviour constituted an attempt to preserve their gender identities. Military masculinity sustained some men in the camps, while other men, who were unfamiliar with this configuration of masculinity, often fared far worse.

The implications of being deported, imprisoned, and tortured in Nazi concentration camps were far-reaching and transcended coping mechanisms within the camps. Maintaining relationships with the outside world was of paramount importance to Jewish men. Trying to sustain their roles as husbands and fathers was a major struggle for these men. Their absence from home and the uncertainties revolving around their families' well-being were agonizing. Yet, as a coping mechanism and method of survival, many men exhibited their manhood by performing the roles of decision makers and advice givers at a distance. Stripped of their provider and protector roles, men found other ways to "give" – typically in the form of written words. In contradiction to the findings of some scholars, men also benefited significantly from their continuing relationship with their families.[116]

Nevertheless, major problems of adjustment to daily life occurred after their release from concentration camps – for example, in the form of "shame culture," when many Jewish men had to deal with disfigured bodies, violated psyches, shattered economic existences, and the prospect of future insecurity resulting from the need for immediate emigration.

Conclusion

In the end, one might ask: What larger conclusions can be drawn from a specific study of German-Jewish men and their gender identities during the Third Reich, and how can we apply and transfer the insights gained to a wider historiographical and contemporary context? One past but recurring critique, echoed even by some Holocaust survivors, revolves around the notion that, ultimately, Jewish men and women perished in equal numbers in the Holocaust, and that ponderings on gender differences might trivialize and distract from the monstrousness of the Nazi genocide. Others have long argued that it is more warranted to turn to the perpetrators and the systemic structures and pervasive ideologies that enabled a crime of such enormity in the first place. But such an undifferentiated approach would relegate all European Jews to the category of passive objects of Nazi despotism who had no control over their lives.

An exclusive focus on the end result, the murder of more than six million human beings, often deflects from historical contingencies that help us better explain the experiences, the reactions, the gradual adaptations, and the different forms of resistance that could precede the Holocaust and that Jews, at different times and places, maintained or developed.[1] In 1933, no German Jew could imagine a place like Auschwitz, and – unlike Jews in many other parts of Europe during World War II – a majority of German Jews never had to, as they were able to emigrate in time. If we want to understand what moved and motivated German Jews in their daily behaviours, in their attempts to survive and cope with the Nazi regime, then gender as an intersectional category of analysis, linked with class, "race," age, and citizenship, becomes an inextricable constituent of an *Alltagsgeschichte* (history of the everyday) that assigns agency to the Nazi victims. This study sheds light on the detailed perceptions and emphatic reactions that German-Jewish men articulated in their countless attempts to live a somewhat normal "everyday life" under Nazi rule.

This study has revealed that the various mundane routines and everyday behaviours of individual German Jews speak to deliberate choices made by them.[2] This work, thus, has attempted to open up to scrutiny some finer lines of inquiry within the source materials. Observations, perceptions, and reactions reveal how German Jews, in this case men, tried to make sense of their lives, how they tried to adapt to their circumstances, to sustain a social-economic existence, and to continue their lives in alignment with gendered and other norms, in the private sphere and beyond. Without heroizing the Nazi victims retroactively, this study has tried to show that despite the overwhelming and unprecedented attack on their livelihoods and lives, German Jews were surprisingly resilient in upholding notions of Jewish masculinity.

Chapter 1 shows how German-Jewish men kept alive canonic, military habits that enabled men to resist their ostracization despite the Nazis' efforts to excommunicate Jewish veterans from things military. Within the historiography of Jewish and Holocaust studies – the two fields this work is embedded in – the German-Jewish experience is somewhat atypical. Prior to World War II, Jews in eastern Europe had not adhered to a type of gender performativity that was predicated on notions of the patriotic, acculturated citizen-soldier. In its early years the Soviet Union was resolved on pushing forward with a clean slate to erect a modern, socialist state, and was disinclined to reminisce about trench-war heroism as German *Freikorps'* and jingoistic veterans' organizations like the *RjF* did. Moreover, though Jews in the Russian empire had also fought in World War I, integration was selective at best, as Benjamin Nathans has shown, and Russian/Soviet Jews were subjected to deportations, pogroms, and other forms of violence during and after the war.[3] The continued performative enactment of military masculinity by German-Jewish men was, thus, a distinctive way of maintaining a gender identity through military norms and German national belonging well into the years of the Nazi era.

In contrast, chapter 2 illustrates what German-Jewish men did not want to be. Nazi propaganda and legislation imposed on Jewish men a false and defamatory characterization as race defilers and vicious rapists of young women. Here, in the wider historiographical context, we can see parallels to the rise in antisemitic language and imagery that sexualized Jews in both eastern and western Europe. Countries like prewar Poland or Vichy France did not shy away from adopting race laws that closely resembled the 1935 Nuremberg Race Laws that outlawed relations between Jews and non-Jews.[4] The discourse of race defilement and the eugenics movement in general were not limited to Germany, especially from 1939 to 1941, and further research is needed into how Jewish masculinities, outside of Germany, altered under such circumstances.

Chapters 3 and 4 demonstrate Jewish men's attempts to preserve the status quo and remain in meaningful employment and positions of authority at home. Defending their roles as primary breadwinners for their families, Jewish men hoped to do more than just make a living. Providing for and protecting their families, as caring husbands and mentoring fathers, Jewish men struggled to adhere to a set of conventional practices of hegemonic masculinity. In these two chapters, striking parallels to the non-German Jewish experience during the years of the Holocaust can be unravelled. In particular, Maddy Carey has highlighted the desperate attempts by Jewish men to uphold the role of the male protector in east-European ghettos and concentration camps. Jewish men tried to keep their families together and as safe as possible, despite their increasingly limited means to do so. She writes that "for the most part, paternal protection in the ghettos particularly was achievable and achieved through traditional methods. Fathers organized housing, found hiding places for children and family members and provided protection for their families through working, smuggling and sustained negotiation and effort."[5]

In terms of the provider role, however, finer differentiations need to be made. One could argue that the ideal of the single male income earner is a Western concept that assimilated Jews had adopted for generations. In the East, however, a more traditional Jewish orthodoxy had lingered into the twentieth century, one that celebrated the Jewish male who devoted his life to the study of the Torah while women took care of the household income. At the same time, other Jews – in the Soviet Union, for instance – followed the more irreligious, socialist path of the state that pushed for a rise in female employment.[6] In short, it was in a particular German context that middle-class assimilated Jewish men identified with their work achievements to uphold their understanding of maleness. Finally, during the years of the Holocaust, the gender role of the income earner dramatically dissipated as Jews were first employed as slave labourers or were murdered outright. In the ghettos, men, women, and often children helped to make ends meet.

While chapters 3 and 4 focus on what Jewish men needed to do to articulate and perform their masculinity – that is, to be providers and protectors – chapters 5 and 6 put the focus again on the violence that the Nazis inflicted upon these men. Jewish men started to adapt and develop strategies of persevering and surviving physical attacks at home, on the street, and in Nazi concentration camps. Here, too, striking parallels can be drawn. Similar to German-Jewish men, Jewish men from Poland and other countries in the initial phases of Nazi occupation were more likely to seek refuge and go into hiding, as *Einsatzgruppen* tended to target men (of higher standings) first.[7] Once the onslaught against all Jews began, Jewish men and women sought refuge in forests, bunkers, or amongst Gentile helpers, as Natalia Aleksiun has shown.[8] Here the parallels end. Chapters 5 and 6 reveal new insights into gender dynamics in the pre-Holocaust era, as there was a visible *disconnect* between Jewish men, the Nazis' early targets, and the witnessing bystanders, Jewish families, wives, children, and friends. Chapter 5 shows how Jewish men in the prewar camps found ways to communicate with the outside world – giving advice, sending notes of care, but also making unilateral decisions. This divide between the incarcerated man and the concerned, waiting families outside was unique to the prewar years, and thus serves as an example of how men's gendered roles were challenged. At the same time, it epitomizes men's unequivocal resilience in maintaining their gender roles.

On the other hand, an analysis of men's attempted reintegration into family and social life following camp imprisonment in the prewar years allows for a further gloss on established Holocaust historiography. The relived traumas, often in physically distorted bodies, and coupled with an associated sense of shame, made Jewish men stand out, especially following the *Kristallnacht* events. Though they hoped to re-establish themselves, if not their social standing, at least their positions within their families, it was an excruciating struggle. To their families, these men appeared emasculated, a disconnect that these men had to endure by themselves.

During the Holocaust, both men and women were subjected to various forms of gendered violence. While Jewish women had to endure rape and in camps could be held as concubines, to name one example, Jewish men also could be singled out to face emasculating violence. The notorious image of the Nazi perpetrator cutting an orthodox Jewish man's beard has persisted in Jewish memory, an example of Nazi mockery and dehumanization that was a less common experience for German-Jewish men, who by their physical appearance – and language! – were less likely to stand out.

It is important to note that the story of German-Jewish men in Nazi Germany does not end in 1942–3 when most Jews had been deported to the East. As I have shown in my previous research, a not-insignificant number of German Jews defied deportation orders and chose to fight the odds of surviving the Third Reich in the "underground."

Hiding from the state and its helpers, approximately 10,000 German Jews (called *U-boote,* as they periodically submerged and disappeared from public life) faced idiosyncratic challenges that were greatly determined by their gender. While a Jewish woman faced fewer challenges – by possibly finding employment as a maid and shelter in a German household while claiming to be a war victim without papers – for a Jewish man, especially one of fighting age not dressed up in uniform, the situation was dramatically different as, for example, a nosy neighbour could report him to the local police. We also need to recall that Jewish men could be identified by their circumcision, another reason to hide. When Jewish men did emerge from their hiding places, to find food or routinely change their shelter as a safety precaution, some resorted to obtaining fake military papers and military uniforms on the black market to disguise their Jewish identity; others benefited from entering into relationships with German women who were lonely in a male-deprived, war-torn social landscape. For Jewish men, therefore, the risk of being detected and denounced was considerably greater than it was for women. There is even evidence that a few Jewish men dressed up as females – an extravagant way of camouflaging one's sexual identity.[9]

A few final words are in order about how some of the findings presented in this study can be used to sharpen our understanding of contemporary issues related to gender. Evidently, the ideas and norms that shaped German hegemonic masculinity in the late nineteenth century and the first half of the twentieth have shifted. Whereas aggrandizing the military and linking it to masculinity was once embedded in German mainstream discourses, social practices, and legal frameworks, a conciliatory, non-martial though still corporeal ideal of masculinity has become the new norm. While a culture of military masculinity saturated with expressions of nationalism continues to hold meaning in many countries, in Germany a more pacifist zeitgeist has emerged, one that expects young men to obtain a university degree or vocational rather than military training. On the other hand, while Wilhelmine Germany may indeed have developed into a militarized society in the late nineteenth century, as Karen Hagemann has pointed out, historians have too often focused exclusively on the role of the military and overlooked what she calls "pacifist masculinity," a critique that Stefanie Schüler-Springorum also voices.[10] This study, as a result, has not universalized German culture in the early twentieth century as having cherished only military doctrines in civil society. Instead, this study has devoted equal space to additional markers and practices of hegemonic masculinity, looking at men in their roles as working income earners and as fathers and husbands. This too constituted (and still constitutes) a hegemonic form of heterosexual masculinity in Germany and beyond.

Though the situation faced by German-Jewish men in the 1930s and early 1940s is not comparable to that in contemporary Germany or any other society, and the apotheosis of German militarism together with its heroes has ended, certain continuities persist. In the early twentieth century, visual and textual discourses of the hyper-sexualized Jewish male, as analysed in chapter 2, were nourished by the fantasies and fears of Germans who harboured radical, *völkisch*, and racist ideas. More than eighty years later, fears of miscegenation and calls for segregation based on allegedly dangerous sexualities by alien men continue to surface in European and other societies. This can be witnessed in the context of rising far-right organizations, xenophobic groups, and political parties in several European countries and of the recurring debates about the alleged numerical overrepresentation of males among refugees from overwhelmingly Muslim countries, debates that imply that foreigners are irremediably distinct in their genetic makeup as well as their culture and social behaviour. Messaging about inappropriate approaches by Muslim men and assaults against German women in public places such as swimming pools closely resembles propaganda perpetrating the myth of the Jewish race defiler.[11]

Outside the context of stigmatizing men from foreign minority groups, masculinity continues to be defined by identification and differentiation. As Germany continues to surprise world economists with its robust economy and low unemployment figures, men, more than women, are still expected to have a paying job. Without proper employment and an income, unable to provide for themselves and their families, men in Germany and elsewhere find themselves at the bottom of a social hierarchy that continues to be governed by gender expectations and conventions. In this regard, the stigma that Jewish men faced as unemployed males (or that they assigned to themselves) in Nazi Germany, though in a radically different context, is akin to contemporary images of unemployed men who find themselves socially marginalized.

Furthermore, men's exposure to a higher risk of violence during conflicts and war continues. As Adam Jones has made clear, able-bodied middle-aged men are typically the first victims in any violent conflict.[12] Starting in 1933, Jewish men were the first Jewish victims of physical harassment, brutalization, and murder. Because men are typically regarded as the greater threat, they continue to be singled out and victimized first. Among contemporary instances, the horrendous Srebrenica massacre, carried out during the Yugoslavian wars in the 1990s, is a stark example of gender-biased violence. All of the more than 8,000 casualties were Muslim men. As important and warranted as it is to raise awareness of the vulnerable position of women when it comes to physical and mental abuse, as well as to tackle systemic oppression that keeps women in inferior positions at work or at home, it is equally crucial to talk about men's vulnerable status as likely victims in cases of crime, war, and genocide, especially when gender intersects with notions of race and religion.

Finally, this book has had much to say about resistance. Many years ago, Werner Ring distinguished several types of resistance during World War II, including symbolic variants.[13] Today much attention in the media continues to focus on physical, armed resistance against repressive regimes. One only needs to think of the Middle East and the Arab Spring. Yet resistance can be subtler. Many of the Jewish men who appeared in this study were able in multiple, pragmatic, but also symbolic ways to resist and defy the Nazis. Jewish men's performative practices, based on social, cultural, and gender norms to which German-Jewish men and women subscribed – such as men's remarkable resilience in maintaining an economic presence – demonstrate how German Jews found ways to resist their ostracization from social, cultural, and economic life without taking up arms. The numerous notes of protest pertaining to Jewish men's exclusion from the military as well as Jews' initially successful intervention in the drafting of the Civil Service Law that allowed thousands of Jewish men to continue in their professions for years provide striking proof of how fruitful persistent, non-violent resistance could be.

In fact, this book has shown that there were even subtler forms of resistance and manifestations of agency. Continuing in their everyday lives with practices and behaviours that we might consider non-relevant and hardly noteworthy was for German Jews in the 1930s an extraordinary achievement. Going out to meet women was a risk that many men continued to take. Working at home, doing unpaid, intellectual work gave fulfilment to some men and prevented them from becoming despondent. Some Jewish men even found some meaning in being productive as essential workers or forced labourers, relying on gender norms to resist the dehumanizing effects of the Nazis' increasing persecution. And as fathers and husbands unexpectedly spent more time at home, they did not appear idle. Many made the best of their situation, developing a new level of affection for their loved ones and taking on new responsibilities as at-home fathers and husbands. Though separated and segregated from Gentile society, Jewish men did not become superfluous as the Nazis might have intended but took on altered roles that heavily counted on a pre-established gender codex.

In the end, a study of Jewish masculinity in Nazi Germany has implications that go beyond a limited geographical or temporal focus and relate to political, social, cultural, and economic issues, discourses, and trends in today's world. Gender studies can serve as a lens to illuminate lingering inequalities and conflicts in the modern world. The marginalization of German-Jewish men in prewar Nazi Germany amplifies the notion that injustice is not only and always the product of guns and laws. As Jewish men were marginalized in the Third Reich, the attacks on their gender identities were far from minor attempts to ridicule and ostracize Jews from mainstream society. In their shifting strategies, the Nazis severely undermined the practices of Jewish manhood. But even the Nazis, in their contempt for human lives, could not prevent Jewish men, while marginalized in their masculinities, from remaining human.

Notes

Abbreviations

GDW   Gedenkstätte Deutscher Widerstand, Berlin (German Resistance Memorial Centre)
JMB   Jüdisches Museum, Berlin
LBINY   Leo Baeck Institute, New York
USHMM United States Holocaust Memorial Museum, Washington, D.C.

Introduction

1 Bendix, *From Berlin to Berkeley*.
2 Anonymous, "Report B333," in Barkow, Gross, and Lenarz, *Novemberpogrom 1938*, 131.
3 Friedländer, *Nazi Germany and the Jews, 1933–1939*, 2.
4 Most notably scholars like Joan Ringelheim, Sybil Milton, Carol Rittner, John K. Roth, Dalia Ofer, Leonore Weitzman, Judith Tylor Baumel, and Marion Kaplan, to name but a few, have shed important light on women's role in the Holocaust, a previously neglected field of study. For an introduction, see Joan Ringelheim, "The Unethical and the Unspeakable: Women and the Holocaust"; Sybil Milton, "Women and the Holocaust: The Case of German and German-Jewish Women"; Ronit Lentin, ed., *Gender and Catastrophe*; Carol Rittner and John Roth, eds, *Different Voices: Women and the Holocaust*; Judith Tylor Baumel, *Double Jeopardy: Gender and the Holocaust*; Dalia Ofer and Lenore Weitzman, eds, *Women in the Holocaust*; Marion Kaplan, *Between Dignity and Despair: Jewish Life in Nazi Germany*. For more recent studies, see Rochelle Saidel and Sonja Hedgepeth, eds, *Sexual Violence against Jewish Women during the Holocaust*; Myrna Goldenberg and Amy Shapiro, eds, *Different Horrors, Same Hell: Gender and the Holocaust*; and Zoe Waxman, *Women in the Holocaust: A Feminist History*.

5　Baader, Gillerman, and Lerner, "German Jews, Gender, and History," 15.
6　Krondorfer, "Introduction," in Krondorfer and Creangă, *The Holocaust and Masculinities*.
7　Tec, *Resistance*, 346.
8　Only recently have scholars begun to examine Jewish masculinity during the time of Nazism. Maddy Carey's pioneering work (2014) on Jewish men during the Holocaust is an important start in the right direction. Kim Wünschmann in her perceptive 2015 study of German-Jewish men and their experiences in German prewar concentration camps further augments this shift toward men's studies. Yet Carey's focus, like that of most Holocaust scholars, including the recent volume by Krondorfer and Creangă, is on the years of genocide, 1941 to 1945, and thus eschews discussions of longer-term developments, changes, and adaptations by Jewish men and their gender identities under Nazi rule. Moreover, although Carey ambitiously looks at many (perhaps too many) countries of distinct cultural and historical backgrounds in eastern and western Europe, she does not include German Jews. Wünschmann's impressive study, on the other hand, goes into detail about German-Jewish masculinity in Nazi camps prior to the Holocaust and men's gendered coping mechanisms. Her study is confined to the microcosm of concentration camps, however, and though this is a key area of research, it does forgo a closer look into Jewish men's gendered experiences under Hitler outside the camps, especially in the years 1933 to 1938. See Carey, *Jewish Masculinity in the Holocaust*; Wünschmann, *Before Auschwitz*. For a recent review of works on German masculinity in Nazi Germany (with a heavy focus on non-Jewish perpetrators) see Kühne, ed., "Masculinity and the Third Reich," in the 2018 special edition of *Central European History*. Björn Krondorfer's and Ovidiu Creangă's notable edition sheds new light on recent research in masculinity studies and brings together perpetrators and victims. Here too the focus is on the years of the Holocaust with a strong emphasis on Nazi concentration camps: Krondorfer and Creangă, *The Holocaust and Masculinities*.
9　Mosse, *The Image of Man*, 6.
10　Connell, *Masculinities*. See also Tosh, "Hegemonic Masculinity and the History of Gender," 46.
11　Kimmel and Messner, *Men's Lives*, xxi.
12　Butler, *Gender Trouble*, 34.
13　Olson and Worsham, "Changing the Subject," 729.
14　Judith Butler, quoted in Olson and Worsham, "Changing the Subject," 730. For a study that relies on the gender performativity concept in the context of Nazi perpetrators, see Westermann, "Tests of Manhood."
15　See Freidenreich, "Gender, Identity and Community."

16 Doris Bergen, in Hajkova, Mailaender, Bergen, Farges, and Grossmann, "Forum: Holocaust and History of Gender and Sexuality," 84.

17 Gardiner, "Theorizing Age with Gender," in *Masculinity Studies and Feminist Theory*.

18 For intersectionality, see Crenshaw, "Mapping the Margins." See also Waxman, "Towards an Integrated History of the Holocaust."

19 Connell, *Masculinities*, 76.

20 Mailaender in Hajkova, Mailaender, Bergen, Farges, and Grossmann, "Forum: Holocaust and History of Gender and Sexuality," 84. For studies of masculinity and homosexuality in the Third Reich, see Plant, *The Pink Triangle*; Heger, *Men with the Pink Triangle*; Jellonnek and Lautmann, *Nationalsozialistischer Terror gegen Homosexuelle*; Giles, "The Institutionalization of Homosexual Panic in the Third Reich"; Marhoefer, *Sex and the Weimar Republic*. For male sexuality and concentration camps, see Sommer, *Das KZ-Bordell Zwangsarbeit in nationalsozialistischen Konzentrationslagern*. For female homosexuality, see Schoppmann, "National Socialist Policies towards Female Homosexuality."

21 Kühne, "Männergeschichte als Geschlechtergeschichte," 23.

22 See Garbarini, *Numbered Days*.

23 A note on the periodization of this study is in order: Though I delve into cultural analyses that pre-date the period of the Third Reich, the focus of this study is on German Jews who lived inside Germany between the years 1933 and 1941, the year deportations began. However, I do make occasional remarks to the 1942–1945 period as not all German Jews were immediately deported; some received deferrals as their work was considered essential, while others lived in "privileged marriages" (meaning they were married to a non-Jewish person) and were supposed to get deported at a later date. Still, the focus is on the 1933–1941 period. For a study on how some German-Jewish men tried to evade deportations and live as "illegals" in the "underground" in wartime Germany, see my article "Disguise and Defiance: German Jewish Men and Their Underground Experiences in Nazi Germany, 1941–1945," *Shofar: An Interdisciplinary Journal of Jewish Studies* 36, no. 3 (January 2018): 110–41.

1. Unsoldierly Men? German Jews and Military Masculinity

1 "Manifesto of Viadrine." In October 1886, twelve Jewish students in Breslau published a manifesto announcing the establishment of Viadrine, the first exclusively Jewish fraternity in Germany. Quoted in Gregory Caplan, "Wicked Sons, German Heroes," 38.

2 Frevert, *A Nation in Barracks*, 3; see also Roche, *Sparta's German Children*.

3 Hagemann, "German Heroes," 123. See also Hagemann, "Military, War and the Mainstreams."

4 Hagemann, "German Heroes," 13.

5 Frevert, *A Nation in Barracks*, 161.

6 Clark, "A Rhetoric of Masculine Citizenship," 5. See also Hagemann, *"Mannlicher Muth und Teutsche Ehre."*

7 Hämmerle, "Back to the Monarchy's Glorified Past?," 154.

8 See Goldmann, *Zwei Kriegsschriften: Über Kriegsziele, Juden und Politik: Der Geist des Militarismus.*

9 For literature on gender and German-Jewish orthodoxy, see Benjamin M. Baader, "Jewish Difference and the Feminine Spirit of Judaism in Mid-19th Century Germany," 60. See also Deborah Hertz, "Männlichkeit und Melancholie im Berlin der Biedermeierzeit." For Jewish cultural militarization, see Gregory Caplan, "Germanizing the Jewish Male," 163.

10 Ernst Schaeffer, "Die Juden als Soldaten," *Nathanael* (1897), quoted in Gregory Caplan, "Wicked Sons," 58.

11 See footnote 8.

12 Hödl, *Die Pathologisierung des jüdischen Körpers im Fin-de-Siecle*, 158, 168–75. See also Hödl, "Genderbestimmungen im Spannungsfeld von Fremd- und Selbstzuschreibung," 88–9.

13 H. Naudh, "Israel im Heere," in *Die Deutsche Wacht: Monatsschrift für nationale Entwicklung* (1879), 12–14, quoted in Gregory Caplan, "Wicked Sons," 38.

14 Armin, *Die Juden Im Heer.*

15 Quoted in Grady, *The German Jewish Soldier of the First World War*, 93.

16 See Frevert, *Ehrenmänner*, and Fetheringill-Zwicker, "Performing Masculinity."

17 Presner, *Muscular Judaism*, 190. See also Brenner, "Introduction: Why Jews and Sports?"; and Friedler, *Makabi Chai, Makkabi Lebt.*

18 The military habitus practices by German-Jewish men continued to resonate meaning even outside of Germany, including émigrés who made it to Palestine in the 1930s. According to Patrick Farges, these men utilized military masculinity as a manifestation of Zionism. Farges, "'Muscle' *Yekkes*?," 469.

19 Mosse, *The Image of Man*, 110.

20 Gregory Caplan, "Wicked Sons," 87.

21 "Der Völkische Beobachter," April 1933, quoted in Comité des Délégations Juives, *Die Lage der Juden in Deutschland 1933* (1984 edition), 166–9. Trans. S. Huebel.

22 Geheran, *Comrades Betrayed*, 63.

23 Hagemann, "German Heroes," 116.

24 Connell, "Masculinity and Nazism," 38

25 Wildmann, *Begehrte Körper*, 131.

26 Kühne, *Kameradschaft*, 85. As an example, the famous German encyclopedia *Das Herder Lexikon* defined the term "man" in 1933 thus: "True manhood

includes strength, bravery, honest decisions (without cunning excuses), farsightedness, initiative, objectivity in regard to people and things (without avoiding reality) and readiness for the serious and dangerous situations in life ... By being a warrior with the task of defending and securing the community body through the exercise of authority, assistance with education and the assumption of leadership and governing roles, the man experiences his natural precedence. The man forges the state, the hardness of which corresponds to the hardness of his own being, bears historical conflicts and wages war." See Frevert, *Mann und Weib, Weib und Mann*, 33. Trans. S. Huebel. See also Theweleit, *Male Fantasies*.

27 Walk, *Das Sonderrecht der Juden in Deutschland*, 17, 146, 154, 254, 290.
28 "B1 (Herr Oppenheim)," in Barkow, Gross, and Lenarz, *Novemberpogrom 1938*, 115.
29 Walk, *Das Sonderrecht der Juden in Deutschland*, 114, 137.
30 Max Rosengart, *Diaries*, LBINY, AR25053, 5.
31 Gregory Caplan, "Wicked Sons," 258–60, 300.
32 Walk, *Das Sonderrecht der Juden in Deutschland*, 259, 390.
33 Nathorff, *Das Tagebuch der Hertha Nathorff*, 70, 71.
34 Tausk, *Breslauer Tagebuch*, 9 March 1933.
35 Julius Meyer, *Verworrene Erinnerungen*, LBINY, ME439 MM55, 7.
36 Whenever possible, I include life dates, including birth and death; if only the birth year is known, I include this information.
37 Ken Baumann, *Memoirs*, LBINY, ME35 MM5, 71.
38 Cohn, *No Justice in Germany*, 275.
39 Alfred Wolf, *Memoirs*, LBINY, ME263 MM82, 229.
40 The *RjF* believed that "athletic training would foster military masculinity, physical exercise, subordination to communal goals, obedience, self-discipline, decisiveness, presence of mind, general command of the body, dexterity, agility, courage, bravery, cold-bloodedness, toughness, endurance, training to reason and moderation. Sport is battle!" See Gregory Caplan, "Wicked Sons," 164. See also Penslar, *Jews and the Military*.
41 Gregory Caplan, "Wicked Sons," 161.
42 Dunker, *Der Reichsbund jüdischer Frontsoldaten*, 27.
43 Though there was an increased output of such works in the 1930s in response to Nazi antisemitism, it is important to note that such efforts represent a continuity and that efforts to counteract antisemitic allegations of Jewish war shirking were made in the 1920s. See for instance Stern, *Angriff und Abwehr*.
44 Leo Löwenstein, "Ich bin ein Deutscher! Ich bin ein Jude!," *Der Schild*, 26 January 1934.
45 In its 17 December 1933 issue, *Der Schild* lists all the locations in Germany where *RjF* chapters had commemorated Jewish war victims.

46 *Die C.V. Zeitung,* 6 April 1933, 117.
47 *Die C.V. Zeitung,* 13 April, 1933, 130.
48 Dunker, *Der Reichsbund jüdischer Frontsoldaten,* 133.
49 Karl Friedländer, "Memoir," in Limberg and Rübsaat, *Sie durften nicht mehr Deutsche sein,* 69–74.
50 Siegfrid Neumann, "Memoir," in Limberg and Rübsaat, *Sie durften nicht mehr Deutsche sein,* 76.
51 Friedländer, *Nazi Germany and the Jews,* 29.
52 Geheran, *Comrades Betrayed,* 71.
53 Gay, *My German Question,* 60.
54 Quoted in Gregory Caplan, "Wicked Sons," 297.
55 Dunker, *Der Reichsbund jüdischer Frontsoldaten,* 136, 140.
56 Ibid., 180. Trans. S. Huebel.
57 Grady, *The German Jewish Soldier of the First World War,* 148.
58 Dunker, *Der Reichsbund jüdischer Frontsoldaten,* 182. Trans. S. Huebel.
59 This number includes members of the affiliated sports groups. Gregory Caplan, "Wicked Sons," 260. See also Mosse, *Image of Man,* 139.
60 Gerson, "Family Matters," 215.
61 Ibid., 21.
62 Edwin Landau, "My Life before and after Hitler," in Richarz, *Jüdisches Leben in Deutschland,* 311.
63 Fritz Ottenheimer, *Hineini – Here I am. Memoir,* LBINY, MMII24, 8.
64 Max Reiner, "Meine Erlebnisse vor und nach dem 30. Januar 1933," in Richarz, *Jüdisches Leben in Deutschland,* 115.
65 Leyens and Andor, *Years of Estrangement,* 10–11.
66 Cohn, *No Justice in Germany,* 7.
67 Ibid., 43.
68 Ibid., 58.
69 Alfred Schwerin, *Memoirs,* LBINY, ME593 MM69, 125.
70 Emil Schorsch, *Memoirs,* LBINY, ME575 MM67, 2.
71 Geheran, *Comrades Betrayed,* 55.
72 Arthur Propp, *Memoirs,* LBINY, ME507 MM62, Folder 2, 105. Trans. S. Huebel.
73 Hermann Pineas, *Memoirs,* LBINY, ME502 MM4 MM61, 1.
74 Klemperer, *I Will Bear Witness: The Diaries of Victor Klemperer, 1942–1945,* 82.
75 Ibid., 64, 114, 161.
76 Herzfeld, *Ein Nichtarischer Deutscher,* 98.
77 What Herzfeld, of course, ignores here is that Germany by 1938 had long ceased to be a democracy; parliamentary elections were no longer held.
78 Max Cohnreich, *Diary,* United States Holocaust Memorial Museum (USHMM), AC 2006.151, 30 March 1939.
79 Edwin Halle, *Kriesgerinnerungen mit Auszügen aus meinem Tagebuch, 1914–1916,* LBINY MM31, 123.

80 Joseph Adler, *The Family of Joseph and Marie Adler. Jews in Germany, German Jews in America*, LBINY, ME971 MMII21, 76.

81 Klemperer, *I Will Bear Witness: The Diaries of Victor Klemperer, 1942–1945*, 53, 121, 303, 363.

82 Ernst Hausmann, *A Family during Troubled Times. The Hausmanns and the Weingartners, 1934–1944*, LBINY, ME886 MMII12, 1.

83 Walter Besser, "Erinnerungen," in Herzberg, *Überleben heißt Erinnern*, 227.

84 Hans Wolfes, *Familiengeschichte, 1936*, in Wolfgang Herzfeld Papers, USHMM, RG10.337, 17. Trans. S. Huebel.

85 Harvey Newton, *Erinnerungen an das KZ Buchenwald Nov.-Dez. 1938*, LBINY MMII22, 1.

86 Ottenheimer, *Memoir*, 1.

87 Aviram, *Mit dem Mut der Verzweiflung*, 9.

88 Orbach, *Soaring Underground*, 21.

89 Martschukat and Stieglitz, *Geschichte der Männlichkeiten*, 57, 75.

90 Nathorff, *Das Tagebuch der Hertha Nathorff*, 98.

91 Spiegel, *Retter in der Nacht*, 56.

92 Elizabeth Freund, *Memoirs*, LBINY, ME153 MM24, 49.

93 Quoted in Leyens and Andor, *Years of Estrangement*, 25. Friedmann's letter gained some popularity, as Hindenburg personally responded by looking into the matter and forwarded the letter to Hitler, who categorically disputed antisemitic violence.

94 Charlotte Hamburger, *Die Familie und das Leben von Hans Hamburger, 1891–1953*, LBINY, ME253 MM31, 12.

95 For a similar argument see Geheran, "Remasculinizing the Shirker," 453.

96 For instance, Horst Geitner was born in 1922 to a Jewish father and raised Jewish. To protect himself from possible antisemitic attacks, however, he was baptized in 1933. He volunteered for the Luftwaffe and received the Iron Cross, an accomplishment that made him proud. "I had proven that I was brave and earned my equality." Geitner felt that the authorities would now see that he was a worthy German and not view him as half-Jewish or as a second-class soldier anymore. "I would be lying to you if I told you I didn't like being a soldier. It was an honor to serve." Rigg, *Lives of Hitler's Jewish Soldiers*, 247.

97 Anna Hájková shows that Jewish men in Theresienstadt talked all day about their World War I memories. See Hájková, "Mutmaßungen über deutsche Juden." Though this cannot be corroborated, two of the sources I studied even claimed that the *RjF* was, as late as 1942, able to prevent their deportations to Auschwitz and arrange for transports to Theresienstadt instead. See Richard Ehrlich, *Tagebuch. The History of our Negative Emigration, 1943–1945*, LBINY ME1101 MM II31, and Edmund Hadra, "Papers," LBINY AR1249.

98 Geheran, *Comrades Betrayed*, 101 and 135–47.

99 Franz Memelsdorff, "Erinnerungsbericht," in Memelsdorff and Heller, *Im KZ: Zwei Jüdische Schicksale, 1938/1945*, 25.

100 Klemperer, *I Will Bear Witness*, 26. Michael Geheran illustrates that Jewish men's preoccupation with things related to World War I continued even after their deportation. In Theresienstadt, for instance, Jewish men organized talks and public lectures on World War I. See Geheran, "Remasculinizing the Shirker," 461.

2. The Question of Race and Sex: Jewish Males and Race Defilement

1 Theweleit, *Male Fantasies*. For contemporary examples, see Artur Dinter, *Die Sünde wider das Blut* (1917) and Guido Kreutzer's *Die Schwarze Schmach: Der Roman des geschändeten Deutschlands* (1921).

2 Adolf Hitler, *Mein Kampf*, quoted in Krüger, "Breeding, Rearing and Preparing the 'Aryan' Body," 58.

3 One of the most widely read anthropologists and later decorated professor Hans F.K. Günther classified "Aryan" manhood as follows: "the Nordic 'Aryan' race is tall, long-legged, and slender … The extremities are strong but slender, as are his neck, feet, and hands … Typical for the Nordic head is the strong back of the skull … The man looks courageous … The skin is white or pink and lets the blood vessels look through … The Nordic man can best be characterized by his superb willpower, his powers of judgment, his cool realism, his trustfulness on a man-to-man basis, his chivalry and justice." Hans F.K. Günther, *Kleine Rassenkunde des Deutschen Volkes*, quoted in Marten, "Racism, Social Darwinism, Antisemitism and Aryan Supremacy," 29.

4 Michaela Haibl, "Juden in der Bildpolitik," 94. See also Heschel, "Sind Juden Männer? Können Frauen jüdisch sein?," 87–8.

5 See also Whitman, *Hitler's American Model*.

6 See Wippermann and Burleigh, *The Racial State*.

7 Gilman, "'Die Rasse ist nicht schön' – 'Nein wir Juden sind keine hübsche Rasse,'" 58. See also Hödl, *Die Pathologisierung des jüdischen Körpers*, 88, and Gilman, *The Jew's Body*.

8 Theodor Fritsch noted already in 1907 that Jews were no longer easily recognizable: "They are not seldom blond and reddish, with water-blue eyes and flat noses, and when they take off the caftan and cut off their side-locks, only a perceptive observer can recognize them as Jews." See Theodor Fritsch, *Handbuch der Judenfrage* (1907). Quoted in Haibl, *Zerrbild als Stereotyp*, 235.

9 Bruns, *Politik des Eros*, 18.

10 von Braun, "Antisemitische Stereotype und Sexualphantasien," 186.

11 Mosse, *Nationalism and Sexuality*, 140.

12 Mosse, *The Image of Man*, 70. See also Chapoutot, *The Law of Blood*.

13 Institut zum Studium der Judenfrage, *Die Juden in Deutschland*, 369.

14 For a study on Streicher, see Ruault, *Tödliche Maskeraden*.

15 Plischke, *Der Jude als Rassenschänder*, 9. Trans. S. Huebel.
16 Ibid., 47.
17 Ibid., 48–50.
18 See Bytwerk, *Julius Streicher*; Welch, *The Third Reich*; and Bytwerk, *Bending Spines*.
19 Gender Killer AG, "Geschlechterbilder im Nationalsozialismus," in *Antisemitismus und Geschlecht*, 58.
20 Haibl, *Zerrbild als Stereotyp*, 107, 289.
21 Przyrembel, "Ambivalente Gefühle," 538.
22 See also Berkowitz, *The Crime of My Very Existence*.
23 Gender Killer AG, "Geschlechterbilder im Nationalsozialismus," 18.
24 See Benz, *Der Ewige Jude*.
25 Friedländer, *The Years of Extermination, 1939–1945*, 99–100.
26 Herzstein, *The War That Hitler Won*, 426. For an analysis of German women portrayed in Nazi films such as *Jud Süß*, see Irina Scheidgen, "Frauenbilder im Spielfilm, Kulturfilm und in der Wochenschau des Dritten Reiches."
27 Gelately, *The Gestapo and German Society*, 129.
28 Przyrembel, *Rassenschande*, 213.
29 Comité des Délégations Juives, *Die Lage der Juden in Deutschland 1933*, 465.
30 Plischke, *Der Jude als Rassenschänder*, 5–6.
31 Welch, *The Third Reich*, 47.
32 Bytwerk, *Julius Streicher*, 143–4.
33 Adolf Hitler, *Mein Kampf*, quoted in Comité des Délégations Juives, *Die Lage der Juden in Deutschland 1933*, 46. Trans. S. Huebel. See also Roos, "Backlash against Prostitutes," 79.
34 For a detailed legal history of the Nuremberg Race Laws, see Essner, *Die Nürnberger Gesetze*. See also Pine, *Nazi Family Policy*.
35 Szobar, "Telling Sexual Stories in the Nazi Courts of Law," 131–2.
36 See Erb, "Der Ritualmord," 74–80; Lefkovitz, "Coats and Tales: Joseph Stories and Myths about Jewish Masculinity," 25; Rohrbacher and Schmidt, *Judenbilder*, 357.
37 Quoted in Przyrembel, *Rassenschande*, 175. Trans. S. Huebel
38 It is not the author's intention, however, to undermine the tremendous pain and suffering that women, Jewish and non-Jewish, had to endure as a result of race defilement accusations and prosecutions. While the law did not expect women to be prosecuted and tried, women could also be subjected to extrajudicial state sanctions. Women, but Jewish women in particular, could be held in protective custody for the duration of and for months following men's trials. See Przyrembel, *Rassenschande*, 257–69; Szobar, "Telling Sexual Stories in the Nazi Courts of Law," 139. For a legal discussion on women's exemption from the law, see Essner, *Die Nürnberger Gesetze*, 226–33. For a primary source of a Jewish woman who was accused and murdered, see Irene Eckler, *Die Vormundschaftsakte*.

39 Szobar, "Telling Sexual Stories in the Nazi Courts of Law," 148.
40 Ibid., 148.
41 Ibid., 139.
42 Wachsmann, *Hitler's Prisons*, 158.
43 Ernst Marcus, "Report," in Limberg and Rübsaat, *Sie durften nicht mehr Deutsche sein*, 191–3. Trans. S. Huebel
44 This sexualization of the public sphere and the concomitant attempts by the Nazis to create a sense of fear of Jewish male assaulters within society started with the Nazis' rise to power in 1933, if not before. For instance, as the print magazine the *Hakenkreuzbanner* wrote in an article titled "The Jewish Aquarium Herweck" on 11 August 1933, "With horn-rimmed glasses making them look intelligent, boldfaced Jewish youth are roaring in the water. From their gazing, the well-mannered girl (there has not been a well-mannered German girl in this pool in a long time) can only flee. We know these mongoloid eyes (*Mongolenaugen*)." See Comité des Délégations Juives, *Die Lage der Juden in Deutschland 1933*, 401. Trans. S. Huebel.
45 See Essner, *Die Nürnberger Gesetze*, 240–3.
46 Gellately, *The Gestapo and German Society*, 136.
47 Kurt Sabatzky, "Report," in Limberg and Rübsaat, *Sie durften nicht mehr Deutsche sein*, 204–5.
48 Jacob Georgsohn, "Antrag auf Anerkennung als Opfer des Faschismus," GDW Berlin.
49 Frederick Weil, *Justitia Fundamentum Regnorum: Mein Leben vor und nach dem 30. Januar 1933*, LBINY ME671 MM 80, 31.
50 Max Augenreich, "Antrag auf Anerkennung als Opfer des Faschismus," GDW Berlin. As a forced labourer, he decided to escape his deportation in 1942 and went underground, where he survived the war.
51 Szobar, "Telling Sexual Stories in the Nazi Courts of Law," 160.
52 Przyrembel, *Rassenschande*, 472. Trans. S. Huebel.
53 The merchant Max Oppenheim (b. 1898) in Würzburg was reported in 1935 for having had sexual relations with German women up to 1930. The grounds for his arrest were that his past behaviour, which had only recently come to light, had caused a public outcry. Allegedly, for his own safety, he was placed in "protective custody." See Gelatelly, *The Gestapo and German Society*, 112.
54 Kaplan, "The Jewish Response to the Third Reich," 83.
55 Herzfeld, *Ein Nichtarischer Deutscher*, 17.
56 Alfred Wolf, *Memoirs*, LBINY ME263 MM82, 238–9.
57 Leyens and Andor, *Years of Estrangement*, 28–9.
58 Comité des Délégations Juives, *Die Lage der Juden in Deutschland 1933. Das Schwarzbuch*, 466. Trans. S. Huebel
59 Ibid., 467.

60 Imprisonment of Jewish race defilers differed from other protective custody cases. For instance, Hans Stein, who was deported to Dachau in 1933, was identified to camp officials as a Jew who had chastised a female employee in his shop after having subjected her to animalistic indecencies. As a result, race defilers suffered harsh treatment once inside the camp. SS guards attacked and beat Lewis Schloss so brutally that he died of his injuries in Dachau (Wünschmann, *Before Auschwitz*, 51–3). Patricia Szobar also revealed cases of torturing Jewish race defilers in Sachsenhausen through suffocation in a broom closet or by being hosed with freezing water, with fatal consequences. See Szobar, "Telling Sexual Stories," 141.

61 Alfred Schwerin, *Memoirs*, LBINY ME 593 MM 69, 2. See also Reuband, "Die Leserschaft des 'Stürmer' im Dritten Reich."

62 Wolf, *Memoirs*, 227.

63 For linguistic violence, see Pegelow Kaplan, *The Language of Nazi Genocide*.

64 Alfred Meyer, *My Attitudes towards Germany*, LBINY AR25075, Box 1, Folder 1, 5.

65 Perel, *Ich war Hitlerjunge Salomon*, 115.

66 Rosenthal, *Zwei Leben in Deutschland*, 19.

67 Max Reiner, "Essay," in Limberg and Rübsaat, *Sie durften nicht mehr Deutsche sein*, 153–6. Trans. S. Huebel.

68 See Canning, "The Body as Method?"

69 Gelately, *The Gestapo and German Society*, 199.

70 Nathorff, *Das Tagebuch der Hertha Nathorff*, 74, 93. Trans. S. Huebel

71 Behar, *Versprich mir, dass Du am Leben bleibst*, 101. It is unclear if his father also knew about Isaak's romance.

72 The age of forty-five was chosen because "Aryan" women of that age were no longer deemed to be of child-bearing age and thus theoretically could not bear a child of mixed Jewish blood. Aryan maids under the age of forty-five, moreover, were only dismissed from a Jewish household if a Jewish male of the age of sixteen or above lived in it. Thus, a Jewish household with men was not determined by the legal age of twenty-one but sixteen, the age when adolescent men were thought to be able to conceive a child. It is estimated that approximately 60,000 "Aryan" women were affected by their forced dismissals from working in Jewish households. See Essner, *Die Nürnberger Gesetze*, 235–40.

73 Gay, *My German Question*, 72.

74 Herzfeld, *Ein Nichtarischer Deutscher*, 30.

75 See for instance zu Uptrup, *Kampf gegen die "Jüdische Weltverschwörung*; and Herf, *The Jewish Enemy*.

76 Kaplan, *Between Dignity and Despair*, 235. See also Kaplan, "The Jewish Response," 71.

77 Timm, "Sex with a Purpose," 223.

78 Wildmann, *Begehrte Körper*, 13.
79 Hödl, *Die Pathologisierung des jüdischen Körpers*, 153.
80 Przyrembel, *Rassenschande*, 349.
81 Szobar, "Telling Sexual Stories in the Nazi Courts of Law," 142.

3. Work until the End? Jewish Men and the Question of Employment

1 Anna-Madeleine Halkes-Carey has ably shown that the few existing
references on this topic suggest that loss of employment led directly
to negative consequences for Jewish men, including sliding into
depression and committing suicide. Such conclusions, according to
the author, are not only reliant on limited research, but, perhaps more
significantly, "they have been drawn in the service of another master.
Written predominantly by historians whose primary interest lies in
understanding the impact of the Holocaust on Jewish female gender
identity, much of what we know about Jewish masculinity is no more
than a corollary of important and successful attempts to show the
significant role that Jewish women played in enabling families and
communities to endure and survive the Holocaust." See Halkes-Carey,
"Jewish Masculinity in the Holocaust," 6.
2 Frevert, *Mann und Weib*, 29. See also Habermas, *Frauen und Männer des
Bürgertums*; Trepp, *Sanfte Männlichkeit und selbständige Weiblichkeit*; Kaplan,
The Making of the Jewish Middle Class.
3 See Schüler-Springorum, *Geschlecht und Differenz*, 37–8, 67; and Richarz,
"Geschlechterhierarchie und Frauenarbeit seit der Vormoderne," 96. See
also Lässig, *Jüdische Wege ins Bürgertum*.
4 See Schüler-Springorum, "A Soft Hero"; see also Lässig, "Religiöse
Modernisierung, Geschlechterdiskurs und kulturelle Verbürgerlichung";
Budde, *Auf dem Weg ins Bürgerleben*; Baader, *Gender, Judaism and Bourgeois
Culture*; Boyarin, *Unheroic Conduct*.
5 Hyman, *Gender and Assimilation in Modern Jewish History*, 153, and Hyman,
"Two Models of Modernization: Jewish Women in the German and
Russian Empires," 41.
6 Ofer and Weitzman, "The Role of Gender in the Holocaust," in Ofer and
Weitzman, *Women in the Holocaust*, 3.
7 For women's roles in the Nazi state, see Steinbacher, *Volksgenossinnen*.
8 Barkai, *Vom Boykott zur Entjudung*, 12.
9 Richarz, *Jewish Life in Germany*, 13–15.
10 See Raphael, "Der Wucherer"; zu Uptrup, *Kampf gegen die "Jüdische
Weltverschwörung."*
11 Barkai, *Vom Boykott zur Entjudung*, 27, 65.

12 Haffner, *The Meaning of Hitler*, 28.
13 Walk, *Das Sonderrecht der Juden in Deutschland*, 119.
14 Schüler-Springorum, *Geschlecht und Differenz*, 138.
15 Barkai, *Vom Boykott zur Entjudung*, 168. For primary sources see James Bachner, whose family had to move to a smaller apartment to save money. Willy Cohn started selling off furniture in 1938 to have some extra money. By 1941, he and his wife and children slept in only one room, a measure to save on the heating costs. Fritz Ottenheimer remembers how his family suffered economically, as the only remaining income was his pension. Bachner, *My Darkest Years*; Cohn, *No Justice in Germany*; Ottenheimer, *Hineini – Here I am: Memoir*, LBINY MMII24.
16 Tec, *Resilience and Courage*, 346.
17 Ibid., 51.
18 Herbert Löwy, "Erlebnisse aus meiner schwersten Zeit, Manuskript 1948," quoted in Kosmala, "Jüdische Väter zwischen Ohnmacht und Überlebenskampf," 9.
19 Krakauer and Krakauer, *Lichter im Dunkeln*, 16.
20 Carl Schwabe, *Mein Leben vor und nach dem 30. Januar 1933*, LBINY, ME586 MM68, 55.
21 Beck, *An Underground Life*, 16–32.
22 Tosh, "What Should Historians Do with Masculinity?," 192.
23 Hilde Honnet-Sichel, "Report," in Limberg and Rübsaat, *Sie durften nicht mehr Deutsche sein. Jüdischer Alltag in Selbstzeugnissen*, 183. Trans. S. Huebel.
24 Kurt Rosenberg, *Tagebücher*, LBINY AR 25279, entry 17 August 1936. Trans S. Huebel. See also Meyer, Bajohr, and Szodrzynski, *Bedrohung, Hoffnung, Skepsis*.
25 Rosenberg, *Tagebücher*, entry 31 August 1933. Trans S. Huebel.
26 Zvi Aviram, *Mit dem Mut der Verzweiflung*, 18.
27 Deutschkron, *Ich trug den gelben Stern*, 19.
28 In 1937, *Das Israelitische Familienblatt* registered three times as many job positions for women as for men. See Schüler-Springorum, *Geschlecht und Differenz*, 114. Memoirs of children also vividly recall how they had to either help out and participate in the family business, such as Rudolf Rosenberg, son of a tobacconist, or find employment outside the home to support their families. Ingeborg Hecht (1921–2011) worked as a babysitter; Lothar Orbach (b. 1924) shovelled snow; Horst Abraham (b. 1917) and his sister found some other work. See Dwork, *Children with a Star*, 11–12; Hecht, *Invisible Walls and To Remember Is to Heal*, 16–17; Orbach, *Soaring Underground*, 31; Horst Abraham, *Lebenserinnerungen Berlin-Shanghai-Chicago*, JMB, Sammlung Familie Abraham, Convolute 43, Folder 1, Inv. Nr. 2010/121/0, 40.

29 Pine, *Nazi Family Policy*, 164.
30 Kwiet and Eschwege, *Selbstbehauptung und Widerstand*, 198. The authors further claim that orthodox Jews far less often resorted to suicide. This supports my point that middle-class Jewish men related to their professions and the status and prestige they associated with their work. Both were fundamental elements of their world-views and identities. For orthodox men, in contrast, religion provided more orientation and meaning in their lives, likely helping them to better process their economic losses.
31 Göschel, *Suicide in Nazi Germany*, 96.
32 Fischer, *Erzwungener Freitod*, 65.
33 Hermann Pineas, *Memoirs*, LBINY ME502 MM4 MM61, 5.
34 Wilhelm Buchheim, *Diaries*, LBINY ME1535 Folder 4, 9
35 Joseph Adler, *The Family of Joseph and Marie Adler. Jews in Germany, German Jews in America*, LBINY ME971 MMII21, 56.
36 Ibid., 51.
37 "Brief des Preußischen Ministerpräsidenten," JMB, Sammlung Familie Badt, Convolute 36, Folder 2, Inv. Nr. 2002/31/22.
38 Fritz Friedländer, "Brief des Oberpräsidenten Berlins an Fritz Friedländer," LBINY AR7201, Box 1.
39 Erich Seligmann, *Letters*, LBYNY, AR4104, Box 1.
40 Adolf Asch, *Memoiren*, LBINY ME18 MM3, 2.
41 Situational ethnicity refers to an ethnic identity such as Jewishness that can be either displayed or concealed depending on its usefulness in a given situation. See van Rahden, *Jews and Other Germans*.
42 Bendix, *From Berlin to Berkeley*, 120.
43 Ibid., 122.
44 Hans Hermann Kuttner, Interview Transcript, Gedenkstätte Sachsenhausen, 2.
45 Fritz Friedländer, *Memoiren*, LBINY ME 760, Box 2, Folder 2, 170. Trans. S. Huebel.
46 Rosenberg, *Tagebücher*, diary entry 25 April 1933. Trans. S. Huebel.
47 Latte, *Und wenn wir nur eine Stunde gewinnen*, 26.
48 Rosenthal, *Zwei Leben in Deutschland*, 34. Trans. S. Huebel.
49 Alfred Meyer, *My Attitudes towards Germany*, LBINY AR 25075 Box 1, Folder 1, 3.
50 Erich Bloch, "Antrag auf Entschädigung wegen Schaden an Körper und Gesundheit," GDW Berlin.
51 Ernst Sachs, "Antrag auf Entschädigung wegen Schaden an Körper und Gesundheit," GDW Berlin.
52 Hans Schwarz, "Antrag auf Entschädigung wegen Schaden an Körper und Gesundheit," GDW Berlin.

53 Kaplan, "The Jewish Response to the Third Reich," 74.
54 Honnet-Sichel, "Report," in Limberg and Rübsaat, *Sie durften nicht mehr Deutsche sein*, 183.
55 Martin Gumpert, *Autobiography*, LBINY ME223 MM31, 216.
56 Gerson, "Family Matters," 221.
57 Frum Family, "Letter 8 July 1940," USHMM, Microfiche RG10.152.
58 "Arbeitszeugnis Salo Rosenthal," JMB, Sammlung Günther Rosenthal, Inv. Nr. 87/1/232.
59 Kaplan, *Between Dignity and Despair*, 30.
60 Cohn, *No Justice in Germany*, 23.
61 Ibid., 354, 379.
62 Wildt, "Victor Klemperer und die Verfolgung der Deutschen Juden," 57.
63 Klemperer, *I Shall Bear Witness, The Diaries of Victor Klemperer, 1933–1941*, 182.
64 Miron, "'Lately, Almost Constantly, Everything Seems Small to Me,'" 131.
65 Erich Hopp, *Drei von Sechs Millionen*. Unpublished Manuscript, 1946. GDW Berlin, 1. Trans. S. Huebel.
66 Camilla Neumann, *Memoirs*, LBINY ME466 MF214 MM59, 3–13.
67 Alfred Elbau Collection, *Erich Frey Diaries*, USHMM RG10.041, 12–13.
68 Beck, *An Underground Life*, 47.
69 Schönhaus, *The Forger*, 3.
70 Yakob Langer, "Letter by Yakob Langer's father to his son," USHMM AC1994 A0322. Trans. S. Huebel.
71 Norbert Neufeld, "Letter," JMB, Sammlung Familie Abraham, Convolute 43, Folder 2, Inv. Nr. 205/149/86. Trans. S. Huebel.
72 Klemperer, *I Will Bear Witness: The Diaries of Victor Klemperer, 1942–1945*, 274.
73 Ernst Wachsner, "Rot Kreuz Brief," JMB, Sammlung Familien Wachsner and Meyerhoff, Convolute 314, K1024, Folder 3, Inv. Nr 2014/194/539. Trans. S. Huebel.
74 Hans Oskar Löwenstein, "Interview Transcript," GDW Berlin, 16.
75 Tosh, "What Should Historians Do with Masculinity?," 192.
76 Messerschmidt, "Varieties of Real Men," 15.
77 Gerson, "Family Matters," 225.
78 Fischer, *Erzwungener Freitod*, 56.

4. Double Burden? Jewish Husbands and Fathers

1 Mosse, *The Image of Man*, 4.
2 Nock, *Marriage in Men's Lives*, 6.
3 Ute Frevert revealed that in eighteenth- and nineteenth-century encyclopedias, definitions of men were taken for granted and could not even be found in such works. See Frevert, *Mann und Weib, Weib und Mann*.

4 See Koonz, *Mothers in the Fatherland*; Czarnowski, "The Value of Marriage for the Volksgemeinschaft"; Pine, *Nazi Family Policy*; Carney, *Marriage and Fatherhood in the SS*.

5 Baader, *Gender, Judaism, and Bourgeois Culture in Germany*, 94.

6 Frevert, *Mann und Weib, Weib und Mann*, 113. For Jewish participation in civil affairs, see van Rahden, *Jews and Other Germans*.

7 Ofer, "The Contribution of Gender to the Study of the Holocaust," 128.

8 Tec, *Resilience and Courage*, 346.

9 Moeller, "The Elephant in the Living Room," 243. Halkes-Carey, "Jewish Masculinity in the Holocaust," 168–9. See also Amesbeger, "Reproduction under the Swastika," 140.

10 See Hagemann, "German Heroes," 127.

11 Veronal was a sleeping medication.

12 Alfred Guttentag, *Diaries*, trans. Erika Guttentag, USHMM, RG10.216, 13–17, 52, 109.

13 Camilla Neumann, Memoirs, LBINY, ME466 MF214 MM59, 14, 17. Trans. S. Huebel.

14 This supports Marion Kaplan's view that women were more inclined to favour emigration because they were not as integrated into the public world. As Kaplan argued, "decisions regarding emigration seem to have been made by husbands despite important role reversal. Both men and women generally clung to traditional roles in responding to the political situations." See Kaplan, *Between Dignity and Despair*, 63, 67.

15 Certainly, the protector role applied to women as well, and Jewish wives and mothers heroically performed this role in the Third Reich, trying to keep families together and keeping their children safe. Under normative conditions, however, men are expected to fulfil the gender role of being the protector. When they were not able to do so in late-1930s Nazi Germany, it was Jewish women who often felt they had to step in. Yet, this does not mean that Jewish men stopped adhering to the protector-role ideal, which warrants a more systematic analysis of Jewish men as fathers and husbands.

16 Julius Guggenheim, *Memoir*, LBINY ME279 MM31, 3.

17 Klemperer, *I Will Bear Witness: The Diaries of Victor Klemperer, 1942–1945*, 408.

18 Ute Frevert showed that starting in the late eighteenth century, the expression of emotions and feelings by educated, cultivated men in Europe was welcomed. According to the *Encyclopedia Britannica* of 1810, "Sensibility is experienced in a much higher degree in civilized than in savage nations and among persons liberally educated than among boors and illiterate mechanics." Increased criticism in the nineteenth century, however, led to fears of male hypersensitivity and thus "educational intervention was needed to prevent youths from becoming mawkish, weak, and doleful." Thus, the role-model male was portrayed as "a citizen

distinguished by his vigilant, lively but also controlled life of emotion, distancing him both from the rough men of the lower strata and also from the blasé dandies of the decadent aristocracy. This also distinguished him from all women, who were not themselves capable of such self-control and reflection on account of their fragile, nervous constitution and character." Frevert "Defining Emotions," 14–30.

19 Bogdal, "Hard-Cold-Fast," 30.
20 Baader, *Gender, Judaism and Bourgeois Culture*, 6. See also 78–95.
21 See Lüdtke, *The History of Everyday Life*.
22 Assmann and Detmers, *Empathy and Its Limits*, 3.
23 Frevert, "Defining Emotions," 5. See also Plamber, *A History of Emotions*, 29.
24 Beck, *An Underground Life*, 47.
25 Klemperer, *I Will Bear Witness: The Diaries of Victor Klemperer, 1942–1945*, 333.
26 Ibid., 329.
27 Ibid.
28 Nock, *Marriage in Men's Lives*, 4.
29 Neumann, *Memoirs*, 13. Trans. S. Huebel.
30 Carl Schwabe, *Memoir*, LBINY, ME586 MM68, 55.
31 Guggenheim, *Memoir*, Diary Entry 17 June 1938.
32 Cohn, *No Justice in Germany*, 2.
33 Ibid., 88.
34 "Letter by Yakob Langer's father to his son," USHMM, AC1994 A0322. Trans. S. Huebel.
35 See Huebel, "Victor Klemperer, 'A Jew but Also a Man.'"
36 Cohn, *No Justice in Germany*, 383.
37 Tosh, "Authority and Nurture in Middle-Class Fatherhood," 50. See also Hobson, *Making Men into Fathers*, 5.
38 The only one I know of is a paper by Beate Kosmala, "Jüdische Väter zwischen Ohnmacht und Überlebenskampf," presented at the Carlebach Conference, Hamburg 2014. The only other studies related to fathers in the Third Reich and the Holocaust are by Anna-Madeleine Halkes-Carey, who devoted one chapter of her dissertation to non-German-Jewish fathers during the Holocaust, and by Amy Beth Carney, who based her research on Nazi fathers in the SS.
39 Tosh, "Authority and Nurture in Middle-Class Fatherhood," 60.
40 Walter Erhart speaks of fatherhood and masculinity that are both acted out and coordinated in numerous individual practices but that, at the same time, are represented and structured along master narratives. Such master narratives provide a template for fatherly behaviour, and according to the psychologist Luigi Zoja, such narratives must be learned in the course of men's lives. See Erhart, "Father Figures in Literature 1900/2000," 64; and Zoja, *The Father*, 12.

41 Josef Zwienicki, "Brief an die Zentralstelle," *Zwienicki Family Papers*, USHMM, AC 2005.122.1.
42 Otto Kollisch, *Diary*, Peter Kollisch Collection, LBINY AR10717, 26.
43 Hermann Pineas, *Memoirs*, LBINY, ME502 MM4 MM61, 9.
44 Hans Alfred Rosenthal, Video Interview 1996, University of Southern California Shoah Foundation.
45 Alfred Elbau Collection, *Erich Frey Diaries*, USHMM RG10.041, 5.
46 Salomon Riemer, "Letter by Salomon Riemer," *Riemer Family Collection*, USHMM, AC 2009.383. Trans. S. Huebel.
47 Hans Berger, *Memoirs*, LBINY, ME46 MM7, 1.
48 Siegmund Weltlinger, "Hast du es schon vergessen? Erlebnisbericht aus der Zeit der Verfolgung," Vortrag Gesellschaft für Christlich-Jüdische Zusammenarbeit, Berln 1954, GDW Berlin, 10.
49 Joseph Adler, *The Family of Joseph and Marie Adler. Jews in Germany, German Jews in America*, LBINY, ME971 MM21, 73.
50 Marion Kaplan has demonstrated this point well in her book *Between Dignity and Despair*.
51 Histories of fatherhood have long focused on two models of fatherhood: the absent father who spent much of his time at work or places of male socialization, and the authoritative, strict-disciplinarian father. See Hagemann, "German Heroes," 128–9. See also Ganaway, "Consuming Masculinity"; and Erhart, "Father Figures in Literature 1900/2000." For an analysis of postwar fatherhood models in Germany, see van Rahden, "Fatherhood, Rechristianization, and the Quest for Democracy in Postwar West Germany.
52 In the 1990s, John Tosh triggered some debate with his thesis of a "flight from domesticity" in nineteenth-century Britain, a thesis that he since, however, has relativized. He claims that there was a growing distance between work and home, yet in their leisure time fathers spent more time at home. Ann-Charlotte Trepp and Rebekka Habermas have also demonstrated that emotion and affection were more common as part of fatherhood in the eighteenth-/nineteenth-century German middle class. John LaRossa in his pioneering work on fatherhood in the nineteenth and twentieth centuries argued that fathers were not the one-dimensional, unemotional/unaffectionate figures they sometimes have been made out to have been. Fathers emerge as men who valued and managed to maintain relations with wives and children that were both affectionate and harmonious. In her study on Wehrmacht soldiers, furthermore, Hester Vaizey shows how affectionate even the German men were who were supposed to exhibit hard masculinity and appear to be fearless and emotionless. Tosh, "Home and Away." See also Trepp, *Sanfte Männlichkeit und selbständige Weiblichkeit*; Habermas, *Frauen und Männer des Bürgertums*;

LaRossa, "The Historical Study of Fatherhood"; and Vaizey, "Husbands and Wives."

53 La Rossa, "The Historical Study of Fatherhood," 38. See also Habermas, *Frauen und Männer des Bürgertums*, 11.

54 Carney, "Victory in the Cradle," 187–218. See also Winter, "Sippengemeinschaft statt Männerbund."

55 Baader, *Gender, Judaism and Bourgeois Culture*, 55, 217.

56 On the other hand, mocking images of the Jewish Hausmann burgeoned. Antisemites such as the social reformer and pedagogue Hans Blüher (1888–1955), prominent member and promoter of the Wandervogel youth, had preached that Jewish men were too domesticated, soft, and effeminate in their physical outlook and behaviour. Such critics claimed that Jewish men spent too much time at home with their families. See Bruns, *Politik des Eros*, 443; and Baader, "Jewish Difference and the Feminine Spirit of Judaism in mid-19th century Germany."

57 Baader, *Gender, Judaism, and Bourgeois Culture*, 212, 55–6. See also Kessel, "The Whole Man," on the importance of nineteenth-century socialization for men in the public sphere. For a recent discussion on the evolving concept of Jewish time in the Third Reich, see Miron, "The 'Lived Time' of German Jews under the Nazi Regime."

58 Alfred Meyer, *My Attitudes towards Germany and Being Jewish*, LBINY AR25075, Box 1, Folder 1, 2.

59 Cohn, *No Justice in Germany*, 382.

60 Ibid., 382.

61 Ibid., 345.

62 Fritz Goldberg, *Mein Leben in Deutschland vor und nach dem 30. Januar 1933*, LBINY ME190, 2.

63 "The Jewish family gained in importance as the place where morality, religiosity and *Bildung* were cultivated and imparted to the next generation." See Baader, *Gender, Judaism, and Bourgeois Culture*, 56.

64 Pine, *Nazi Family Policy*, 168.

65 Klemperer, *I Will Bear Witness: The Diaries of Victor Klemperer 1942–1945*, 240.

66 Garbarini, *Numbered Days*, 104.

67 Albert Rose, "Letter by Albert Rose to his son," *Sammlung Familie Rose*, JMB, Convolute 169, Inv. Nr. 2013/430/129. Trans. S. Huebel.

68 Ibid., Inv. Nr. 2013/430/130.

69 Inge Deutschkron remembered how her father was teaching foreign students German under the table. Even after the war began, Yakob Langer's father taught literature to fourteen- and fifteen-year-old Jewish boys to further their education. See Deutschkron, *Ich trug den gelben Stern*, 19; see also "Letter by Yakob Langer's father to his son" (previously cited note 34).

70 Kurt Rosenberg, *Tagebücher*, LBINY, AR 25279, entry 7 June 1934. Trans. S. Huebel.
71 Cohn, *No Justice in Germany*, 9.
72 Krakauer and Krakauer, *Lichter im Dunkeln*, 67.
73 Max Cohnreich, *Diaries*, USHMM, AC 2006.151. Entry 9 February 1939.
74 Alfred Schwerin, *Memoirs*, LBINY, ME593 MM69, 103. Trans. S. Huebel.
75 Ibid., 103.
76 Hans Winterfeldt, USC Digital Video Testimony Archive.
77 Cohn, *No Justice in Germany*, 205.
78 Jalowicz Simon, *Untergetaucht. Eine junge Frau überlebt in Berlin, 1940–1945*.
79 Nathorff, *Tagebuch*, 76.
80 See also Amkraut, *Between Home and Homeland*.
81 Pine, *Nazi Family Policy*, 166.
82 Kollisch, *Diary*, Box 1, Folder 2, 34. For Kindertransporte, see Craig-Norton, *The Kindertransport*.
83 Cohn, *No Justice in Germany*, 6, 22, 31, 40, 48, 52, 53, 116, 164, 196, 240, 276, 338.
84 Weltlinger, *Hast Du es schon vergessen?*, 15. Trans. S. Huebel.
85 Gustav Meyer, "Brief," *Sammlung Familie Meyer*, JMB, Convolute 395, Folder 2, Inv. Nr. 2003/197/28.
86 "Letter by Yakob Langer's father to his son." Trans. S. Huebel.
87 Frey, *Diaries*, 36.
88 Ibid., 5–6. Trans. S. Huebel.
89 Pine, *Nazi Family Policy*, 154.
90 Bachner, *My Darkest Years*, 48.
91 Tec, *Resistance*, 55.
92 Schwerin, *Memoir*, 5–6.
93 On this topic, see Wenk and Eschenbach, "Soziales Gedächntis und Geschlechterdifferenz," 13–38.
94 Raffaella Sarti argues rightly that for too long domesticity has been understood by historians as a female arena. See also her edited special issue, "Men at Home: Domesticities, Authority, Emotions and Work."
95 See also Schüler-Springorum, "A Soft Hero," 103. See also Breuer, "Competing Masculinities."
96 Werner Angress argued that "fathers were caught up in the relentless economic pressures exerted upon their dwindling business activities by party and state ... In the evening after work, [they] revealed to their families what in fact they had become – broken men. Indecision, fear, frustration, all these led to endless bickering between the parents and thereby made the home for their children a place to be avoided, to be fled." Angress, *Between Fear and Hope*, 33. My empirical evidence does not support this argument.

97 Arthur Katz-Kamer, "Eidesstattliche Erklärung," GDW Berlin.

98 Joseph Adler, *The Family of Joseph and Marie Adler*, 89; Schwabe, *Memoir*, 89; Alexander Szanto, *Memoir*, LBINY, ME638 MM76, 107; Alfred Wolf, *Memoir*, LBINY, ME263 MM82, 250.

99 Behar, *Versprich mir, dass Du am Leben bleibst*, 86.

100 Schönhaus, *The Forger*, 17.

5. Outside the *KZ*: Jewish Masculinities and the Rise of Nazi Violence

1 Jones, "Gender and Genocide," 234.

2 See for instance, Bock, *Zwangssterilisation im Nationalsozialismus*; Saidel, *The Women of Ravensbrück*; Bock, *Genozid und Geschlecht*; Saidel and Hedgepeth, *Sexual Violence against Jewish Women during the Holocaust*; Halbmayer, "Sexualisierte Gewalt gegen Frauen."

3 Lentin, "Introduction: (En)gendering Genocides," 7.

4 Ibid., 9.

5 Wünschmann, *Before Auschwitz*, 102.

6 Wachsmann, "The Dynamics of Destruction," 28.

7 Milton, "Women and the Holocaust"; Ringelheim, "Genocide and Gender," 23.

8 Koonz, *Mothers in the Fatherland*, 349.

9 Kaplan, *Between Dignity and Despair*, 235.

10 This is not a criticism. Touching new ground back then, feminist historians had good reason to focus their attention on women, who previously had often been left out by general historians.

11 Marion Kaplan similarly argued that "Nazi propaganda put the emphasis on Jewish men, the Jew or *der Jude* – usually strangely distorted males with huge noses and stomachs. These rulers of the world were occasionally accompanied by an obese woman bedecked in jewelry and her grotesque children, but generally it was the Jewish male whom the Nazis caricatured and vilified." See Kaplan, "The Jewish Response to the Third Reich," 71.

12 See also Walter, *Antisemitische Kriminalität und Gewalt*.

13 Ringelheim, *Genocide and Gender*, 21, 24. Nechama Tec also argued that "because Jewish men rather than women were perceived as the chief enemies of the Third Reich, most of the terror was directed against them." See Tec, *Resistance*, 26.

14 Comité des Délégations Juives, *Die Lage der Juden in Deutschland 1933*. See especially chapter 9, "Violent Acts," 492–508.

15 Hermann Pressmann, *Diaries*, Trans. H. Pressmann, USHMM RG 10.481. Accessed English translation at http://www.museumoffamilyhistory .com/ce/pd-main.htm. Diary entries 5 March, 23 March, 22 April 1933.

16 Pressmann, *Diaries*, 20 April 1933.

17 Ibid., Diary entry 18 June 1933.
18 Nathorff, *Das Tagebuch der Hertha Nathorff*, 54. Trans. S. Huebel.
19 Martin Gumpert, "Report," in Limberg and Rübsaat, *Sie durften nicht mehr Deutsche sein*, 161–3. Trans. S. Huebel.
20 Pfeffer's inclusion of the lawyer's previous war service again underlines how military masculinity had become integral to gender relations and how it was acquired and performed by women and men. See chapter 1.
21 Gerta Pfeffer, "Report," in Limberg and Rübsaat, *Sie durften nicht mehr Deutsche sein*, 36–8.
22 Hermann Tuggelin, "Report," in Limberg and Rübsaat, *Sie durften nicht mehr Deutsche sein*, 28–30. Trans. S. Huebel.
23 Barnay, "Report," in Limberg and Rübsaat, *Sie durften nicht mehr Deutsche sein*, 44. Trans. S. Huebel.
24 See Comité des Délégations Juives, *Die Lage der Juden in Deutschland 1933*, 298–9.
25 Sometimes, however, violence stood in a somewhat rational correlation to economic motives, as many memoirs recall. Even though this was technically illegal, many Jews were arrested and extorted with more violence unless they complied with the Nazis' demands, most notoriously for the selling, liquidation, or transferring of their properties, businesses, and assets. Alan Steinweis illustrates cases when Jews were brutalized until they agreed to transfer large sums of money to local SA chapters. See Steinweis, *Kristallnacht*, 78.
26 Anonymous, "B7," in Barkow, Gross, and Lenarz, *Novemberpogrom 1938*, 323. The abbreviation "B" likely stands for *Bericht*, or report.
27 Anonymous, "B35," in Barkow, Gross, and Lenarz, *Novemberpogrom*, 158.
28 Anonymous, "B1001," in Barkow, Gross, and Lenarz, *Novemberpogrom*, 289.
29 Anonymous, "B64," in Barkow, Gross, and Lenarz, *Novemberpogrom*, 160.
30 Anonymous, "B190," in Barkow, Gross, and Lenarz, *Novemberpogrom*, 815.
31 Weltlinger, *Hast du es schon vergessen?*, 9. Trans. S. Huebel.
32 Adolf Riesenfeld, *Diaries*, LBINY ME787, 87.
33 Walter Besser, "Vernehmungsprotokoll des Zeugen Walter Besser, 9.5.1963, Der Generalstaatsanwalt der Deutschen Demokratischen Republik," *File Walter Besser*, GDW Berlin. Trans. S. Huebel.
34 Gerhard Bry, *Resistance Memoir*, LBINY ME73 MM12 273, 71. Bry moved legally to Britain in 1935.
35 Monika Joseph, "Letter by Monika Joseph to Beate Kosmala," *File Egon Joseph*, GDW Berlin. Trans. S. Huebel.
36 Nathorff, *Tagebücher*, 77. Trans. S. Huebel.
37 Cohn, *No Justice in Germany*, 7.
38 Kurt Rosenberg, *Diaries*, 1916–1939, LBINY, AR25279, 14 April 1933.
39 Tausk, *Breslauer Tagebuch, 1933–1940*, 164. Trans. S. Huebel.

40 Alexander Szanto, *Memoir*, LBINY, ME638 MM76, 105.
41 Riesenfeld, *Diaries*, 49.
42 Cohn, *No Justice in Germany*, 193.
43 Elizabeth Freund, *Memoir*, LBINY, ME153 MM24, 48. It turned out to be a friend of the couple who had knocked on the door.
44 Koonz, *Mothers for the Fatherland*, 349.
45 Hauser, *Wege jüdischer Selbstbehauptung*, 51. Trans. S. Huebel.
46 Julius Goldstein, "Oral Interview," USC Shoah Foundation Visual History Archive.
47 Dünner, *Zu Protokoll gegeben*, 71.
48 Hermann Zimmermann, "Oral Interview," USC Shoah Foundation Visual History Archive.
49 Neurath, *The Society of Terror*, 54–65.
50 The so-called *Juni-Aktion* was Himmler's plan, first in the former Austria, then nationwide, to arrest Jewish asocial males (loosely defined as unemployed, homeless, etc.) and Jewish males who had a "criminal record" of more than four weeks of prison. However, the targeted number was overreached by a close execution of the order. Over 12,000 people were arrested, including some 2,300 Jewish prisoners who were deported to Buchenwald and Sachsenhausen. The overall goal of the arrests was to increase pressure on these individuals and German Jews in general to expedite their emigration from Germany. As a result of these large-scale arrests, the number of cases of recorded maltreatment, suicide, and murder in concentration camps skyrocketed. See Faludi, *Die Juni Aktion 1938*. For a primary account, see Frederick Weil, *Justitia Fundamentum Regnorum: Mein Leben vor und nach dem 33. Januar 1933*, LBINY ME671 MM80. See also Fromm, *Blood and Banquets*, 273; and Tichauer, "Der Schafstall," 282.
51 Reichmann, *Deutscher Bürger und verfolgter Jude*, 90.
52 Paul Steiner, *Diaries*, LBINY, AR25208, Diary 7. Entry 15 June 1938.
53 Bachner, *My Darkest Years*, 48.
54 Anonymous, "Report B307," in Barkow, Gross, and Lenarz, *Novemberpogrom 1938*, 409. Trans. S. Huebel.
55 Anonymous, "Report B220," in Barkow, Gross, and Lenarz, *Novemberpogrom*, 123. Trans. S. Huebel.
56 Anonymous, "Report B333," in Barkow, Gross, and Lenarz, *Novemberpogrom*, 131. Trans. S. Huebel.
57 Langnas, *Tagebücher und Briefe einer jüdischen Krankenschwester in Wien*, 66.
58 Ernst Eisenmayer, "Oral Interview," USC Shoah Foundation Visual History Archive.
59 Louis Srulowitz, *Memoirs*, LBINY ME1329 MMIII3, 4.
60 Klaus Loewald, *My Kristallnacht*, LBINY, ME1203 MMII39, 2–5.

61 Nathorff, *Tagebücher*, 122.
62 Weltlinger, *Hast Du es schon vergessen?*, 10.
63 Burkhard, *Tanz mal Jude*, 15.
64 Otto Kollisch, *Diary*, Peter Kollisch Collection, LBINY AR10717, Box 1, Folder 2, 9.
65 Alfred Schwerin, *Memoirs*, LBINY, ME593 MM69, 9. Trans. S. Huebel.
66 Kollisch, *Diary*, 9. Trans. S. Huebel.
67 Hermann Pineas, *Memoir*, LBINY ME502 MM4 MM61, 16.
68 Riesenfeld, *Diaries*, 48.
69 Memelsdorff, "Erinnerungsbericht," in Memelsdorff and Heller, *Im KZ*, 16–17. Trans. S. Huebel.
70 For gender construction in (auto)biographies see Dausien, "Erzähltes Leben – erzähltes Geschlecht?"
71 Joseph Adler, *The Family of Joseph and Marie Adler*, 83. Trans. S. Huebel.
72 Ernst Hochsinger, quoted in Wünschmann, "Die Konzentrationslagererfahrungen deutsch-jüdischer Männer nach dem Novemberpogrom 1938," 48.

6. Inside the *KZ*: Jewish Masculinities in Prewar Nazi Concentration Camps

1 Wünschmann, "Männlichkeitskonstruktionen jüdischer Häftlinge in NS Konzentrationslagern," 205.
2 Ibid., 235. See also Steinweis, *Kristallnacht*, 61. On the other hand, Kim Wünschmann asserts that about 4 to 10 per cent of camp prisoners were Jewish and non-Jewish women during this time and that there is no recorded killing of a female prisoner prior to 1939. See Wünschmann, *Before Auschwitz*, 7.
3 Jane Caplan, "Gender and the Concentration Camps," 99.
4 Women in Nazi concentration camps had to face specific forms of violence and after-effects that pertained to women only, including rape, abortion, pregnancy, and childbirth and the sheer impossibility of keeping newborns alive in camp environments. See endnote 3 in the Introduction for further readings.
5 Bock, *Genozid und Geschlecht*, 8.
6 Goldenberg and Shapiro, *Different Horrors, Same Hell*.
7 Wachsmann, "The Dynamics of Destruction," 25. An early account of Jews being tortured in 1933–4 is by the theatre director Wolfgang Langhoff (1901–66), who was imprisoned in the concentration camps Börgermoor and Lichtenburg. See Langhoff, *Die Moorsoldaten*.
8 See Arnold Bernstein, "Das Ende der Bernstein Linie," in Limberg and Rübsaat, *Sie durften nicht mehr Deutsche sein*, 104–14.

9 Wünschmann, *Before Auschwitz*, 43–5. For arbitrary arrests of Jewish men see pages 45–53. For instance, Korman Rosenbusch of Dettelbach, a village in Franconia, was arrested in March 1933, years before the passing of the Nuremberg Race Laws, because of his behaviour as a Jew toward the female sex. Allegedly, he had outraged the public, and he was sentenced to two years of imprisonment in Dachau "for his own protection."

10 Harvey Newton (formerly known as Hermann Neustadt) recalled the verbal abuse of the people on the street who were watching the arrested march through town. See *Erinnerungen an das KZ Buchenwald November-Dezember 1938*, LBINY MMII22, 4.

11 Wallner, *By Order of the Gestapo*. See also Anonymous, "B82," in Barkow, Gross, and Lenarz, *Novemberpogrom*.

12 Emil Schorsch, *Memoirs*, LBINY, ME575 MM67, 8.

13 Technically, SS guards had no legal authority to kill camp prisoners except to prevent an escape. Guards, therefore, fabricated on death certificates that the perished prisoner was trying to escape.

14 Early accounts of concentration camp mistreatment were written by former inmates and escapees and typically published outside of Germany and smuggled back into Germany. They include Seger, *Oranienburg*; Abraham, *Juda Verrecke*; Anonymous, *Konzentrationslager*; Langhoff, *Die Moorsoldaten*; Mühsam, *Der Leidensweg Erich Mühsams*. In the early years, the Nazis were so preoccupied with their international reputation that they in turn published (unsuccessful) rebuttals to these first-generation witness accounts, including Werner Schäfer, *Konzentrationslager Oranienburg*, and Jakob Trachtenberg, who selectively cites accounts by Jewish organizations such as the veterans organization *RjF* that in 1933 addressed foreign governments and dignitaries, defending Germany's new government and trying to improve Germany's international standing. See Trachtenberg, *Die Greuelpropaganda ist eine Lügenpropaganda sagen die Juden selbst!* See also Moore, "'The Truth about the Concentration Camps.'"

15 The drastic loss of weight was experienced by all prisoners. Frederick Weil asserted that he had lost forty-two pounds in four weeks. See Frederick Weil, *Justitia Fundamentum Regnorum: Mein Leben vor und nach dem 33. Januar 1933*, LBINY ME671 MM80, 109.

16 Herbert Luft, "Report," USHMM RG10.028, 5–6. Trans. S. Huebel.

17 Anonymous, "B77," in Barkow, Gross, and Lenarz, *Novemberpogrom*, 520.

18 Anonymous, "B323," in Barkow, Gross, and Lenarz, *Novemberpogrom*, 605. See also Schwerin, *Memoir*, 68.

19 Anonymous, "B174," in Barkow, Gross, and Lenarz, *Novemberpogrom*, 81. Buchenwald was located in a forested, elevated area (near Weimar) and was cut off from direct water sources. Water had to be brought in daily by water trucks. Thus, water was severely restricted for prisoner consumption.

20 Kienitz, "Body Damage."
21 Forth, *Masculinity in the Modern West*, 69.
22 Max Tabaschnik, "Königsstein," in Anonymous, *Konzentrationslager: Ein Appell an das Gewissen der Welt. Ein Buch der Greuel. Die Opfer klagen an*, 141.
23 Reichmann, *Deutscher Bürger und Verfolgter Jude*, 122. Trans. S. Huebel.
24 Anonymous, "B77," in Barkow, Gross, and Lenarz, *Novemberpogrom*, 572.
25 Memelsdorff and Heller, *Im KZ*, 38.
26 Ibid., 49. Trans. S. Huebel.
27 Siegfried Oppenheimer, *Meine Erlebnisse am 10. November 1938 und mein Aufenthalt in Buchenwald bis zu meiner Rückkehr am 14.12. nach Bad Nauheim*, LBINY ME448 MM61, 5.
28 Memelsdorff, "Erinnerungsbericht," in Memelsdorff and Heller, *Im KZ*, 74. Trans. S. Huebel. See also Schwerin *Memoirs*, 80.
29 Carl Schwabe, *Memoir*, LBINY, ME586 MM68, 76–7. Trans. S. Huebel.
30 Anonymous, "B82," in Barkow, Gross, and Lenarz, *Novemberpogrom*, 493. Trans. S. Huebel.
31 Anonymous, "B184," in Barkow, Gross, and Lenarz, *Novemberpogrom*, 558.
32 Anonymous, "B328," in Barkow, Gross, and Lenarz, *Novemberpogrom*, 53. Trans. S. Huebel.
33 Ibid.
34 Schwerin, *Memoir*, 45.
35 Anonymous, "B340," in Barkow, Gross, and Lenarz, *Novemberpogrom*, 623. Trans. S. Huebel.
36 Christopher Dillon, "'Tolerance Means Weakness,'" 386.
37 Anonymous, "B328," in Barkow, Gross, and Lenarz, *Novemberpogrom*, 54. Trans. S. Huebel.
38 Jane Caplan, "Gender and the Concentration Camps," 99.
39 See Bock, *Genozid und Geschlecht*, 19.
40 Kühne, *Kameradschaft*. English edition *The Rise and Fall of Comradeship*. For a primary source, see *Handbuch der SA*.
41 Schroer, "Civilization, Barbarism, and the Ethos of Self-control among the Perpetrators."
42 Dillon, "'Tolerance Means Weakness,'" 385. See also Haynes, "Ordinary Masculinity."
43 Dillon, "'Tolerance Means Weakness,'" 386. See also Ettelson, "The Nazi New Man."
44 Anonymous, "B194," in Barkow, Gross, and Lenarz, *Novemberpogrom*, 654.
45 Wünschmann, "Die Konzentrationslagererfahrungen deutsch-jüdischer Männer nach dem Novemberpogrom 1938," 54. See also Becker and Bock, "Muselmänner in Nazi Concentration Camps."
46 Dillon, "Tolerance Means Weakness," 388. Central to conceptualizing a generic model of masculinity is a trial of tests that men must pass, according to David Gilmore in his seminal work *Manhood in the Making*.

47 Wünschmann, "Die Konzentrationslagererfahrungen deutsch-jüdischer Männer," 42–9.

48 In a related case, Brian Feltman has argued that German POWs in the post-World War I period "believed their response to captivity would say much about their national character and identity as men." See Feltman, *The Stigma of Surrender*, 106.

49 Schwerin, *Memoir*, 36. Trans. S. Huebel.

50 Ibid., 46. Trans. S. Huebel.

51 For instance, reports recalled that when Jews were arrested in 1938 (both in March and November), Jewish men had to perform military exercises and gymnastics on the street. Often groups of Jewish men were also organized in military formations to march to the train stations. The Nazi pressure to conform to military expectations, therefore, was not necessarily restricted to the sealed-off concentration camps. See Anonymous, "B189," in Barkow, Gross, and Lenarz, *Novemberpogrom*, 736–9.

52 Schorsch, *Memoirs*, 8.

53 Newton, *Erinnerungen*, 6. Trans. S. Huebel.

54 Anonymous, "B82," in Barkow, Gross, and Lenarz, *Novemberpogrom*, 496. Trans. S. Huebel.

55 Anonymous, "B175," in Barkow, Gross, and Lenarz, *Novemberpogrom*, 551.

56 Harry Ross, "Interview Transcript," Gedenkstätte und Museum Sachsenhausen, 8. Veronika Springmann has similarly argued that age, bodily strength, and health were crucial factors for camp survival. See Springmann, "Boxen im Konzentratinslager."

57 Theweleit, *Male Fantasies*.

58 Anonymous, "B340," in Barkow, Gross, and Lenarz, *Novemberpogrom*, 635.

59 Karl Guggenheim, quoted in Gregory Caplan, "Wicked Sons, German Heroes," 313.

60 See for instance, Newton, *Erinnerungen*, 10; and Siegfried Oppenheimer, *Meine Erlebnisse*, 13.

61 Schwerin, *Memoirs*, 87.

62 Kaplan, *Between Dignity and Despair*, 140. In my own research, I came across the case of Siegbert Freiberg, who in an interview recalled that his stepmother, who was Jewish, gave her ticket to go abroad to a Jewish man who, like her husband, had been imprisoned in concentration camps. Siegbert's father survived the war in Shanghai. Siegbert (b. 1923) managed, with much luck, to survive an illegal underground existence in Berlin. His stepmother was killed in Auschwitz. See Siegbert Freiberg, "Oral Interview," USC Shoah Foundation Visual History Archive.

63 Reichmann, *Deutscher Bürger und verfogter Jude*, 164.

64 Kaplan, *Between Dignity and Despair*, 140. My own research corroborates Kaplan's findings. See Harry Kuttner, "Interview Transcript," P3 Hans Hermann Kuttner, Gedenkstätte Sachsenhausen; Inge Rose, "Letter to

Erich Rose," *Sammlung Familie Rose*, JMB, Dok. 2013/430/274, K790, Folder 10.

65 Weil, *Justitia*, 82.

66 Abraham, *Juda Verrecke*, 138. Trans. S. Huebel.

67 Otto Schenkelbach, "Letter to Father, 11 September 1938," Schenkelbach/ Feldbau Collection, USHMM AC2006.359.1. Trans. S. Huebel. For a similar argument about Jewish men imprisoned in concentration camps and being powerless to fulfil the protector role, see Pine, "The Experiences and Behavior of Male Holocaust Victims at Auschwitz."

68 Tabaschnik, "Königstein," in Anonymous, *Konzentrationslager*, 94.

69 Kosmala, "Jüdische Väter zwischen Ohnmacht und Überlebenskampf," 10.

70 Bendix, *From Berlin to Berkeley*, 154.

71 In contemporary reports, men often acknowledged the fact that their wives had been left in ignorance of their fate and whereabouts and how tormenting this uncertainty had been for their families. See Anonymous, "B99," "B114," in Barkow, Gross, and Lenarz, *Novemberpogrom;* and Schorsch, *Memoirs*, 9. Utilizing dramatic language, in a contemporary account written in 1939 and published in 1945, the Austrian Julius Freund wrote that following his deportation to Buchenwald in the spring of 1938, his children were crying and looking for their father. His wife was missing her husband and provider (*Ernährer*). See Freund, *O Buchenwald*, 17.

72 Marum, *Briefe aus dem KZ Kislau*, 50.

73 Oskar Richter, "Letters," *Edith Bredehoft Collection*, USHMM, AC1993.136.

74 Günther Rosenthal, "Letter to His Wife," *Sammlung Günther Rosenthal*, JMB, Doc. Nr. 87/1/147.

75 Fechenbach, *Mein Herz schlägt weiter*, 12–13. The manuscript was originally published in 1936 by the Kultur Verlag St Gallen. Supposed to be transferred to Dachau in August 1933, Fechenbach was murdered by SA/ SS men in a forest.

76 Mühsam, *Der Leidensweg Erich Mühsams*, 25.

77 Marum, *Briefe aus dem KZ Kislau*, 50. Trans. S. Huebel.

78 Ibid., 74. He repeated his zest for working and providing for his family a few weeks later, in early June. See page 76. In early July, he stated that he was looking forward to working again, as he was getting "rusty." See page 84. Marum was murdered in *KZ* Kislau in March 1934.

79 Ibid., 77, 82.

80 Fechenbach, *Mein Herz schlägt weiter*, 51. In a similar fashion, Hertha Nathorff, according to the diary, responded to her child's recurring questions about her father's whereabouts, following his arrest in November 1938, by explaining that her father was participating in a major military exercise that could last a few weeks. Nathorff, *Tagebücher*, 125–7.

81 Anonymous, "B253," in Barkow, Gross, and Lenarz, *Novemberpogrom*, 663. Similar letters to the *Kinderkommittee* or the royal family in the

Netherlands include "B260," and "B262." "B279" explicitly refers to imprisoned, unemployed men and starving children. Trans. S. Huebel.

82 Hirsch Schulmann, "Letter from Dachau to Daughter, 15 January 1939." *Sonja Schulmann Schwartz Collection*, USHMM AC1993.124.19.
83 Fechenbach, *Mein Herz schlägt weiter*, 23.
84 Ibid., 18. Trans. S. Huebel.
85 Marum, *Briefe aus dem KZ Kislau*, 68. Trans. S. Huebel.
86 Julius Einstein, "Letter to His Children," *Julius and Selma Einstein Papers*, USHMM, AC1998.162.1. Trans. S. Huebel.
87 Reichmann, *Deutscher Bürger und verfolgter Jude*, 233. For an interesting exchange of love letters between Ruth Grabowski (b. 1907) and her boyfriend, Werner Cohn (1912–42), who was arrested and imprisned in 1938 for various delinquencies, see Sammlung Familie Grabwoski, JMB, Convolute 224.
88 Oppenheimer, *Meine Erlebnisse*, 15.
89 Schwerin, *Memoirs*, 95.
90 Ibid., 96.
91 Deutschkron, *Ich trug den gelben Stern*, 54.
92 Fromm, *Blood and Banquets*, 249.
93 Schwabe, *Memoirs*, 82, 84.
94 Kuttner, "Interview Transcript," 5.
95 Ernst Hausmann, *A Family during Troubled Times. The Hausmanns and the Weingartners, 1934–1944*, LBINY, ME886 MMII12, 12.
96 Szalet, *Barracke 38*, 470. Trans. S. Huebel.
97 Werner Tabaschnik, "Ein Kind erzählt vom Dritten Reich," in Anonymous, *Konzentrationslager*, 115. Trans. S. Huebel.
98 Max Tabaschnik, "Königstein," in Anonymous, *Konzentrationslager*, 108. Trans. S. Huebel.
99 See also Pine, *Nazi Family Policy*, 162.
100 See, for instance, Oppenheimer, *Meine Erlebnisse*, 14.
101 Hecht, *Invisible Walls and To Remember Is to Heal*, 58.
102 Kaplan, *Between Dignity and Despair*, 123.
103 For shame culture, see Kühne, *Belonging and Genocide*, 28–9.
104 Schorsch, *Memoirs*, 11. Trans. S. Huebel.
105 Ibid., 12.
106 Nathorff, *Tagebücher*, 157. Trans. S. Huebel.
107 Weltlinger, *Hast du es schon vergessen?*, 13.
108 Schwerin, *Memoirs*, 162. Trans. S. Huebel.
109 Walter Besser, in Herzberg, *Überleben heißt erinnern*, 229. Trans. S. Huebel.
110 Moritz Mandelkern, "In Our Hope," in Boehm, *We Survived*, 222.
111 Anonymous, "B136," in Barkow, Gross, and Lenarz, *Novemberpogrom*, 818. See also the witness account "B116" for a list of more suicides. For suicides within concentration camps, see "B152."

112 Reichmann, *Deutscher Bürger und verfolgter Jude*, 246. Trans. S. Huebel.
113 Ofer and Weitzman, "The Role of Women in the Holocaust," in *Women in the Holocaust*, 6.
114 Steinweis, *Kristallnacht*, 5.
115 Jane Caplan, "Gender and the Concentration Camps," 83.
116 Falk Pingel, for instance, has argued that "it seems that the men who were in contact with their families or who still had communication with the outside world experienced much greater difficulties in adjusting to daily life within the concentration camps. They tried to subdue their feelings and emotions, in the belief that such behaviour would weaken their ability to survive the harsh conditions." See Pingel, "Social Life in an Unsocial Environment," 69. Pingel's argument resembles a "hypothesis," and the author himself acknowledges that "to date we have neither interviews nor reports from survivors on this subject, nor [have we] seen a methodical approach that might confirm such a theory." Yet, this study suggests that a closer look at Jewish men's memoirs and reports of their *prewar* internment, when Jewish women were generally not interned, is a suitable approach to study the dynamics of such gender relations.

Conclusion

1 For a discussion on space and gender, see Huebel, "Nazi KZs as Gendered Jewish Spaces?"
2 For the pioneering work on the history of everyday life, see Lüdtke, *The History of Everyday Life*.
3 Nathans, *Beyond the Pale*; Lohr, *Nationalizing the Russian Empire*. See also Rozenblit and Karp, eds, *World War I and the Jews*.
4 Friedländer, *Nazi Germany and the Jews*.
5 Halkes-Carey, "Jewish Masculinity in the Holocaust," 181.
6 See Veidlinger, *In the Shadow of the Shtetl*.
7 Ofer and Weitzman, "The Role of Women in the Holocaust," in *Women in the Holocaust*, 6.
8 Aleksiun, "Gender and the Daily Lives of Jews in Hiding in Eastern Galicia."
9 Huebel, "Disguise and Defiance."
10 Hagemann, "Military, War and the Mainstreams," 72; Schüler-Springorum, "A Soft Hero," 102.
11 Such as during New Year's Eve celebrations in German cities like Cologne and Hamburg on 31 December 2015.
12 Jones, "Gender and Genocide."
13 Ring, *Life with the Enemy*.

Bibliography

Primary Sources

Archives

Leo Baeck Institute, New York (LBINY)
United States Holocaust Memorial Museum: (USHMM)
Jüdisches Museum Berlin: (JMB)
USC Shoah Foundation, Visual History Archive
Gedenkstätte Deutscher Widerstand (GDW)
Gedenkstätte und Museum Sachsenhausen
Goethe University Frankfurt a. M. Library, Digital Online Collections

Printed

Abraham, Max. *Juda Verrecke. Ein Rabbiner im Konzentrationslager.* Berlin:
 Verlagsanstalt, 1934.
Anonymous. *Konzentrationslager: Ein Appell an das Gewissen der Welt! Ein Buch
 der Greuel. Die Opfer klagen an.* Karlsbad: Graphia Verlag, 1934.
Armin, Otto. *Die Juden im Heer: Eine statistische Untersuchung nach amtlichen
 Quellen.* Munich, 1919.
Aviram, Zvi. *Mit dem Mut der Verzweiflung: Mein Widerstand im Berliner
 Untergrund, 1943–1948.* Ed. Beate Kosmala and Patrick Siegele. Berlin:
 Metropol Verlag, 2015.
Bachner, James. *My Darkest Years: Memoirs of a Survivor of Auschwitz, Warsaw
 and Dachau.* Jefferson, NC: MacFarland Press, 2007.
Barkow, Ben, Raphael Gross, and Michael Lenarz, eds. *Novemberpogrom 1938 –
 Die Augenzeugenberichte der Wiener Library.* Berlin: Suhrkamp Verlag, 2008.
Beck, Gad. *An Underground Life: Memoirs of a Gay Jew in Nazi Berlin.* Madison:
 University of Wisconsin Press, 1999.

Behar, Isaak. *Versprich mir, dass Du am Leben bleibst: Ein jüdisches Schicksal.* 4th ed. Berlin: List Verlag, 2013.

Bendix, Reinhard. *From Berlin to Berkeley: German Jewish Identities.* New Brunswick, NJ: Transaction Publishers, 1986.

Benz, Angelika, ed. *Im KZ: Zwei Jüdische Schicksale, 1938/1945.* Frankfurt: Fischer, 2012.

Boehm, Erich, ed. *We Survived: Fourteen Histories of the Hidden and Hunted in Nazi Germany.* New York: Basic Books, 2003.

Burkhard, Hugo. *Tanz mal Jude. Von Dachau bis Shanghai. Meine Erlebnisse in den Konzentrationslagern Dachau, Buchenwald, Ghetto Shanghai, 1933–1948.* Nuremberg: Druck und Verlag Richard Reichenbach, 1967.

Cohn, Willy. *No Justice in Germany: The Breslau Diaries, 1933–1941.* Ed. Nobert Conrads. Trans. Kenneth Kronenberg. Palo Alto, CA: Stanford University Press, 2012.

Comité des Délégations Juives, ed. *Die Lage der Juden in Deutschland 1933: Das Schwarzbuch – Tatsachen und Dokumente.* 1st ed. Paris 1934. Reprint, Frankfurt: Ullstein, 1984.

Deutschkron, Inge. *Ich trug den gelben Stern.* 2nd ed. Cologne: Verlag Wissenschaft und Politik, 1979.

Dünner, Joseph. *Zu Protokoll gegeben: Mein Leben als Deutscher und Jude.* Munich: Kurt Desch Verlag, 1971.

Eckler, Irene. *Die Vormundschaftsakte, 1935–1958: Verfolgung einer Familie wegen "Rassenschande."* Schwetzingen: Horneburg Verlag, 1996.

Fechenbach, Felix. *Mein Herz schlägt weiter. Briefe aus der Schutzhaft.* Ed. Walter Victor. 1st ed. St Gallen: Kultur Verlag, 1936. Passau: Alexander-Haller Verlag, 1987.

Frauenfeld, Rudolf. "Wir Illegalen." *Der Weg: Zeitschrift für Fragen des Judentums,* 1, no. 4 (March 1946).

Freund, Julius. *O Buchenwald.* Klagenfurt: Selbstverlag, 1945.

Fromm, Bella. *Blood and Banquets: A Berlin Social Diary.* Trans. Bella Fromm. New York: Harper and Brothers, 1943.

Gay, Peter. *My German Question: Growing up in Nazi Berlin.* New Haven, CT: Yale University Press, 1998.

Goldmann, Nachum. *Zwei Kriegsschriften: Über Kriegsziele, Juden, und Politik: Der Geist des Militarismus & Aus der weltkulturellen Bedeutung und Aufgabe des Judentums.* Bremen: Faksimile Verlag Roland, 2001.

Handbuch der SA. Berlin: Verlag Offene Worte, 1939.

Hauser, Martin. *Wege jüdischer Selbstbehauptung: Tagebuchaufzeichnungen 1929–1967.* Bonn: Bundeszentrale für Politische Bildung, 1992.

Hecht, Ingeborg. *Invisible Walls and To Remember Is to Heal: A German Family under the Nuremberg Laws.* Evanston, IL: Northwestern University Press, 1984.

Heger, Heinz. *Men with the Pink Triangle: The True, Life-And-Death Story of Homosexuals in the Nazi Death Camps*. Boston: Alyson Books, 1986.

Herman-Friede, Eugen. *Für Freudensprünge keine Zeit: Erinnerungen an Illegalität und Aufbegehren, 1942–1948*. 3rd ed. Afterword by Barbara Schieb. Berlin: Metropol, 1994.

Herzberg, Wolfgang, ed. *Überleben heisst erinnern: Lebensgeschichten deutscher Juden*. Berlin: Aufbau Verlag Berlin, 1990.

Herzfeld, Albert. *Ein Nichtarischer Deutscher: Die Tagebücher des Albert Herzfeld, 1935–1939*. Düsseldorf: Triltsch Verlag, 1982.

Institut zum Studium der Judenfrage. *Die Juden in Deutschland*, 8th ed. Munich: Franz Eher Verlag, 1939.

Jalowicz Simon, Marie. *Untergetaucht. Eine junge Frau überlebt in Berlin, 1940– 1945*. Ed. Irene Statenwerth and Hermann Simon. Frankfurt: Fischer, 2014.

Johnson, Erich A., and Karl-Heinz Reuband, eds. *What We Knew: Terror, Mass Murder and Everyday Life in Nazi Germany. An Oral History*. New York: Basic Books, 2006.

Klemperer, Victor. *I Shall Bear Witness, The Diaries of Victor Klemperer, 1933– 1941*. Trans. Martin Chalmers. London: Weidenfeld & Nicolson, 1998.

– *I Will Bear Witness: The Diaries of Victor Klemperer, 1942–1945*. Trans. Martin Chalmers. New York: Modern Library, 2001.

Krakauer, Max, and Karoline Krakauer. *Lichter im Dunkeln. Flucht und Rettung eines jüdischen Ehepaars im Dritten Reich*. Stuttgart: Calwer Verlag, 1994.

Langhoff, Wolfgang. *Die Moorsoldaten: 13 Monate KZ*. Zurich: Schweizer Spiegel Verlag, 1935.

Langnas, Mignon. *Tagebücher und Briefe einer jüdischen Krankenschwester in Wien, 1937–1949*. Ed. Elizabeth Fraller. Innsbruck: Studienverlag, 2010.

Latte, Konrad. *Und wenn wir nur eine Stunde gewinnen … Wie ein jüdischer Musiker die Nazi Jahre überlebte*. Ed. Peter Schneider. Berlin: Rowohlt, 2001.

Leyens, Erich, and Lotte Andor. *Years of Estrangement*. Trans. Brigitte Goldstein. Evanston, IL: Northwestern University Press, 1996.

Limberg, Margarete, and Hubert Rübsaat, eds. *Sie durften nicht mehr Deutsche sein: Jüdischer Alltag in Selbstzeugnissen, 1933–1938*. Frankfurt: Campus Verlag, 1990.

Marum, Ludwig. *Briefe aus dem KZ Kislau*. Ed. Elisabeth Marum-Lunau and Jörg Schadt. Karlsruhe: Müller Verlag, 1988.

Memelsdorff, Franz, and Georg Heller. *Im KZ: Zwei jüdische Schicksale, 1938/1945*. Ed. Angelika Benz. Frankfurt: Fischer, 2012.

Mühsam, Kreszentia. *Der Leidensweg Erich Mühsams*. Zurich: Mopr Verlag, 1935.

Nathorff, Hertha. *Das Tagebuch der Hertha Nathorff*. Ed. Wolfgang Benz. Munich: Oldenbourg Verlag, 1987.

Neuman, Ralph. *Memories from My Early Life in Germany, 1926–1946*. Berlin: GDW, 2006.

Neurath, Paul Martin. *The Society of Terror. Inside the Dachau and Buchenwald KZ Camps*. Ed. Christian Fleck and Nico Stehr. Boulder, CO: Paradigm Publishers, 2005.

Orbach, Larry. *Soaring Underground: Autobiographie eines jüdischen Jugendlichen im Berliner Untergrund, 1938–1945*. Berlin: Kowalke and Co Verlag, 1998.

Perel, Sally. *Ich war Hitlerjunge Salomon*. 10th ed. Munich: Heyne Verlag, 1992.

Plischke, Kurt. *Der Jude als Rassenschänder Eine Anklage gegen Juda und eine Mahnung an die deutschen Frauen und Mädchen*. Berlin: NS-Druck und Verlag, 1934.

Propp, Arthur. "November, 1938 in Königsberg." Ed. Christopher R. Friedrichs. *Midstream, 33*, no. 2 (February 1987): 49–54.

Reichmann, Hans. *Deutscher Bürger und verfolgter Jude: Novemberpogrom und KZ Sachsenhausen 1937–1939*. Ed. Michael Wildt. Munich: Oldenbourg, 1998.

Richarz, Monika, ed. *Jüdisches Leben in Deutschland, Vol 3: 1918–1945*. Stuttgart: DVA, 1982.

Rosenthal, Hans. *Zwei Leben in Deutschland*. Bergisch Gladbach: BasteiLuebbe, 1982.

Schäfer, Werner. *Konzentrationslager Oranienburg: Das Anti-Braun Buch über das erste deutsche Konzentrationslager*. Berlin, 1934.

Schönhaus, Cioma. *The Forger. An Extraordinary Story of Survival in Wartime Berlin*. Cambridge, MA: Da Capo Press, 2007.

Seger, Gerhardt. *Oranienburg. Erster Authentischer Bericht eines aus dem KZ Geflüchteten*. Karlsbad, 1934.

Spiegel, Marga. *Retter in der Nacht. Wie eine Jüdische Familie in einem münsterländischen Versteck überlebte*. 3rd ed. Münster: Lit Verlag, 1999.

Stern, Heinemann. *Angriff und Abwehr: Ein Handbuch der Judenfrage*. Berlin: Philo Verlag, 1924.

Strauss, Herbert. *In the Eye of the Storm*. New York: Fordham University Press, 1999.

Szalet, Leon. *Barracke 38: 237 Tage in den Judenblocks von Sachsenhausen*. Berlin: Metropol Verlag, 2006.

Tausk, Walter. *Breslauer Tagebuch, 1933–1940*. 4th ed. Berlin: Rütten and Loening, 1988.

Trachtenberg, Jakob. *Die Greuelpropaganda ist eine Lügenpropaganda sagen die Juden selbst!* Berlin: Jakob Trachtenberg Verlag, 1933.

von Leers, Johann. *Die Verbrechernatur der Juden*. Berlin: P. Hochmuth Verlag, 1944.

– *Juden sehen Dich an!* Berlin: Nationalsozialistisches Druck- und Verlagshaus, 1933.

– *Judentum und Gaunertum. Eine Wesens- und Lebensgemeinschaft*. Berlin: Theodor Fritsch Verlag, 1940.

Wallner, Peter. *By Order of the Gestapo. A Record of Life in Dachau and Buchenwald Concentration Camps.* London: Murray, 1941.

Weltlinger, Siegmund. *Hast du es schon vergessen? Erlebnisbericht aus der Zeit der Verfolgung.* Berlin: Gesellschaft für Christlich-Jüdische Zusammenarbeit, 1954.

Secondary Sources

Aleksiun, Natalia. "Gender and the Daily Lives of Jews in Hiding in Eastern Galicia." *NASHIM: A Journal of Jewish Women's Studies and Gender Issues,* 27 (Fall 2014): 38–61.

Amesbeger, Helga. "Reproduction under the Swastika: The Other Side of the Nazi Glorification of Motherhood." In *Sexual Violence against Jewish Women during the Holocaust,* ed. Sonja Hedgepeth and Rochelle Saidel, 139–55. Waltham, MA: Brandeis University, 2010.

Amkraut, Brian. *Between Home and Homeland: Youth Aliyah from Nazi Germany.* Tuscaloosa: University of Alabama Press, 2006.

Angress, Werner T. "The German Army's 'Judenzählung' of 1916: Genesis – Consequences – Significance." *Leo Baeck Institute Yearbook,* 23, no. 1 (1978): 117–38.

– *Between Fear and Hope: Jewish Youth in the Third Reich.* New York: Columbia University Press, 1988.

Assmann, Aleida, and Ines Detmers. *Empathy and Its Limits.* New York: Palgrave Macmillan, 2016.

Baader, Benjamin M. *Gender, Judaism, and Bourgeois Culture in Germany, 1800–1870.* Bloomington: Indiana University Press, 2007.

– "Jewish Difference and the Feminine Spirit of Judaism in Mid-19th Century Germany." In *Jewish Masculinities: German Jews, Gender, and History,* ed. Benjamin M. Baader, Sharon Gillerman, and Paul Lerner, 50–71. Bloomington: Indiana University Press, 2012.

Baader, Benjamin M., Sharon Gillerman, and Paul Lerner. "German Jews, Gender and History." In *Jewish Masculinities: German Jews, Gender, and History,* ed. Benjamin M. Baader, Sharon Gillerman, and Paul Lerner, 1–22. Bloomington: Indiana University Press, 2012.

Barkai, Avraham. *Vom Boykott zur Entjudung. Der wirtschaftliche Existenzkampf der Juden im Dritten Reich 1933–1943.* Frankfurt: got Verlag, 1988.

Baumel, Judith Tylor. *Double Jeopardy: Gender and the Holocaust.* Elstree, Herts: Vallentine Mitchell Publishers, 1998.

Becker, Michael, and Dennis Bock. "Muselmänner in Nazi Concentration Camps: Thinking Masculinity at the Extremes." In *The Holocaust and Masculinities: Critical Inquiries into Presence and Absence of Men,* ed. Björn

Krondorfer and Ovidiu Creangă, 129–46. New York: State University of New York Press, 2020.

Benz, Wolfgang. *Der Ewige Jude: Metaphern und Methoden Nationalsozialistischer Propaganda.* Berlin: Metropol Verlag, 2010.

Berkowitz, Michael. *The Crime of My Very Existence: Nazism and the Myth of Jewish Criminality.* Berkeley: University of California Press, 2007.

Bock, Gisela. *Zwangssterilisation im Nationalsozialismus: Studien zur Rassenpolitik und Frauenpolitik.* Opladen: Westdeutscher Verlag, 1986.

– *Genozid und Geschlecht. Jüdische Frauen im nationalsozialistischen Lagersystem.* Frankfurt: Campus Verlag, 2005.

Bogdal, Klaus-Michael. "Hard-Cold-Fast: Imagining Masculinity in the German Academy, Literature, and the Media." In *Conceptions of Postwar German Masculinity,* ed. Roy Jerome, 13–43. Albany: State University of New York Press, 2001.

Boyarin, Daniel. *Unheroic Conduct: The Rise of Heterosexuality and the Invention of the Jewish Man.* Oakland: University of California Press, 1997.

Brenner, Michael. "Why Jews and Sports?" In *Emancipation through Muscles: Jews and Sports in Europe,* ed. Michael Brenner and Gideon Reuveni, 1–12. Lincoln: University of Nebraska Press, 2006.

Breuer, Karin. "Competing Masculinities: Fraternities, Gender and Nationality in the German Confederation, 1815–30." *Gender & History,* 20, no. 2 (2008): 270–87.

Brod, Harry, ed. *A Mensch among Men: Explorations in Jewish Masculinity.* Berkeley, CA: The Crossing Press, 1988.

Bruns, Claudia. *Politik des Eros: Der Männerbund in Wissenschaft, Politik und Jugendkultur, 1880–1934.* Cologne: Böhlau, 2008.

Budde, Gunilla. *Auf dem Weg ins Bürgerleben: Kindheit und Erziehung in deutschen und englischen Bürgerfamilien, 1840–1914.* Göttingen: Vandenhoeck and Ruprecht, 1994.

Butler, Judith. *Gender Trouble.* New York: Routledge, 1990.

Bytwerk, Randall. *Bending Spines: The Propagandas of Nazi Germany and the German Democratic Republic.* East Lansing: Michigan State University Press, 2004.

– *Julius Streicher. Nazi Editor of the Notorious Anti-Semitic Newspaper Der Stürmer.* 2nd ed. New York: Stein and Day Publishers, 1983.

Canning, Kathleen. "The Body as Method? Reflections on the Place of the Body in Gender History." *Gender & History,* 11, no. 3 (November 1999): 499–513.

Caplan, Gregory. "Wicked Sons, German Heroes: Jewish Soldiers, Veterans and Memoirs of World War I in Germany." PhD diss., The University of Washington, 2001.

– "Germanizing the Jewish Male: Military Masculinity as the Last Stage of Acculturation." In *Towards Normality? Acculturation of Modern German*

Jewry, ed. Rainer Liedtke and David Rechter, 159–84. Tübingen: Mohr Siebeck Verlag, 2003.

Caplan, Jane. "Gender and the Concentration Camps." In *Nazi Concentration Camps in Nazi Germany: The New Histories*, ed. Nikolaus Wachsmann and Jane Caplan, 82–107. London: Routledge, 2009.

Carey, Maddy. *Jewish Masculinity in the Holocaust: Between Destruction and Construction*. London: Bloomsbury, 2017.

Carney, Amy Beth. "Victory in the Cradle: Fatherhood and the Family Community in the Nazi Schutzstaffel." PhD diss., Florida State University, 2010.

– *Marriage and Fatherhood in the SS*. Toronto: University of Toronto Press, 2018.

Chapoutot, Johann. *The Law of Blood: Thinking and Acting as a Nazi*. Cambridge, MA: Belknap Press, 2018.

Clark, Anna. "The Rhetoric of Masculine Citizenship: Concepts and Representations in Modern Western Political Culture." In *Representing Masculinity*, ed. Stefan Dudink, Karen Hagemann, and Anna Clark, 3–23. New York: Palgrave MacMillan, 2007.

Connell, R.W. *Masculinities*. 2nd ed. Berkeley: University of California Press, 2005.

– "Masculinity and Nazism." In *Männlichkeitskonstruktionen im National-sozialismus. Formen, Funktionen und Wirkungsmacht von Geschlechterkonstruktionen im Nationalsozialismus und ihre Reflexion in der pädagogischen Praxis*, ed. Anette Dietrich and Ljiljana Heise, 37–42. Frankfurt am Main: Peter Lang Verlag, 2013.

Craig-Norton, Jennifer. *The Kindertransport: Contesting Memory*. Bloomington: Indiana University Press, 2019.

Crenshaw, Kimberlé. "Mapping the Margins: Intersectionality, Identity Politics, and Violence against Women of Color Source." *Stanford Law Review*, 43, no. 6 (1991): 1241–99.

Crim, Brian E. "Was It All Just a Dream? German-Jewish Veterans and the Confrontation with volkisch Nationalism in the Interwar Period." In *Sacrifice and National Belonging in Twentieth-Century Germany*, ed. Marcus Funck, Mathew Paul Berg, and Greg Eghigian, 64–89. College Station: Texas A&M University Press, 2002.

Czarnowski, Gabriele. "The Value of Marriage for the Volksgemeinschaft: Policies toward Women and Marriage under National Socialism." In *Fascist Italy and Nazi Germany: Comparisons and Contrasts*, ed. Richard Bessel, 94–111. Cambridge: Cambridge University Press, 1996.

Dausien, Bettina. "Erzähltes Leben – erzähltes Geschlecht? Aspekte der narrativen Konstruktion von Geschlecht im Kontext der Biographieforschung." *Feministische Studien*, 19, no. 2 (2001): 57–73.

Diehl, Paula. *Macht, Mythos, Utopie: Die Köperbilder der SS-Männer*. Berlin: Akademie Verlag, 2004.

Dietrich, Anette, and Ljiljana Heise, eds. *Männlichkeitskonstruktionen im Nationalsozialismus: Formen, Funktionen und Wirkungsmacht von Geschlechterkonstruktionen im Nationalsozialismus und ihre Reflexion in der pädagogischen Praxis.* Frankfurt: Peter Lang Verlag, 2013.

Dillon, Christopher. "Tolerance Means Weakness: The Dachau SS, Militarism, and Masculinity." *Historical Research*, 86, no. 232 (2013): 373–89.

Dunker, Ulrich. *Der Reichsbund jüdischer Frontsoldaten, 1919–1938: Geschichte eines jüdischen Abwehrvereins.* Düsseldorf: Droste Verlag, 1977.

Dwork, Deborah. *Children with a Star: Jewish Youth in Nazi Europe.* New Haven, CT: Yale University Press, 1991.

Erb, Rainer. "Der Ritualmord." In *Bilder der Judenfeindschaft: Antisemitismus, Vorurteile und Mythen*, ed. Julius Schoeps, 74–9. Eltville: Bechtermüntz, 1999.

Erhart, Walter. "Father Figures in Literature 1900/2000." In *Fatherhood in Late Modernity: Cultural Images, Social Practices, Structural Frames*, ed. Mechtild Oechsle, Ursula Müller, and Sabine Hess. Opladen: Verlag Barbara Budrich, 2014.

Essner, Cornelia. *Die Nürnberger Gesetze oder die Verwaltung des Rassenwahns, 1933–1945.* Paderborn: Ferdinand Schöningh, 2002.

Ettelson, Todd R. "The Nazi New Man: Embodying Masculinity and Regulating Sexuality in the SA and SS, 1930–1939." PhD diss., University of Michigan, 2004.

Faludi, Christian. *Die Juni Aktion 1938: Eine Dokumentation zur Radikalisierung der Judenverfolgung.* Frankfurt: Campus Verlag, 2013.

Farges, Patrick. "'Muscle' *Yekkes*? Multiple German-Jewish Masculinities in Palestine and Israel after 1933." *Central European History*, 51 (2018): 446–87.

Feltman, Brian. *The Stigma of Surrender – German Prisoners, British Captors and Manhood in the Great War and Beyond.* Chapel Hill: University of North Carolina Press, 2015.

Fetheringill-Zwicker, Lisa. "Performing Masculinity: Jewish Students and the Honor Code at German Universities." In *Jewish Masculinities: German Jews, Gender and History*, ed. Benjamin M. Baader, Sharon Gillerman, and Paul Lerner, 114–37. Bloomington: Indiana University Press, 2012.

Fischer, Anna. *Erzwungener Freitod, Spuren und Zeugnisse in den Freitod getriebener Juden der Jahre 1938–1945 in Berlin.* Berlin: Textverlag, 2007.

Forth, Christopher. *Masculinity in the Modern West. Gender, Civilization, and the Body.* Basingstoke, Hants: Palgrave, 2008.

Foucault, Michel. *The History of Sexuality, Vol. 1.* New York: Vintage Books, 1990.

Freidenreich, Harriet Pass. "Gender, Identity, and Community: Jewish University Women in Germany and Austria." In *In Search of Jewish Community: Jewish Identities in Germany and Austria, 1918–1933*, ed. Derek

Penslar and Michael Brenner, 154–75. Bloomington: Indiana University Press, 1999.

Frevert, Ute. *A Nation in Barracks: Modern Germany, Military Conscription and Civil Society.* Oxford: Berg Publishers, 2004.

– *Mann und Weib, Weib und Mann: Geschlechterdifferenzen in der Moderne.* Munich: C.H. Beck, 1995.

– *Ehrenmänner: Das Duell in der bügerlichen Gesellschaft.* Munich: DTV, 1995. English translation: *Men of Honour: A Social and Cultural History of the Duel.* Cambridge: Cambridge University Press, 1995.

– "Defining Emotions: Concepts and Debates over Three Centuries." In *Emotional Lexicons: Continuity and Change in the Vocabulary of Feeling, 1700–2000*, ed. Ute Frevert and Thomas Dixon, 1–31. Oxford: Oxford University Press, 2014.

Friedländer, Saul. *Nazi Germany and the Jews, 1933–1939.* New York: Harper Perennial: 1998.

– *The Years of Extermination, 1939–1945. Nazi Germany and the Jews.* New York: Harper Collins, 2007.

Friedler, Eric. *Makabi Chai, Makkabi Lebt. Die Jüdische Sportbewegung in Deutschland, 1898–1998.* Vienna: Verlag Christian Brandstätter, 1998.

Ganaway, Bryan. "Consuming Masculinity: Toys and Boys in Wilhelmine Germany." In *Edinburgh German Yearbook Volume 2: Masculinities in German Culture*, ed. Sarah Colvin and Peter Davies, 97–112. Rochester, NY: Camden House, 2008.

Garbarini, Alexandra. *Numbered Days: Diaries and the Holocaust.* New Haven, CT: Yale University Press, 2006.

Gardiner, Judith Kegan, ed. *Masculinity Studies and Feminist Theory.* New York: Columbia University Press, 2002.

Geheran, Michael. "Remasculinizing the Shirker: The Jewish Frontkämpfer under Hitler." *Central European History*, 51 (2018): 440–65.

– *Comrades Betrayed: Jewish World War I Veterans under Hitler.* Ithaca, NY: Cornell University Press, 2020.

Gelatelly, Robert. *The Gestapo and German Society: Enforcing Racial Policy, 1933–1945.* Oxford: Calderon Press, 1991.

Geller, Jay. *The Other Jewish Question: Identifying the Jew and Making Sense of Modernity.* New York: Fordham University Press, 2011.

Gender Killer AG, ed. *Antisemitismus und Geschlecht. Von maskulinierten Jüdinnen und effeminierten Juden und anderen Geschlechterbildern.* Münster: Unrast Verlag, 2005.

Gerson, Judith. "Family Matters: German Jewish Masculinities among Nazi Era Refugees." In *Jewish Masculinities: German Jews, Gender and History*, ed. Benjamin M. Baader, Sharon Gillerman, and Paul Lerner, 210–31. Bloomington: Indiana University Press, 2012.

Giles, Geoffrey. "The Institutionalization of Homosexual Panic in the Third Reich." In *Social Outsiders in Nazi Germany*, ed. Robert Gellately and Nathan Stolzfus, 233–55. Princeton, NJ: Princeton University Press, 2001.

Gilman, Sander. *The Jew's Body*. London: Routledge, 1991.

– "'Die Rasse ist nicht schön' – 'Nein, wir Juden sind keine hübsche Rasse.' Der schöne und der hässliche Jude." In *Der schejne Jid: Das Bild des Jüdischen Körpers in Mythos und Ritual*, ed. Sander Gilman and Robert Jütte, 57–74. Vienna: Picus Verlag, 1998.

Gilmore, David. *Manhood in the Making: Cultural Concepts of Masculinity*. New Haven, CT: Yale University Press, 1991.

Goldberg, Amos. "Empathy, Ethics, and Politics in Holocaust Historiography." In *Empathy and Its Limits*, ed. Aleida Assmann and Ines Detmers, 52–77. New York: Palgrave Macmillan, 2016.

Goldenberg, Myrna, and Amy Shapiro, eds. *Different Horrors, Same Hell: Gender and the Holocaust*. Seattle: Washington University Press, 2012.

Göschel, Christian. *Suicide in Nazi Germany*. Oxford: Oxford University Press, 2009.

Grady, Tim. *The German Jewish Soldier of the First World War in History and Memory*. Liverpool: Liverpool University Press, 2011.

Grossmann, Atina. "The Survivors Were Few and the Dead Were Many: Jewish Identity and Memory in Occupied Berlin." In *Jüdische Welten: Juden in Deutschland vom 18. Jahrhundert bis in die Gegenwart*, ed. Beate Meyer and Marion Kaplan, 317–35. Göttingen: Wallstein Verlag, 2005.

Habermas, Rebekka. *Frauen und Männer des Bürgertums. Eine Familiengeschichte, 1750–1850*. Göttingen: Vandenhoeck & Ruprecht, 2000.

Hackett, David. A., ed. *Der Buchenwald-Report. Berichte ueber das KZ Buchenwald bei Weimar*. Munich: Beck Verlag, 2002.

Haffner, Sebastian. *The Meaning of Hitler*. 13th ed. Trans. Ewald Osers. Cambridge, MA: Harvard University Press, 2004.

Hagemann, Karen. *"Mannlicher Muth und Teutsche Ehre": Nation, Militär und Geschlecht zur Zeit der Antinapoleonischen Kriege Preußens*. Paderborn: Schöningh, 2002.

– "German Heroes: The Cult of the Death for the Fatherland in Nineteenth-Century Germany." In *Masculinities in Politics and War: Gendering Modern History*, ed. Stefan Dudink, Karen Hagemann, and John Tosh, 116–34. Manchester: Manchester University Press, 2004.

– "Military, War and the Mainstreams: Gendering Modern German Military History." In *Gendering Modern German History*, ed. Karen Hagemann and Jean Quataert, 63–85. New York: Berghahn Books, 2007.

Haibl, Michaela. "Juden in der Bildpolitik: Vom antijüdischen zum antisemitischen Judenstereotyp in der populären Druckgraphik des 19. Jahrhunderts." In *Abgestempelt. Judenfeindliche Postkarten auf der Grundlage der Sammlung Wolfgang Haney*, ed. Helmut Gold and Georg Heuberger, 79–97. Frankfurt: Umschau Buchverlag, 1999.

– *Zerrbild als Stereotyp: Visuelle Darstellung von Juden, zwischen 1850 und 1900.* Berlin: Metropol, 2000.

Hájková, Anna. "Mutmaßungen über deutsche Juden: Alte Menschen aus Deutschland im Theresienstädter Ghetto." In *Alltag im Holocaust: Jüdisches Leben im Großdeutschen Reich 1941–1945*, ed. Andrea Löw, Doris Bergen, and Anna Hájková, 179–98. Berlin: de Gruyter, 2014.

Hajkova, Anna, Elissa Mailaender, Doris Bergen, Patrick Farges, and Atina Grossmann. "Forum: Holocaust and History of Gender and Sexuality." *German History*, 36 (2018): 78–100.

Halbmayer, Brigitte. "Sexualisierte Gewalt gegen Frauen." In *Nationalsozialismus und Geschlecht. Zur Politisierung und Ästhetisierung von Körper, Rasse und Sexualität im Dritten Reich und nach 1945*, ed. Elke Frietsch and Sybille Herkommer, 141–55. Bielefeld: Transcript Verlag, 2009.

Halkes-Carey, Anna-Madeleine. "Jewish Masculinity in the Holocaust." PhD diss., Royal Holloway, University of London, 2015.

Hämmerle, Christa. "Back to the Monarchy's Glorified Past? Military Discourses on Male Citizenship and Universal Conscription in the Austrian Empire 1868–1914." In *Representing Masculinity*, ed. Stefan Dudink, Karen Hagemann, and Anna Clark, 151–68. New York: Palgrave MacMillan: 2007.

Hausen, Karin. "Family and Role Division: The Polarization of Sexual Stereotypes in the 19th century. An Aspect of the Dissociation of Work and Family Life." In *The German Family. Essays on the Social History of the Family in 19th- and 20th-century Germany*, ed. Richard Evans, 51–83. London: Croom Helm, 1981.

Haynes, Stephen R. "Ordinary Masculinity: Gender Analysis and Holocaust Scholarship." *The Journal of Men's Studies*, 10, no. 2 (Winter 2002): 143–63.

Herf, Jeffrey. *The Jewish Enemy: Nazi Propaganda during World War II and the Holocaust.* Cambridge, MA: Belknap Press, 2008.

Hertz, Deborah. "Männlichkeit und Melancholie im Berlin der Biedermeierzeit." In *Deutsch-Jüdische Geschichte als Geschlechtergeschichte*, ed. Stefanie Schüler-Springorum and Kirsten Heinsohn, 276–92. Göttingen: Wallstein, 2006.

Herzstein, Robert. *The War That Hitler Won: Goebbels and the Nazi Media Campaign.* New York: Paragon House, 1986.

Heschel, Susanna. "Sind Juden Männer? Können Frauen jüdisch sein? Die gesellschaftliche Definition des männlichen/weiblichen Körpers." In *Der schejne Jid: Das Bild des Jüdischen Körpers in Mythos und Ritual*, ed. Sander Gilman and Robert Jütte, 86–96. Vienna: Picus Verlag, 1998.

Hillenbrand, Klaus. *Nicht mit Uns. Das Leben von Leonie und Walter Frankenstein.* Frankfurt: Suhrkamp Verlag, 2008.

Hobson, Barbara, ed. *Making Men into Fathers. Men, Masculinities and the Social Politics of Fatherhood*. Cambridge: Cambridge University Press, 2002.

Hödl, Klaus. *Die Pathologisierung des jüdischen Körpers im Fin-de-Siecle*. Vienna: Picus Verlag, 1997.

– "Genderbestimmungen im Spannungsfeld von Fremd- und Selbstzuschreibung: Der verwichlichte Jude im diskursiven Spannungsfeld im Zentraleuropäischen Fin-de-Siecle." In *Antisemitismus und Geschlecht. Von maskulinierten Jüdinnen und effeminierten Juden und anderen Geschlechterbildern*, ed. Gender Killer AG, 81–101. Münster: Unrast Verlag, 2005.

Horowitz, Sara. "Women in Holocaust Literature: Engendering Trauma Memory." In *Women in the Holocaust*, ed. Dalia Ofer and Leonore Weitzman, 364–77. New Haven, CT: Yale University Press, 1999.

Hortzitz, Nicoline. "Die Sprache der Judenfeindschaft." In *Bilder der Judenfeindschaft*, ed. Julius Schoeps, 19–40. Eltville: Bechtermüntz, 1999.

Huebel, Sebastian. "Victor Klemperer, A Jew but Also a Man: The Importance of Understanding German-Jewish Masculinities in the Third Reich." *Women in Judaism: A Multidisciplinary E-Journal*, 12, no. 2 (November 2015): 1–28.

– "Disguise and Defiance: German Jewish Men and Their Underground Experiences in Nazi Germany, 1941–45." *Shofar: An Interdisciplinary Journal of Jewish Studies*, 36, no. 3 (January 2018): 110–41.

– "Nazi KZs as Gendered Jewish Spaces? German-Jewish Masculinity and the Negotiation of Gender Practices in Prewar Nazi Concentration Camps." *Jewish Culture and History*, 21, no. 1 (2020): 24–41.

Hyman, Paula. *Gender and Assimilation in Modern Jewish History: The Roles and Representations of Women*. Seattle: University of Washington Press, 1995.

– "Two Models of Modernization: Jewish Women in the German and Russian Empires." In *Jews and Gender: The Challenge to Hierarchy*, ed. Jonathan Frankel, 39–53. Oxford: Oxford University Press, 2000.

Jacobs, Peter. *Victor Klemperer: Im Kern ein deutsches Gewächs*. 2nd ed. Berlin: Aufbau Verlag, 2000.

Jellonnek, Burkhard, and Rüdiger Lautmann, eds. *Nationalsozialistischer Terror gegen Homosexuelle: Verdrängt und ungesühnt*. Schöningh: Paderborn, 2002.

Johnson, Eric A., and Karl-Heinz Reuband. *What We Knew: Terror, Mass Murder, and Everyday Life in Nazi Germany*. New York: Basic Books, 2006.

Jones, Adam. "Gender and Genocide." In *The Historiography of Genocide*, ed. Dan Stone, 228–52. London: Palgrave Macmillan, 2008.

Kaplan, Marion. *The Making of the Jewish Middle Class: Women, Family and Identity in Imperial Germany*. Oxford: Oxford University Press, 1991.

– *Between Dignity and Despair: Jewish Life in Nazi Germany*. Oxford: Oxford University Press, 1998.

– "The Jewish Response to the Third Reich: Gender at the Grassroots." In *Jews and Gender: The Challenge to Hierarchy*, ed. Jonathan Frankel, 70–87. Oxford: Oxford University Press, 2000.

Kessel, Martina. "The Whole Man: The Longing for a Masculine World in Nineteenth-Century Germany." *Gender & History*, 15, no. 1 (2003): 1–31.

Kienitz, Sabine. "Body Damage: War Disability and Constructions of Masculinity in Weimar Germany." In *Home/Front: The Military, War and Gender in Twentieth-Century Germany*, ed. Karen Hagemann and Stefanie Schüler-Springorum, 181–204. Oxford: Berg Publishers, 2002.

Kimmel, Michael, and Michael Messner. *Men's Lives*. 7th ed. London: Pearson, 2007.

Koonz, Claudia. *Mothers in the Fatherland: Women, the Family and Nazi Politics.* New York: St Martin's Press, 1987.

Kosmala, Beate. "Robert Eisenstädt's Flucht aus dem KZ Majdanek: Über Frankfurt am Main in die Schweiz." In *Überleben im Dritten Reich*, ed. Wolfgang Benz, 287–99. Munich: Beck Verlag, 2003.

– "Facing Deportation in Germany, 1941–1945: Jewish and Non-Jewish Responses." In *Facing the Nazi Genocide: Non-Jews and Jews in Europe*, ed. Beate Kosmala and Feliks Tych, 17–40. Berlin: Metropol, 2004.

– "Jüdische Väter zwischen Ohnmacht und Überlebenskampf." Conference Paper, Carlebach Conference, Hamburg 2014.

– "Überlebensstrategien jüdischer Frauen in Berlin – Flucht vor Deportation, 1941–1943." In *Alltag im Holocaust: Jüdisches Leben im Großdeutschen Reich 1941–1945*, ed. Andrea Löw, Doris Bergen, and Anna Hájková, 29–47. Munich: Oldenbourg Verlag 2014.

Krondorfer, Björn, ed. *Men and Masculinities in Christianity and Judaism: A Critical Reader.* London: SCM Press, 2009.

Krondorfer, Björn, and Ovidiu Creangă, eds. *Holocaust and Masculinities: Critical Inquiries into the Presence and Absence of Men.* New York: State University of NewYork Press, 2020.

Krüger, Arnd. "Breeding, Rearing and Preparing the 'Aryan' Body: Creating Supermen the Nazi Way." In *Shaping the Superman: Fascist Body as Political Icon*, ed. J.P. Mangan, 42–68. London: Frank Cass Publishers, 1999.

Kühne, Thomas. "Männergeschichte als Geschlechtergeschichte." In *Männergeschichte – Geschlechtergeschichte: Männlichkeit im Wandel der Moderne*, ed. Thomas Kühne, 7–30. Frankfurt: Campus Verlag, 1996.

– *Kameradschaft: Soldaten des nationalsozialistischen Krieges und das 20. Jahrhundert*. Göttingen: Vandenhoeck & Ruprecht, 2006. English Edition *The Rise and Fall of Comradeship: Hitler's Soldiers, Male Bonding and Mass Violence in the Twentieth Century*. Cambridge: Cambridge University Press, 2017.

– *Belonging and Genocide: Hitler's Community, 1918–1945.* New Haven, CT: Yale University Press, 2010.

Kühne, Thomas, ed. "Masculinity and the Third Reich." *Central European History*, Special Edition, 51, no. 3 (September 2018): 335–522.

Kwiet, Konrad. "Ich habe mich durchs Leben geboxt: Die unglaubliche Geschichte des Bully Salem Schott." In *Jüdische Welten – Juden in Deutschland vom 18. Jahrhundert bis in die Gegenwart*, ed. Beate Meyer and Marion Kaplan, 231–47. Göttingen: Wallstein, 2005.

Kwiet, Konrad, and Hermann Eschwege. *Selbstbehauptung und Widerstand. Deutsche Juden in Kampf um Existenz und Menschenwürde*. 2nd ed. Hamburg: Christians Verlag, 1986.

LaRossa, John. "The Historical Study of Fatherhood: Theoretical and Methodological Considerations." In *Fatherhood in Late Modernity: Cultural Images, Social Practices, Structural Frames*, ed. Mechtild Oechsle, Ursula Müller, and Sabine Hess, 37–58. Opladen: Verlag Barbara Budrich, 2012.

Lässig, Simone. *Jüdische Wege ins Bürgertum. Kulturelles Kapital und Sozialer Aufstieg im 19. Jahrhundert*. Göttingen: Vandenhoeck & Ruprecht, 2004.

– "Religiöse Modernisierung, Geschlechterdiskurs und kulturelle Verbürgerlichung." In *Deutsch-Jüdische Geschichte als Geschlechtergeschichte*, ed. Stefanie Schüler-Springorum and Kirsten Heinsohn, 46–84. Göttingen: Wallstein Verlag, 2006.

Lefkovitz, Lori. "Coats and Tales: Joseph Stories and Myths about Jewish Masculinity." In *A Mensch among Men: Explorations in Jewish Masculinity*, ed. Harry Brod, 19–29. Berkeley: The Crossing Press, 1988.

Lentin, Ronit, ed. *Gender and Catastrophe*. London: Zed Books, 1997.

Lohr, Eric. *Nationalizing the Russian Empire: The Campaign against Enemy Aliens during World War I*. Cambridge, MA: Harvard University Press, 2003.

Lüdtke, Alf. *The History of Everyday Life: Reconstructing Historical Experiences and Ways of Life*. Princeton, NJ: Princeton University Press, 1995.

Lutjens, Richard. "Vom Untertauchen: U-Boote und der Berliner Alltag, 1941–1945." In *Alltag im Holocaust: Jüdisches Leben im Großdeutschen Reich 1941–1945*, ed. Andrea Löw, Doris Bergen, and Anna Hájková, 49–63. Munich: Oldenbourg Verlag, 2014.

Marhoefer, Laurie. *Sex and the Weimar Republic: German Homosexual Emancipation and the Rise of the Nazis*. Toronto: University of Toronto Press, 2015.

Marten, Heinz-Georg. "Racism, Social Darwinism, Antisemitism and 'Aryan' Supremacy." In *Shaping the Superman: Fascist Body as Political Icon*, ed. J.P. Mangan, 23–41. London: Frank Cass Publishers, 1999.

Martschukat, Jürgen, and Olaf Stieglitz. *Geschichte der Männlichkeiten*. Frankfurt: Campus Verlag, 2008.

Messerschmidt, James. "Varieties of Real Men." In *Men's Lives*, ed. Michael Kimmel and Michael Messner, 3–20. 7th ed. London: Pearson, 2007.

Meyer, Beate, Joachim Bajohr, and Joachim Szodrzynski, eds. *Bedrohung, Hoffnung, Skepsis: Vier Tagebücher des Jahres 1933*. Göttingen: Wallstein Verlag, 2013.

Milton, Sybil. "Women and the Holocaust: The Case of German and German-Jewish Women." In *When Biology Became Destiny: Women in Weimar and Nazi Germany*, ed. Renate Bridenthal, Atina Grossman, and Marion Kaplan, 297–333. New York: Monthly Review Press, 1984.

Miron, Guy. "'Lately, Almost Constantly, Everything Seems Small to Me': The Lived Space of German Jews under the Nazi Regime." *Jewish Social Studies*, 20, no. 1 (Fall 2013): 121–49.

– "The 'Lived Time' of German Jews under the Nazi Regime." *The Journal of Modern History*, 90 (March 2018): 116–53.

Moeller, Robert. "The Elephant in the Living Room: Or Why the History of 20th-century Germany Should Be a Family Affair." In *Gendering Modern German History: Rewritings of the Mainstream*, ed. Karen Hagemann and Jean Quataert, 228–49. New York: Berghahn Books, 2007.

Moore, Paul. "'The Truth about the Concentration Camps': Werner Schäfer's Anti-Brown Book and the Transnational Debate on Early Nazi Terror." *German History*, 34, no. 4 (December 2016): 579–607.

Mosse, George. *The Image of Man: The Creation of Modern Masculinity*. Oxford: Oxford University Press, 1996.

– *Nationalism and Sexuality: Respectability and Abnormal Sexuality in Modern Europe*. New York: Howard Fertig, 1997.

Nathans, Benjamin. *Beyond the Pale: The Jewish Encounter with Late Imperial Russia*. Berkeley: University of California Press, 2002.

Nock, Steve. *Marriage in Men's Lives*. Oxford: Oxford University Press, 1998.

Ofer, Dalia. "The Contribution of Gender to the Study of the Holocaust." In *Gender and Jewish History*, ed. Marion Kaplan and Deborah Dash Moore, 120–35. Bloomington: Indiana University Press, 2010.

Ofer, Dalia, and Lenore Weitzman, eds. *Women in the Holocaust*. New Haven, CT: Yale University Press, 1999.

Olson, Gary A., and Lynn Worsham. "Changing the Subject: Judith Butler's Politics of Radical Resignification." *JAC: A Journal of Rhetoric, Culture and Politics*, 20, no. 4 (2000): 727–65.

Paxton, Robert. *The Anatomy of Fascism*. New York: Vintage Press, 2005.

Pegelow Kaplan, Thomas. *The Language of Nazi Genocide: Linguistic Violence and the Struggle of Germans of Jewish Ancestry*. Cambridge: Cambridge University Press, 2009.

Penslar, Derek. *Jews and the Military: A History*. Princeton, NJ: Princeton University Press, 2013.

Philipps, Carson. "Post-Holocaust Conceptualizations of Masculinity in Germanophone and Jewish Men." PhD diss., York University, 2013.

Pine, Lisa. *Nazi Family Policy, 1933–1945*. Oxford: Berg Publishers, 1997.
– "The Experiences and Behavior of Male Holocaust Victims at Auschwitz."
   In *The Holocaust and Masculinities: Critical Inquiries into the Presence and
   Absence of Men*, ed. Björn Krondorfer and Ovidiu Creangă, 77–98. New
   York: State University of New York Press, 2020.
Pingel, Falk. "Social Life in an Unsocial Environment: The Inmates' Struggle
   for Survival." In *Nazi Concentration Camps in Nazi Germany: The New
   Histories*, ed. Nikolaus Wachsmann and Jane Caplan, 58–81. London:
   Routledge, 2009.
Plamber, Jan. *A History of Emotions: An Introduction*. Oxford: Oxford University
   Press, 2015.
Plant, Richard. *The Pink Triangle. The Nazi War against Homosexuals*. New York:
   New Public Book, 1986.
Presner, Todd Samuel. *Muscular Judaism: The Jewish Body and the Politics of
   Regeneration*. London: Routledge, 2007.
Przyrembel, Alexandra. *Rassenschande: Reinheitsmythos und
   Vernichtungslegitimation im Nationalsozialismus*. Göttingen: Vandenhoeck &
   Ruprecht, 2003.
– "Ambivalente Gefühle: Sexualität und Antisemitismus während des
   Nationalsozialismus." *Geschichte und Gesellschaft*, 39, no. 4 (December 2013):
   527–54.
Raphael, Freddy. "Der Wucherer." In *Bilder der Judenfeindschaft*, ed. Julius
   Schoeps, 103–18. Eltville: Bechtermüntz, 1999.
Reuband, Karl-Heinz. "Die Leserschaft des 'Stürmer' im Dritten Reich:
   Soziale Zusammensetzung und antisemitische Orientierungen." *Historical
   Social Research*, 33, no. 4 (2008): 214–54.
Richarz, Monika, ed. *Jüdisches Leben in Deutschland, Vol 3: 1918–1945*. Stuttgart:
   DVA, 1982.
– *Jewish Life in Germany: Memoirs from Three Centuries*. Bloomington: Indiana
   University Press, 1991.
– "Geschlechterhierarchie und Frauenarbeit seit der Vormoderne." In
   *Deutsch-Jüdische Geschichte als Geschlechtergeschichte. Studien zum 19. und
   20. Jahrhundert*, ed. Stefanie Schüler–Springorum and Kirsten Heinesohn,
   87–104. Göttingen: Wallstein Verlag, 2006.
Rigg, Bryan Mark. *Hitler's Jewish Soldiers: The Untold Story of Nazi Racial Laws
   and Men of Jewish Descent in the German Military*. Lawrence: University of
   Kansas Press, 2002.
– *Lives of Hitler's Jewish Soldiers: Untold Tales of Men of Jewish Descent Who
   Fought for the Third Reich*. Lawrence: University of Kansas Press, 2009.
Ring, Werner. *Life with the Enemy: Collaboration and Resistance in Hitler's Europe,
   1939–1945*. New York: Doubleday, 1982.

Ringelheim, Joan. "The Unethical and the Unspeakable: Women and the Holocaust." *Simon Wiesenthal Center Annual*, 1 (1984).

– "Genocide and Gender: A Split Memory." In *Gender and Catastrophe*, ed. Ronit Lentin, 18–33. London: Zed Books, 1997.

Rittner, Carol, and John K. Roth, eds. *Different Voices: Women and the Holocaust*. New York: Paragon House, 1998.

Roche, Helen. *Sparta's German Children: The Ideal of Ancient Sparta in the Royal Prussian Cadet Corps, 1818–1920, and in National Socialist Elite Schools (the Napolas), 1933–1945*. Swansea: Classical Press of Wales, 2013.

Rohrbacher, Stefan, and Michael Schmidt. *Judenbilder: Kulturgeschichte antijüdischer Mythen und antisemitischer Vorurteile*. Hamburg: Rowohlt Verlag, 1991.

Roos, Julia. "Backlash against Prostitutes: Rights, Origins, and Dynamics of Nazi Prostitution Policies." In *Sexuality and German Fascism*, ed. Dagmar Herzog, 67–94. New York: Berghahn Books, 2004.

Rozenblit, Marsha L., and Jonathan Karp, eds. *World War I and the Jews: Conflict and Transformation in Europe, the Middle East, and America*. New York: Berghahn Books, 2018.

Ruault, Franco. *Tödliche Maskeraden: Julius Streicher und die "Lösung der Judenfrage."* Frankfurt: Peter Lang, 2009.

Saidel, Rochelle. *The Women of Ravensbrück*. Madison: University of Wisconsin Press, 2004.

Saidel, Rochelle, and Sonja Hedgepeth, eds. *Sexual Violence against Jewish Women during the Holocaust*. Waltham, MA: Brandeis University Press, 2010.

Sarti, Raffaella, ed. "Men at Home: Domesticities, Authority, Emotions and Work." *Gender & History*, 27, no. 3 (2015): 521–886.

Scheidgen, Irina. "Frauenbilder im Spielfilm, Kulturfilm und in der Wochenschau des Dritten Reiches." In *Nationalsozialismus und Geschlecht. Zur Politisierung und Ästhetisierung von Körper, Rasse und Sexualität im Dritten Reich und nach 1945*, ed. Elke Frietsch and Christina Herkommer, 259–82. Bielefeld: Transcript Verlag, 2009.

Schoeps, Julius, ed. *Bilder der Judenfeindschaft*. Eltville: Bechtermüntz, 1999.

Schoppmann, Claudia. "National Socialist Policies towards Female Homosexuality." In *Gender Relations in German History: Power, Agency and Experience from the 16th to the 20th Century*, ed. Lynn Abrams and Elizabeth Harvey, 177–88. London: University College of London Press, 1996.

– "Flucht in den Untergrund: Zur Situation der jüdischen Bevölkerung in Deutschland, 1941–1945." In *Nationalsozialismus und Geschlecht: Zur Politisierung und Ästhetisierung von Körper, "Rasse" und Sexualität im "Dritten Reich" und nach 1945*, ed. Elke Frietsch and Christina Herkommer, 285–97. Bielefeld: Transcript Verlag, 2009.

Schrafstetter, Susanna. *Flucht und Versteck: Untergetauchte Juden in München – Verfolgungserfahrung nach Nachkriegsalltag.* Göttingen: Wallstein Verlag, 2015.

Schroer, Timothy L. "Civilization, Barbarism, and the Ethos of Self-control among the Perpetrators." *German Studies Review,* 25, no. 1 (2012): 33–54.

Schüler-Springorum, Stefanie. "A Soft Hero: Male Jewish Identity in Imperial Germany through the Autobiography of Aron Liebeck." In *Jewish Masculinities: German Jews, Gender, and History,* ed. Benjamin M. Baader, Sharon Gillerman, and Paul Lerner, 90–113. Bloomington: Indiana University Press, 2013.

– *Geschlecht und Differenz: Perspektiven deutsch-jüdischer Geschichte.* Paderborn: Ferdinand Schoeningh Verlag, 2014.

Sommer, Robert. *Das KZ-Bordell Zwangsarbeit in nationalsozialistischen Konzentrationslagern.* Paderborn: Schöningh, 2009.

Springmann, Veronika. "Boxen im Konzentrationslager. Erzählmuster und Interpretationen." In *Männlichkeitskonstruktionen im Nationalsozialismus: Formen, Funktionen und Wirkungsmacht von Geschlechterkonstruktionen im Nationalsozialismus und ihre Reflexion in der pädagogischen Praxis,* ed. Anette Dietrich and Ljiljana Heise, 185–99. Frankfurt: Peter Lang, 2013.

Steinbacher, Sybille, ed. *Volksgenossinen: Frauen in der NS-Volksgemeinschaft.* Wallstein: Göttingen, 2007.

Steinweis, Alan. *Kristallnacht.* Cambridge, MA: Belknap Press of Harvard University Press, 2009.

Szobar, Patricia. "Telling Sexual Stories in the Nazi Courts of Law: Racial Defilement in Germany, 1933 to 1945." In *Sexuality and German Fascism,* ed. Dagmar Herzog, 131–63. New York: Berghahn Books, 2004.

Tec, Nechama. *Resilience and Courage: Women, Men, and the Holocaust.* New Haven, CT: Yale University Press, 2003.

– *Resistance: Jews and Christians Who Defied Nazi Terror.* Oxford: Oxford University Press, 2013.

Theweleit, Klaus. *Male Fantasies.* Minnesota: University of Minneapolis Press, 1987.

Timm, Anette. "Sex with a Purpose: Prostitution, Venereal Disease and Militarized Masculinity in the Third Reich." In *Sexuality and German Fascism,* ed. Dagmar Herzog, 223–55. New York: Berghahn Books, 2004.

Tosh, John. "What Should Historians Do with Masculinity? Reflections on Nineteenth Century Britain." *History Workshop,* 38, no. 1 (1994): 179–202.

– "Authority and Nurture in Middle-Class Fatherhood: The Case of Early and Mid-Victorian England." *Gender & History,* 8, no. 1 (April 1996): 48–64.

– "Hegemonic Masculinity and the History of Gender." In *Masculinities in Politics and War: Gendering Modern History,* ed. Stefan Dudink, Karen

Hagemann, and John Tosh, 41–58. Manchester: Manchester University Press, 2004.

– "Home and Away: The Flight from Domesticity in Late 19th-century England Revisited." *Gender & History*, 27, no. 3 (2015): 561–75.

Trepp, Anne-Charlott. "Männerwelten privat: Vaterschaft im späten 18. und beginnenden 19. Jahrhundert." In *Männergeschichte – Geschlechtergeschichte: Männlichkeit im Wandel der Moderne*, ed. Thomas Kühne, 31–50. Frankfurt: Campus Verlag, 1996.

– *Sanfte Männlichkeit und selbständige Weiblichkeit: Männer und Frauen im Hamburger Bürgertum zwischen 1770–1840*. Göttingen: Vandenhoeck & Ruprecht, 1996.

Vaizey, Hester. "Husbands and Wives: An Evaluation of the Emotional Impact of World War Two in Germany." *European History Quarterly*, 40, no. 3 (2010): 389–411.

van Rahden, Till. *Jews and Other Germans: Civil Society, Religious Diversity and Urban Politics in Breslau, 1860–1925*. Trans. Marcus Brainard. Madison: University of Wisconsin Press, 2008.

– "Fatherhood, Rechristianization, and the Quest for Democracy in Postwar West Germany." In *Raising Citizens in the "Century of the Child,"* ed. Dirk Schuhmann, 141–64. New York: Berghahn, 2010.

Veidlinger, Jeffrey. *In the Shadow of the Shtetl: Small-Town Jewish Life in Soviet Ukraine*. Bloomington: Indiana University Press, 2013.

von Braun, Christina. "Antisemitische Stereotype und Sexualphantasien." In *Die Macht der Bilder: Antisemitische Vorurteile und Mythen*, ed. Jüdisches Museum der Stadt Wien, 180–91. Vienna: Picus Verlag, 1995.

– "Der sinnliche und übersinnliche Jude." In *Der schejne Jid. Das Bild des Jüdischen Körpers in Mythos und Ritual*, ed. Sander Gilman and Robert Jütte. Vienna: Picus Verlag, 1998.

– "Blut und Blutschande: Zur Bedeutung des Blutes in der antisemitischen Denkwelt." In *Bilder der Judenfeindschaft*, ed. Julius Schoeps and Joachim Schlör, 80–95. Eltville: Bechtermüntz Verlag, 1999.

Wachsmann, Nikolaus. *Hitler's Prisons*. New Haven, CT: Yale University Press, 2004.

– "The Dynamics of Destruction: The Development of the Concentration Camps, 1933–1945." In *Nazi Concentration Camps in Nazi Germany: The New Histories*, ed. Nikolaus Wachsmann and Jane Caplan, 17–43. London: Routledge, 2009.

Walk, Joseph. *Das Sonderrecht der Juden in Deutschland*. Heidelberg: C.F. Müller Verlag, 1981.

Walter, Dirk. *Antisemitische Kriminalität und Gewalt: Judenfeindschaft in der Weimarer Republik*. Bonn: Verlag Dietz, 1999.

Waxman, Zoe. "Towards an Integrated History of the Holocaust: Masculinity, Femininity and Genocide." In *Years of Persecution, Years of Extermination: Saul Friedlander and the Future of Holocaust Studies,* ed. Christian Wiese, Alan Kramer, Paul Betts, Richard Bessel, Paul Betts, Alon Confino, et al., 311–22 London: Bloomsbury, 2010.

– *Women in the Holocaust: A Feminist History.* Oxford: Oxford University Press, 2017.

Welch, David. *The Third Reich: Politics and Propaganda.* London: Routledge, 1993.

Wenk, Silke, and Insa Eschenbach. "Soziales Gedächntis und Geschlechterdifferenz. Eine Einführung." In *Gedächtnis und Geschlecht,* ed. Insa Eschebach, Sigrid Jacobeit, and Silke Wenk, 13–38. Frankfurt: Campus Verlag, 2002.

Westermann, Edward B. "Tests of Manhood: Alcohol, Sexual Violence and Killing in the Holocaust." In *The Holocaust and Masculinities: Critical Inquiries into the Presence and Absence of Men,* ed. Björn Krondorfer and Ovidiu Creangă, 147–70. New York: State University of New York Press, 2020.

Wetzel, Juliane. "Karriere nach der Rettung: Charlotte Knobloch's Weg zur Vizepräsidentin der Juden in Deutschland." In *Überleben im Dritten Reich,* ed. Wolfgang Benz, 301–11. Munich: Beck Verlag, 2003.

Whitman, James Q. *Hitler's American Model: The United States and the Making of Nazi Race Laws.* Princeton, NJ: Princeton University Press, 2017.

Wildmann, Daniel. *Begehrte Körper: Konstruktion und Inszenierung des 'arischen' Männerkörpers im Dritten Reich.* Würzburg: Könighausen und Neumann, 1998.

Wildt, Michael. "Victor Klemperer und die Verfolgung der Deutschen Juden." In *Im Herzen der Finsternis: Victor Klemperer als Chronist der NS-Zeit,* ed. Hannes Heer, 49–72. Berlin: Aufbau Verlag, 1997.

Winter, Sebastian. "Sippengemeinschaft statt Männerbund: Die historische Genese der Männlichkeitsentwürfe in der SS und die ihnen unterliegende Psychodynamik." In *Männlichkeitskonstruktionen im Nationalsozialismus Formen, Funktionen und Wirkungsmacht von Geschlechterkonstruktionen im Nationalsozialismus und ihre Reflexion in der pädagogischen Praxis,* ed. Anette Dietrich and Ljiljana Heise, 65–81. Frankfurt: Peter Lang, 2013.

Wippermann, Wolfgang, and Michael Burleigh. *The Racial State: Germany 1933–1945.* Cambridge: Cambridge University Press, 1993.

Wünschmann, Kim. "Die Konzentrationslagererfahrungen deutsch-jüdischer Männer nach dem Novemberpogrom 1938: Geschlechtergeschichtliche Überlegungen zu männlichem Selbstverständniss und Rollenbild." In *"Wer bleibt opfert seine Jahre, vielleicht sein Leben:" Deutsche Juden, 1938–1941,* ed. Susanne Heim, Beate Meyer, and Francis Nikosia, 39–58. Göttingen: Wallstein, 2010.

– "Männlichkeitskonstruktionen jüdischer Häftlinge in NS Konzentrationslagern." In *Männlichkeitskonstruktionen im Nationalsozialismus: Formen, Funktionen und Wirkungsmacht von Geschlechterkonstruktionen im Nationalsozialismus und ihre Reflexion in der pädagogischen Praxis*, ed. Anette Dietrich and Ljiljana Heise, 201–19. Frankfurt: Peter Lang, 2013.

– *Before Auschwitz: Jewish Prisoners in the Prewar Concentration Camps*. Cambridge, MA: Harvard University Press, 2015.

Zoja, Luigi. *The Father: Historical, Psychological and Cultural Perspectives*. Trans. Henry Martin. London: Brunner-Routledge, 2001.

zu Uptrup, Wolfram Meyer. *Kampf gegen die "Jüdische Weltverschwörung": Propaganda und Antisemitismus der Nationalsozialisten, 1919–1945*. Berlin: Metropol Verlag, 2003.

Image and Photo Credits

1 Courtesy of NS Documentation Centre of the City of Cologne.
2 Public Domain.
3 Public Domain. Retrieved from the Web.
4 Public Domain. Retrieved from http://www.bytwerk.com/gpa /images/kladder/kd33-31a.jpg. Courtesy of Randal Bytwerk.
5 Public Domain. Retrieved from http://www.bytwerk.com/gpa /posters/garant.jpg. Courtesy of Randal Bytwerk.
6 Public Domain. Reichsbund jüdischer Frontsoldaten, *Gefallene Deutsche Juden: Frontbriefe 1914–1918* (Berlin: Vortrup Verlag, 1935), i–ii.
7 Public Domain. Kurt Plischke, *Der Jude als Rassenschänder: Eine Anklage gegen Juda und eine Mahnung an die deutschen Frauen und Mädchen* (Berlin: NS Druck & Verlag, 1934), 46.
8 Public Domain. Retrieved from http://research.calvin.edu /german-propaganda-archive/images/sturmer/ds16a.jpg. Courtesy of Randal Bytwerk.
9 Public Domain. Retrieved from http://research.calvin.edu /german-propaganda-archive/images/sturmer/sturm06.jpg. Courtesy of Randal Bytwerk.
10 Public Domain. Retrieved from https://research.calvin.edu /german-propaganda-archive/images/giftpilz/scan10.jpg.
11 Public Domain. Retrieved from http://research.calvin.edu /german-propaganda-archive/images/fuchs/fuchs13.jpg. Courtesy of Randal Bytwerk.
12 Public Domain. Courtesy of Archives of Contemporary History, Eidgenössische Technische Hochschule Zürich.
13 Courtesy of Historisches Museum Hannover.
14 Public Domain. Retrieved from http://cuxpedia.de/index.php ?title=Datei:Rassenschande_in_Cuxhaven.jpeg.

15   Courtesy of Institut für Stadtgeschichte, Gelsenkirchen. Photo ISG
     FS I 6018.
16   Courtesy of German Historical Institute, German History in
     Documents and Images, Washington, DC. Retrieved from http://
     germanhistorydocs.ghi-dc.org/sub_image.cfm?image_id=2331.
17   Public Domain. Retrieved from http://research.calvin.edu
     /german-propaganda-archive/images/fuchs/fuchs3.jpg.
     Courtesy of Randal Bytwerk.
18   Public Domain. Retrieved from http://www.spurensuche
     -bremen.de/stadt-und-land-hand-in-hand/.
19   Courtesy of Jewish Museum Berlin, Collection Familie Klotzsch,
     K291 Inv.-Nr 2003/145/24. Gift by Miriam und Irving Klothen;
     photo: Roman Marz.
20   Courtesy of Jewish Museum Berlin, Collection Familien
     Wachsner/Meyerhoff, Convolute 314. K1024, Folder 3,
     Inv.-Nr 2014/194/539. Gift by Marianne Meyerhoff; photo:
     Kai-Annett Becker.
21   Courtesy of Danièle Cohn.
22   Courtesy of Danièle Cohn.
23   Courtesy of Yad Yashem Photo Archive, Jerusalem, FA192_3.
24   Courtesy of Sonia Pressmann Fuentes.
25   Public Domain. Courtesy of Archives of Contemporary History,
     Eidgenössische Technische Hochschule Zürich.
26   Courtesy of the Leo Baeck Institute, New York.
27   United States Holocaust Memorial Museum. Photo #79914.
     Courtesy of Robert A. Schmuhl. Retrieved from https://
     collections.ushmm.org/search/catalog/pa1054522.

Index

A page reference in *italics* indicates an illustration.

German and European Studies

General Editor: Jennifer L. Jenkins